The Strategic Community-Based Firm

The Strategic Community-Based Firm

Mitsuru Kodama
Professor of Information and Management
College of Commerce and Graduate School of Business Administration
Nihon University

palgrave
macmillan

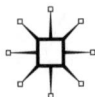

First published 2007 by
PALGRAVE MACMILLAN
Houndmills, Basingstoke, Hampshire RG21 6XS and
175 Fifth Avenue, New York, N.Y. 10010
Companies and representatives throughout the world

PALGRAVE MACMILLAN is the global academic imprint of the Palgrave
Macmillan division of St. Martin's Press, LLC and of Palgrave Macmillan Ltd.
Macmillan® is a registered trademark in the United States, United Kingdom
and other countries. Palgrave is a registered trademark in the European
Union and other countries.

ISBN-13: 978–0–230–00685–0   hardback
ISBN-10: 0–230–00685–X   hardback

This book is printed on paper suitable for recycling and made from fully
managed and sustained forest sources.

A catalogue record for this book is available from the British Library.

Library of Congress Cataloging-in-Publication Data

Kodama, Mitsuru, 1957–
    The strategic community-based firm / Mitsuru Kodama.
       p. cm.
    Includes bibliographical references (p.) and index.
    ISBN 0–230–00685–X (cloth)
       1. Strategic alliances (Business) 2. Strategic alliances (Business)—
    Japan—Case studies. 3. Business networks. 4. Business networks—
    Japan—Case studies. 5. Knowledge management. 6. Knowledge
    management—Japan—Case studies. I. Title.

    HD69.S8.K63 2007
    338.8'7—dc22   2006046019

10   9   8   7   6   5   4   3   2   1
16   15 14 13 12 11 10 09 08 07

Printed and bound in Great Britain by
Antony Rowe Ltd, Chippenham and Eastbourne

Contents

List of Figures

Acknowledgements

This book is the product of deep, extensive observation and analysis over many years of activity in the business arena. I majored in electronics engineering and then joined NTT, Japan's largest telecommunications carrier. Today, global telecommunications carriers are constantly facing new strategies and organizational reforms as they work toward creating broadband businesses in the severe environment of technological innovations, deregulation, and global competition.

At NTT, I worked with exciting businesses involving the development of new products and services and internal corporate ventures in the rapidly changing field of IT and communications. As a result of this, I become deeply aware that the structure itself between strategies and organizations in a corporation is a dynamic living entity in the flow of time from the past, through the present and on to the future, and I feel very strongly that the source of dynamic strategies and organizations is based on the people, groups, and networks of all these entities. In other words, it is 'the importance of people' and 'the importance of nurturing people.' The research issues in this book are to capture realistically along a time axis the dynamics and processes of constantly changing strategies and organizations and to derive a new theoretical framework by which corporations can give birth to new knowledge and innovation. As a practitioner and researcher, my primary goal for the research in this book is how to find a bridge between theory and practice.

To achieve this goal, I have analyzed in considerable detail the thoughts and behavior of partner companies and a large number of actors including customers. In the pursuit of such research issues as how a corporation actually forms strategies and implements them or how corporations rebuild their organization and acquire new organizational capabilities, I conducted a penetrating qualitative study as seen through my own eyes and experiences. Through long periods of field research, I gained many insights and encouragement concerning 'the creation of a future' and 'the realization of a vision' from actors and their lives out in the dynamic business arena. There is also drama in various business activities (from the macro to the micro and in cases of success and failure) where actors' convictions and ideas bring strategies to reality and actors acquire capabilities for their organizations. The deep qualitative study rooted in workplaces in the field identifies the dynamic strategies and movements of organizations and the various values of actors in a way that is not possible with a quantitative study that conducts detailed analyses of statistical results obtained from snapshot-type questionnaires.

This book could not be completed without the thorough and strict inter-action that I have had with many practitioners and I would like to extend my gratitude to these practitioners. Among them, I would like to express my deep gratitude to Mr Shigeru Ikeda, former Senior Executive Vice-President of NTT and former President of CIAJ. I learned a great deal about methods of change management from Mr Ikeda. I would also like to give deep thanks to the late Mr Norioki Morinaga (former NTT DoCoMo Vice-President) and Mr Shiro Tsuda (former President and former CEO of Vodafone K.K. and a former Vice-President of NTT DoCoMo). Both these people were my immediate superiors (managers at NTT's head office) at the time I joined NTT. They also warmly welcomed me when I was transferred from NTT East to NTT DoCoMo. I also wish to thank my family who sup-ported me when I made the transition from the business world to the aca-demic world. Concerning the publication of this book, the author wishes to extend his appreciation to Mrs Kippenberger, Senior Commissioning Editor, and Ms Pash, Assistant Editor of Palgrave Macmillan, who provided tremendous support.

I still have a considerable quantity of important data, particularly relating to change management that I could only mention briefly here due to the limited space of this book, and I would like to offer these new ideas to readers on another occasion. Finally, I have used material some previously published, and I am deeply appreciative to the following publishers for their permission to reproduce this.

Permission has been received from Sage Publications to use the following papers:

Kodama, M. (2003) 'Strategic innovation in traditional big Business', *Organization Studies*, Vol. 24, No. 2, 235–68.

Permission has been received from Wiley Interscience to use the fol-lowing papers:

Kodama, M. (2004) 'Strategic community-based theory of firms – case study of dialectical management of NTT DoCoMo', *Systems Research and Behavioral Science*, Vol. 21, No. 6.

Permission has been received from Elsevier Science to use the following papers:

Kodama, M. (2005) 'Knowledge creation through the networks strategic communities: case studies on new product development in Japanese companies', *Long Range Planning*, Vol. 38, No. 1.

Kodama, M. (2007) 'Innovation through boundary management – case study in reforms at Matsushita Electric', *Technovation*, Vol. 26, No. 1.

List of Abbreviations

A/V products	Audio and Visual products
ASP/ISP	Application Service Provider/information Service Provider
AVC	Audio Visual Corporation
CCD	Charge Coupled Devices
CDMA 1X WIN	Brand name of 3G service by KDD1
CEO	Chief Executive Officer
CFT	Cross-functional Team
CPU	Central Computational Unit
DIGA	Branding name of DVD recorder in Matsushita
DRAMs	Digital Random Access Memory
DVD	Digital Video Disc
EDA	Electronic Design Automation
FMC	Fixed and Mobile Convergence
FOMA	Freedom of Mobile Multimedia Access; service of brand name in NTT DoCoMo
FTTH	Fiber-to-the-home Broadband Network
GBD	Gateway Business Department
H.263/G71X, MPEG4/AMR	Technical terms
ICT	Information and Communication Technology
IM	Instant Messenger
i-mode FeliCa	Brand name of mobile e-commerce by NTT DoCoMo
IMT-2000	Name of 3G (Third generation) mobile phone service
IP	Information Providers
IP	Intellectual Property
ISDN	Integrated Subscriber Digital Network
IT	Information Technology
ITS	Intelligence Transport System
ITU	International Telecommunication Union
JAVA	Operating system developed by SUN
LSC	Leadership-based Strategic Community
LSI	Large Scale Integrated
MBD	Multimedia Business Department

NTT	Nippon Telegraph and Telephone Corporation
NTT DoCoMo, KDDI, Matsushita Electric, Fujitsu	Name of the company
OEM	Original Equipment Manufacturing
PDA	Personal Digital Assistance
PHS	Personal Handyphone System
R&D	Research and Development
SC	Strategic Community
3G	Third Generation
TQM	Total Quality Management
W-CDMA, CDMA	Name of system architecture of 3G (Third generation) mobile phone service

1
Introduction – Creating New Business Models Across Different Technologies and Industries

With the advances in Information Technology (IT) recently in a knowledge-based society, there is a growing need to merge different technologies, to develop products and services that span different industries, and to build business models. In the past, innovations in technology have developed through the deep pursuit of specialized knowledge. Now, there are numerous cases in which the technology of one field had to be merged with the technology of another field in order to develop new products based on new ideas.

Superior core technologies are continuing to be dispersed and reformed throughout the world in such advanced business fields as IT, telecommunications, e-business, content, electronics, automobile, and biotechnology. Under the conditions of existing hierarchical organizations and closed autonomous systems in the age of mass production, many corporations are increasingly experiencing difficulties in their attempts to fully control innovation on their own (e.g. Sawhney and Prandelli, 2000; Chesbrough, 2003). On the other hand, a style of management that utilizes networked organizations to integrate superior knowledge from multiple aspects, knowledge that is dispersed both within and outside organizations including customers in an open environment, is likely to become increasingly important for corporations aiming to generate competitive advantage in a networked economy. Needless to say, however, corporations must at the same time maintain and further nurture their own core competences that are difficult for other parties to imitate (e.g. Hamel and Prahalad, 1994).

Japanese industries such as the mobile phone and automobile industries, which are at a top level in technology and service by international standards are today continuing to give birth to new products and services by integrating different knowledge beyond the organizational boundaries of various industries. They are thus continuing to form a value chain that becomes a new framework. In the area of 3G mobile phone services, for example, NTT DoCoMo, KDDI, and other world-class Japanese mobile phone carriers are actively developing strategic alliances that transcend the boundaries of industry in order to bring out new products and services. These alliances are being formed with mobile handset manufacturers, computer manufacturers, communications device manufacturers, semiconductor vendors, content providers, overseas telecommunications carriers, financial institutions, automobile manufacturers, and others (Figure 1.1). At the same time, automobile manufacturers such as Toyota, Nissan, and Honda are looking to establish strategic alliances with such diverse industries as the IT, electric appliance, semiconductor, software, computer, steel, and the biotechnology industries in order to develop new vehicles and services that bring greater convenience and comfort for the 21st century through enhanced safety, environmental friendliness, and use of information (Figure 1.2).

Along with pursuing profits for their existing businesses, while considering risk in an environment of uncertainty, these companies in the mobile phone and automobile industries have a dynamic view of strategy (e.g. Markides, 1997; Eisenhardt and Sull, 2001) that, through a process of integrating new knowledge, deliberately forms new market positions, such as new products and services or new business models, that transcend their own particular core capabilities.

An important issue facing corporations as they seek to achieve future innovation is not just to respond to changes in the environment but also to follow a process of creating an environment in which they can deliberately form a new market position. Particularly in the high-tech industry, where corporations must continue to introduce new products and services in rapidly changing environments, corporations also need the dynamic capability through a dynamic view of strategy for creating their own changes in the environment as they respond to external environmental changes (Markides, 1997, 1999; Chakravarty, 1997).

However, more than ever before, the strategic advantage of corporations depends on mobilizing, combining, integrating and transforming knowledge into new high value-added products and services in a highly complex environment. At the same time, this advantage is increasingly threatened by discontinuities in the very knowledge base which is critical to long-term business success. Today's managers are thus faced with a paradox: their organizations are increasingly reliant on knowledge at a time when any knowledge-based advantage is eroding rapidly.

The research question that this book aims to address is 'What is the source of organization capability required by a corporation when it faces

3

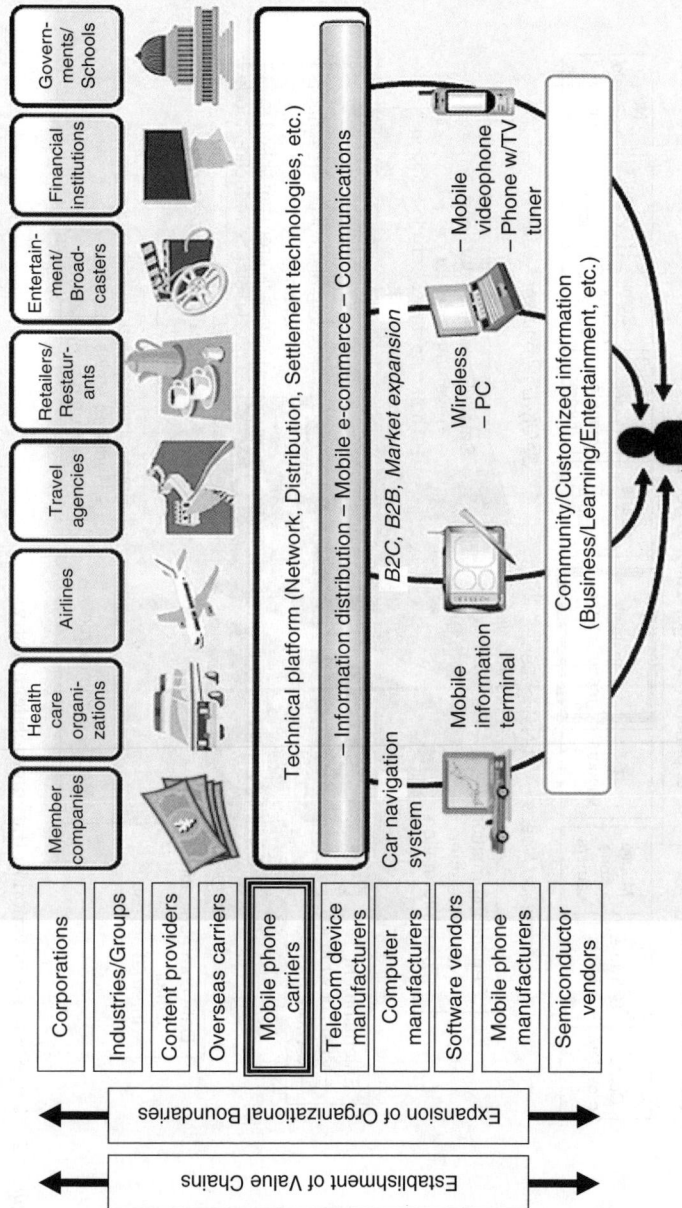

Figure 1.1 Value chain innovation in the mobile phone industry

4

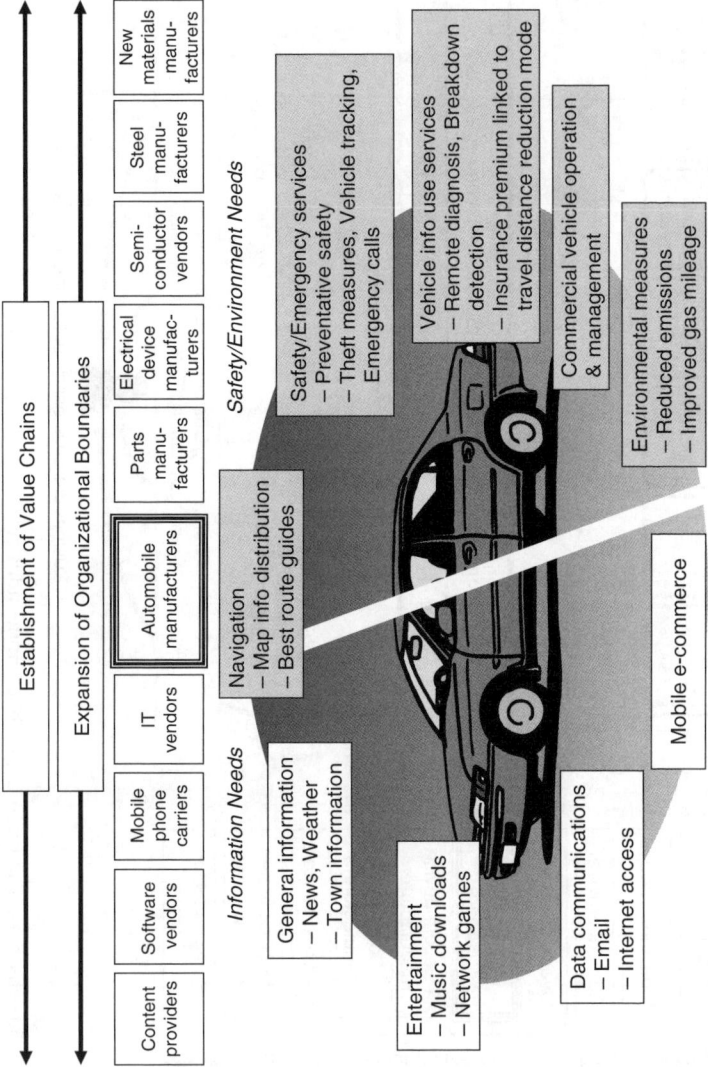

Figure 1.2   Value chain innovation in the automobile industry

the issue of creating a completely new market that has never existed before?' In particular, the author believes it is important for corporations to acquire organizational capability as it considers what process to use in integrating diverse new knowledge, both inside and outside the corporation, that emerges through new product and service development efforts aimed at creating new markets.

To establish and maintain competitive advantage, it is important for companies to have a process of accessing, sharing, and integrating knowledge in diverse areas concerning technology, business processes, and others that is spread out both within and outside the company. The process of accessing diverse knowledge that is dispersed inside and outside the corporation (Grant and Baden-Fuller, 2004), sharing knowledge (Davenport and Prusak, 1998), and integrating knowledge (Grant, 1996b) is thus vital for corporations. In an environment of turbulent change and uncertainty, a dynamic strategy-making process in which the corporation goes beyond its own core capability and always deliberately forms new market positions (new products, services, and business models, etc.) is an issue of daily importance for managers and practitioners.

Recent leading-edge high-tech organizations are turning to projects or teams in collaborations both inside and outside the corporations across organizational boundaries as a way of dealing with this paradox. Managing through projects or teams in collaboration with other organizations such as external partners including customers has the advantage of speed and focus.

This book describes a framework (the 'strategic community' concept) concerning a process that dynamically shares and integrates knowledge possessed by people, groups, or organizations across organizational boundaries, and creates new knowledge, such as developing new products and services or new business models. The author would like to suggest, through detailed case studies of Japanese high-tech industries including joint product innovation with US-based companies, that strategy, organization and leadership in corporations that realize dynamic knowledge integration at multiple organizational boundaries represent the dynamic view of strategy that a company needs in order to obtain organizational capability with a competitive edge.

In particular, the author addresses the following topics relevant to academic researchers and practitioners around the world:

- knowledge-based view of corporate strategy;
- the distinctive challenges of managing through strategic communities in particular sectors;

- evaluating success in managing through strategic communities;
- the role of strategic communities and networked strategic communities as focal points of knowledge creation and integration;
- the role of strategic communities in cross-sectoral collaboration;
- the leadership behavior of corporate managers, including members of top management, regarding their formation of strategic communities;
- the strategy-making process that corporations should adopt and how they should formulate and implement the timing of strategic communities' formation and the process of distributing resources. (Details are analyzed by individual divisions or at the project level.);
- changing the organisation's strategic position by managing strategic communities and networked strategic communities (e.g. by entering new markets, undertaking a joint product development);
- the impact of managing strategic communities on the dynamics of competition in particular sectors;
- new organizational architectures through networked strategic communities.

In the knowledge-based society of the 21st century, the diverse knowledge that people have (not just related to technology) represents a source for creating new products and services of value to customers who bring new competitiveness. Strategic community creation may be key to generating the knowledge that is essential for tackling technological, market, and business discontinuities. The author believes that the concepts of 'strategic community' offers new and valuable insight for many researchers and practitioners aiming to realize innovation.

In Chapter 2, the theoretical framework that forms the core of the book obtained from longitudinal qualitative research is described. The new concepts proposed in this chapter concern a dynamic, practical method that corporate managers can use to integrate diverse knowledge distributed on networks, whether real or virtual, in order to develop new products or business models. At the core of the framework in this book is a concept known as the strategic community (SC), a theory for a practical method of accelerating innovation in a corporation. To obtain diverse knowledge of value, it is important to have a process in which managers from various strata of management both inside and outside the corporation can dynamically form strategic communities with internal and external managers without being restricted to existing formal organizations. In this chapter, the author wishes to define a theoretical framework concerning the dynamism of SC formation, a dynamic view of strategy through networked SCs, and the acquisition of integrative competences in SC-based firms derived from the most recent in-depth case studies in high-tech fields.

In Chapter 3, the dialectical management in a large corporation is described, through the in-depth case study. As a case study, the author examines NTT DoCoMo, the major Japanese communications carrier that gave birth to i-mode, a mobile internet service that has been enjoying strong growth in Japan and now around the world. The author analyzes the strategic and organizational dynamism that generated the innovation for NTT DoCoMo to become the first in the world to offer i-mode, and subsequently their 3G mobile phone service called FOMA, by integrating traditional organizations with organizations that have different cultures within the company and by forming networked SCs with external partners including customers.

In Chapter 4, the author describes the radical innovation process in a large corporation. As a case study here, the author analyzes and discusses the process of innovation from the strategic and organizational point of view at NTT, Japan's largest communications carrier where the author has observed this process for some 10 years in the past. Along with strong leadership in top management for reforms in traditional organizations, knowledge management resulting from the formation of SCs at all layers of management across organizations as well as creative abrasion and productive friction are major drivers promoting corporate reforms.

In Chapter 5, the framework of the strategy-making process for executing and continuing both the building of a new, ongoing market position and the acquisition of new capabilities so that a corporation could achieve innovation in the future is discussed. The author would like to present a new viewpoint on knowledge-based theory of the firm based on data obtained from qualitative research into the time series strategy-making process over the past six years. NTT Group corporations successfully introduced new products and services to the market through a spiraling knowledge-integrating approach through networked SCs as a dynamic view of strategy aimed at deliberately and continually creating new markets.

Chapter 6 analyzes the case of change management at Matsushita Electric. In fiscal 2001, Matsushita Electric, a traditional Japanese manufacturer of general electrical appliances, recorded the largest loss in its history. Then, following drastic structural reforms, the company's business results experienced a rapid V-shaped recovery. By transforming its product development strategy from the old technology-led type to a customer-led type and implementing far-reaching organizational reforms, Matsushita emerged as a global leader in the field of digital household appliances. The source of Matsushita's new product development capability was founded on the formation of a number of SCs, which represent the organizational boundaries within and outside Matsushita Group companies, and the organizational integration of these SCs.

In Chapter 7, the author analyzes the case of new product development at Fujitsu. The dynamism through which improvisationally networked SCs of organizations both inside and outside the company, including customers and external partners, are formed in order to integrate knowledge possessed by many players so that they can develop new products in the industry's rapidly-changing broadband and mobile multimedia markets and technologies. It is important for project leaders involved in product development at a corporation to gain new insight by exercising dialectical leadership to integrate diverse knowledge and leadership styles inside and outside the company.

In Chapter 8, a new theoretical framework and insight derived from the in-depth case studies is presented. In order to achieve ongoing innovation, companies need to continually create new intellectual capital. The viewpoint of a SC-based firm is different from that of conventional corporate or strategic theory in that it basically focuses on ways to pursue new value in the age of knowledge. SC-based firms need a systemized practical framework that will let them create business concepts for products and services with absolute value that has never existed before. This systemized framework is referred to as 'knowledge architecture.' In acquiring integrative competences, companies form a 'knowledge concept platform' through the building of 'strategic architecture' and 'organizational architecture,' and then create and put into practice new businesses. By building in the knowledge architecture framework both within and outside the company, the company is able to acquire resources and capabilities that bring ongoing value and competitive advantage and to create and put into practice new business concepts. The concepts of the knowledge architecture and the strategies and organizations at a SC-based firm that realizes these concepts are discussed in this chapter.

In Chapter 9, the author wishes to mention the implications to researchers and practitioners. The first implication aims to propose – from the theoretical and practical viewpoints of strategy, leadership, organizational culture, competences, knowledge management, and business process management – the nature of organizations that enable large corporations to give birth to radical innovation. The second implication concerns the leadership behavior of corporate managers, including members of top management, regarding their formation of strategic communities. What sort of pattern or style of leadership do managers think is required? What sort of thinking or behavior should managers adopt? The author wishes to point out that managers consider dialectical leadership to be a vital capability in their efforts to synthesize diverse knowledge within and outside the corporation.

In the Appendix, the author touches on the method of field research in this book. A qualitative research methodology is adopted due to the need for rich data that could facilitate the generation of theoretical categories that could not be derived satisfactorily from existing theory. In particular, due to the exploratory nature of this research and an interest in identifying the main people, events, activities and influences that affect the progress of innovation, the author selected the grounded theory-based study of data interpretation, which was blended with the case study design and with ethnographic approaches and participant observation.

2
Theoretical Framework of the Research

Innovation and organizational boundaries

To establish and maintain competitive advantage, it is important for companies to have a process of accessing, sharing, and integrating knowledge in diverse areas concerning technology, business processes, and others that is spread out both within and outside the company.

The process of accessing diverse knowledge that is dispersed inside and outside the corporation (Grant and Baden-Fuller, 2004), sharing knowledge (Davenport and Prusak, 1998), and integrating knowledge (Grant, 1996b) is thus vital for corporations. In an environment of turbulent change and uncertainty, a dynamic strategy-making process in which the corporation goes beyond its own core capability and always deliberately forms new market positions (new products, services, business models and so on) is an issue of daily importance for managers and practitioners.

The author believes that the knowledge of individuals, groups, and organizations within and outside the company, obtained from his business experience over the past 20 years (developing products and services, providing marketing and customer support, and launching new ventures in the fields of IT and info-communications), forms the basis of a framework for analyses aimed at a dynamic view of strategy.

The knowledge-based view of companies thus far gives us valuable insights into how they can strategically create new knowledge and establish their target market position, from the viewpoint of corporate activities gained from the process of generating intangible assets known as knowledge. The process of integrating diverse core knowledge within and outside the company and obtaining new knowledge for new products, services, and business models is also a vital element from the viewpoint of a dynamic strategy (e.g. Markides, 1997, 1999; Chakravarty, 1997;

Eisenhardt and Sull, 2001) for quickly establishing the company's own market position as a new market or technology.

Though the starting point of corporate strategy may be knowledge possessed by people, tacit knowledge such as skills and know-how is embedded in individual people (Brown and Duguid, 1991). In particular, in the process of knowledge integration, the knowledge possessed by various people within and outside the company must be integrated beyond the boundaries between organizations. At the organizational boundaries, however, friction and conflicts that hinder knowledge integration among actors that possess different knowledge may sometimes occur (Leonard-Barton, 1995). This is because actors with different backgrounds and experience are governed by individual mental models (e.g. Markides, 1999) or path dependencies (Rosenberg, 1982; Hargadon and Sutton, 1997), and they feel uncomfortable or express resistance when faced with a different type of knowledge at organizational boundaries. Companies and organizations that are governed by individual mental models, however, cannot avoid competency traps (Levitt and March, 1988; Martines and Kambil, 1999) or core rigidities (Leonard-Barton, 1992, 1995), and they may lose their opportunities for innovation (Christensen, 1997).

On the other hand, the new knowledge or different knowledge that actors become aware of at the organizational boundaries can serve as a source that enables innovation. Knowledge boundaries that result from differences in domain-specific knowledge (Weber, 1924/1947), such as the actors' various values, specializations, and their individual thought worlds (Dougherty, 1992), are present at the organizational boundaries in the cross-functional teams across the organization and at the organizational boundaries dispersed within and outside the corporation (Carlile, 2002, 2004). The existence of these knowledge boundaries can become enablers of knowledge integration and the innovation that follows, and at the same time the knowledge boundaries can become constraints, too. In the process of forming a business model, actors become aware of many knowledge boundaries as they form organizational boundaries across different industries. However, constructive, creative dialog or friction among actors at pragmatic organizational boundaries becomes a trigger for the creation of new knowledge that leads to innovation (Leonard-Barton, 1995; Hagel III and Brown, 2005).

Many organizational boundaries that envelop different industries are present in the business models of the mobile phone and automobile industries in Chapter 1. In their aim to realize a complex business model in service development, actors commit themselves to many knowledge boundaries, bridge multiple knowledge boundaries with different contexts and knowledge, and realize knowledge integration. The idea and action of networking organizational boundaries by project leaders and team members lead to the realization of new services and business models.

This author believes that an understanding of the mechanisms of knowledge integration that crosses organizational boundaries (which are also knowledge boundaries between actors) within and outside the corporation – boundaries that comprise the complexities of business models such as those in mobile phone services – will propose beneficial implications to many practitioners not only from an academic viewpoint but from a practical one as well.

Five basic concepts in strategic communities: *ba*, community of practice, pragmatic boundaries, networks, integrative competences

In their daily business activities, practitioners become aware of a variety of organizational boundaries. 'Organizational boundaries' is being referred to here as the boundaries between work tasks in formal organizations dedicated to such areas as research, development, production, or sales; boundaries between layers of management within the company; or boundaries between customers, external partners, or various industries. Boundaries are configured by actors of different backgrounds or with different knowledge. The characteristics of these boundaries mainly consist of the following three layers in stages (Shannon and Weaver, 1949; Jantsch, 1980; Carlile, 2002, 2004). (Figure 2.1)

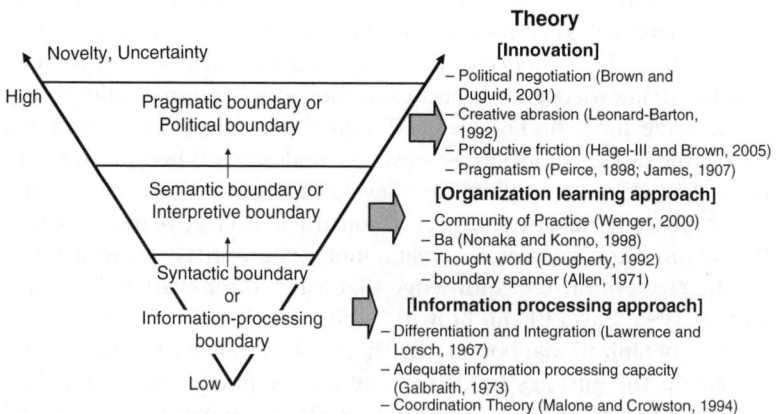

Figure 2.1   Characteristics of organizational boundary (knowledge boundary)
Source: Based on Carlile (2002, 2004).

The first layer is the syntactic or information-processing boundary for ensuring that information or knowledge is accurately transferred between actors. Specifically, this layer may be the commercialization of a product through development and production methods or routines that have already been established as a business process. The aim of syntactic boundaries within a company is to focus on rules such as internal procedures or manuals governing predetermined work tasks or operations as the means to establishing a more efficient, productive process.

The second layer represents the semantic or interpretive boundary whose aim is to generate new meaning and to translate new knowledge. Specifically, an organization's incremental action aimed at further improving existing business processes or development and production methods occurs at the semantic boundary. Though internal procedures and other rules that are important in the syntactic boundary are also important in the semantic boundary within a company, a series of organizational learning such as total quality management (TQM) aimed at promoting best practice or improving business tasks within the company are also encouraged at the semantic boundary.

The third layer consists of the pragmatic or political boundary whose aim is to transform existing knowledge through friction or conflicts among actors or through political pressure so that actors can address completely new issues and achieve new goals. Specifically, this refers to the realization of completely different business concepts, such as the development of products and services that realize new business models, the development of new technology architectures and components, and new development and production methods. It is highly possible that the new knowledge that becomes the source of innovation is generated from this sort of pragmatic boundary.

These three layers of boundaries, however, are mutually dependent, and their characteristics change significantly according to changes in the environment, such as customer needs or the competitive environment, or to the intentions or interests of actors (syntactic boundary → semantic boundary → pragmatic boundary). Especially if changes in the environment or actors' intentions aimed at innovation or corporate reform are more strongly influential, the relationships between actors will shift to a more pragmatic boundary (syntactic boundary → semantic boundary → pragmatic boundary) (Carlile, 2004).

This new knowledge that emerges from the various organizational boundaries both inside and outside the company is the very source of organizational capability. The integration of new knowledge that emerges from various pragmatic boundaries within and outside the company, including customers and partners (or the integration of pragmatic boundaries existing within and outside the company), in particular is the source that generates innovation, which as a result is the organizational capability that generates ongoing competitiveness.

The new ideas this author wishes to propose in this book concern a dynamic, practical method that corporate managers can use to integrate diverse knowledge distributed on networks, whether real or virtual, in order to develop new products or business models. At the core of the framework is a concept known as the strategic community (SC) (Kodama, 2003, 2005a), a theory for a practical method of accelerating innovation in a corporation. To obtain diverse knowledge of value, it is important to have a process in which managers from various strata of management both inside and outside the corporation can dynamically form SCs as pragmatic boundaries with internal and external actors without being restricted to existing formal organizations.

The SC is made up of five basic concepts. The first is that the SC possesses the element of 'ba' as a constantly changing shared context in motion that allows corporations to respond to dynamic changes in market and technology environments, or to spontaneously create new market and technology environments (Nonaka and Konno, 1998). Ba is a place that offers a shared context. Knowledge needs a context to be created, as it is context-specific. The context defines the participants and the nature of the participation. The context is social, cultural, and even historical, providing a basis for one to interpret information, thus creating meaning and becoming knowledge. Ba is not necessarily just a physical space or even a geographical location or virtual space through Information and Communication Technology (ICT) but a time-space nexus as much as a shared mental space. Any form of new knowledge can be created regardless of the business structure, as Ba transcends formal business structures. Bennett (2001) reported as follows by examining the Japanese characters of 'Ba': 'The top right character represents the sun; the character on the left the earth; and the bottom right (loosely) "rays of light falling to the ground".' Thus to the Western (though not the Japanese) eye, Ba is interpretable as a 'place of illumination, where sun and earth unite and enlightenment happens.'

The second concept is that the SC is a community of practice (Wenger, 2000) rooted in the resonance of value (Kodama, 2001, 2002) among the actors that form the SC. This aspect promotes mutual learning within the community by gaining an understanding of mutual contexts among members and resonating value, and continually generates new knowledge. In the SC, the community membership and the community leader at the center of activities are gradually established, and these people dynamically produce the context in which they work toward fulfilling the community's mission. In this case, it involves the development of new products and services, and community members create new knowledge by learning from one another and sharing.

The third concept is that the SC possesses a nature of being a pragmatic boundary so that actors with different contexts can transform existing knowledge (Carlile, 2002, 2004). (Since pragmatic boundaries are positioned above the syntactic and semantic boundary layers, SCs are not necessarily endowed with the nature only of pragmatic boundaries.) The pragmatic approach, with its roots in the philosophies of Peirce (1989/1992) and James(1907), highlights the importance of understanding the consequences that exist between things that are different and dependent on each other. The concepts of Ba and the community of practice cause new meaning to be generated and shared among members at the boundaries (e.g. Dougherty, 1992), and they promote organizational learning and best practice (equivalent to the semantic boundary, the second layer, mentioned above) (Figure 2.1).

At the organizational boundaries that generate the high-level novelty or uncertainty inherent in innovation, however, new meaning must be generated through the sharing of contexts within the Ba or practical communities, new knowledge that transcends organizational learning must be created, and existing knowledge must be transformed (equivalent to the pragmatic boundary, the third layer, mentioned above). Various problems and issues are raised at the pragmatic boundary, and actors must face the challenge to find solutions and create new knowledge. Actors at the organizational boundaries need to have more practical, creative abrasion (Leonard-Barton, 1992), productive friction (Hagel III and Brown, 2005) as well as political negotiations (Brown and Duguid, 2001) (Figure 2.1).

The fourth concept is that in which the actors, as hubs or connectors in an organization, dynamically bridge multiple different SCs (or pragmatic boundaries) and form networks (or links) among the SCs (Barabasi, 2002; Watts, 2003; Kodama, 2005a, b). In this way, multiple SCs (or pragmatic boundaries) become integrated and enable corporations to create new knowledge. In order to build new product development or business models, the actors then consciously network the SCs that are pragmatic boundaries among various organizations in the corporation and integrate multiple organizational boundaries. If needed, the actors also form SCs through strategic alliances with external entities including customers and bind them deeply with SCs within the corporation (Kodama, 2005b). (Figure 2.2)

The fifth concept refers to the integrative competences that the SCs and networked SCs possess. This author wishes to define 'integrative competences' as the capability of a corporation to respond quickly to changes in the environment (market) by forming SCs and networked SCs, or the capability for it to acquire the capabilities needed to create a new environment (market) at the same time and realize the optimum overall management. In other words, integrative competences possess the dual aspects of passively changing capabilities to make them suitably respond to changes in the environment (environmental responsiveness) on the one hand and acquiring new capabilities required to create new environments (environmental creation) on the other.[1]

Exercising integrative competences enables a company to generate new products, services and business models on an ongoing basis. To achieve this, companies need to create new knowledge. At the foundation of new knowledge creation lies the integration of different knowledge (knowledge transformation), and this is achieved by forming SCs and networked SCs. In addition, dialectical thought and action represent a vital viewpoint for actors who are in charge of forming SCs and networked SCs.[2]

The important dialectic that the author is referring to in the context of daily business activities represents the synthesis of holistic thinking that captures diverse knowledge from an overall point of view and analytical thinking that captures things in a logical manner.[3] Holistic thinking is the source that creates new ideas and business concepts from various contexts and viewpoints such as lifestyles, culture, society, or economics, while analytical thinking is the source that embodies ideas and concepts from the business viewpoint of technology integration and profit models. The author wishes to refer to the leadership that organizational actors need to exercise in order to realize integrative competences as 'dialectical leadership' (Kodama, 2005a, b).

The companies in Figure 2.2 form SCs through strategic alliances with various external partners and customers, including leading corporate users in particular. For example, mobile phone companies form SCs with external partners such as handset manufacturers and content providers, while automobile manufacturers forms SCs with external partners such as IT vendors and electrical appliance manufacturers. The individual SCs are made up of managers with different corporate cultures and values who are capable of engaging in fierce debates over difficult business challenges, and different context and knowledge are shared, created, and innovated within the SCs.

In order to build new business models or value chains at the mobile phone companies or automobile manufacturers mentioned in Chapter 1, each SC needs to integrate the different knowledge that was created. However, members playing central roles at individual companies, especially upper and middle managers, commit to a number of SCs, bridge SCs with different context and knowledge, and consciously create networks among them. (Capable managers are aware of the importance of networking boundaries based on past experience.) The idea and action of networking organizational boundaries by managers lead to the realization of new business models and value chains.

A number of problems and issues in the integration of knowledge, however, occur in the knowledge boundaries between managers. Struggles and conflicts are common occurrences within SCs and among networked SCs. These elements are harmful factors in the effort to synthesize the knowledge possessed by the SCs. This synthesis is thus promoted by the leadership-based strategic community (LSC) which the author describes below. Actors need to build a platform for resonating values and creating relationships of mutual trust while also engaging in ongoing mutual exchanges, deep collaboration at the boundaries of multiple, different SCs. Doing this successfully can establish the LSC between actors (leaders) and produce the integrative competences of their dialectical leadership.

Dialectical leadership is required of leaders that make up the LSC. The LSC is an informal SC made up of leaders from the various SCs, positioned

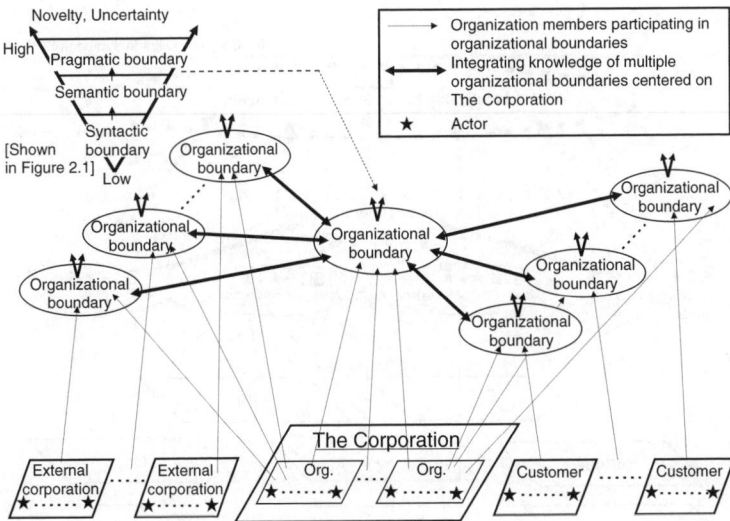

Figure 2.2 Integration of multiple organizational boundaries – networked strategic communities

above the layer of networked SCs (Figure 2.3). LSC synthesizes the knowledge of all SCs in the network that were formed by leaders (made up of personnel from various levels of participating organizations: top management, middle management, and others) and generates integrative competences through dialectical leadership. the LSC actively analyzes problems and resolves issues, forms an arena for the resonance of new values (Kodama, 2001), and creates a higher level of knowledge.

The LSC promotes dialectical dialogue and discussion among leaders in order to cultivate a thorough understanding of problems and issues. By communicating and collaborating with each other, leaders become aware of the roles and values of each other's work. As a result, leaders are able to transform the various conflicts that have arisen among them into constructive conflicts (Robbins, 1974). This process requires leaders to follow a pattern of dialectical thought and action in which they ask themselves what sorts of actions they themselves would take, what sorts of strategies or tactics they would adopt, and what they could contribute toward achieving the large project and the innovation of a new knowledge creation. The combined synergy and dialectical leadership among the leaders resulted in the high levels of integrative competences that have enabled companies to realize innovation.

The LSC strengthens the cross-functional or inter-corporate integration characteristics of the SCs and networked SCs. The LSC's role is to boost

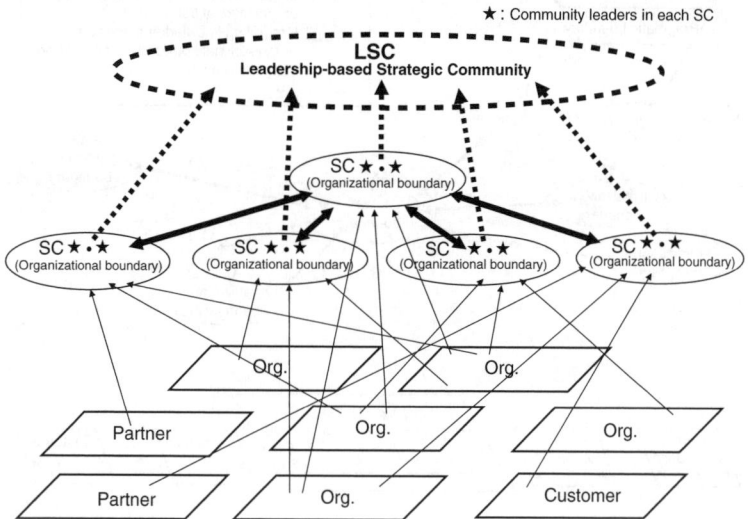

Figure 2.3   Formation of LSC

the performance of knowledge sharing and integration, and to do so, the leaders in the LSC need to have the element of dialectical leadership. In other words, dialectical leadership embodies the leadership of leaders that promotes a management capable of integrating a variety of knowledge in the different SCs. The leaders must balance various paradoxes in the areas of corporate culture, human resources, technology, business models and others in order to successfully integrate the knowledge of these SCs. A solid LSC and the dialectical leadership of leaders give birth to high integrative competences, and this can give birth to new product and service development, a platform of new business models.

At the corporate level, an organizational capability can be thought of as a collection of different combinations of various competencies that can be used to share and assess knowledge across the various types of boundaries. From the standpoint of strategies, instead of seeing the firm as an integration of resources, it can be more completely described as an integration of different types of boundaries (SCs) where knowledge must be shared and integrated. Thus, in a rapidly changing and highly uncertain business environment, it is most important for corporations to dynamically form SCs (or rebuild SCs as needed) and, by way of their integrated (networked) links, to stimulate the desired new knowledge through the process of integration and transformation.

Comparison of SC, networked SCs and existing theories

Comparison of SCs and other management theories

The author wishes to focus on the following three viewpoints in this comparison of SCs and existing management theories. The first viewpoint involves the information processing model and related product development theory, the second viewpoint concerns the theory of traditional organizations, and the third viewpoint involves corporate reform models in international business research. These viewpoints are discussed below.

Concerning the first point, the integration of SCs that are organizational boundaries is different from the organizational information processing model that is a representative contingency theory. For example, theories such as Lawrence and Lorsch's 'differentiation and integration' (Lawrence and Lorsch, 1967) or Galbraith's 'adequate information processing capacity' (Galbraith, 1973) or 'coordination theory' (Malone and Crowston, 1994) are based on an information processing model, and are used to describe greater efficiency of product development or business processes through the coordination of communication or links among members in formal organizations within the corporation or in other corporations.

In addition, many existing studies on successful new product development (e.g. Allen, 1977; Tushman, 1977; Tushman and Nadler, 1978; Clark and Fujimoto, 1991; Brown and Eisenhardt, 1995) have pointed out the importance of smooth communication or boundary spanners at cross-functional boundaries. The central concepts of these theories focused on functions such as the efficient processing, transfer (and translate), storage, and retrieval of large quantities of information or knowledge (Davenport and Prusak, 1998). The Ba or community of practice is a trigger that gives birth to new meaning to information or knowledge, causes actors at organizational boundaries (semantic boundaries) to share new context, and promotes incremental organizational behavior. Figure 2.1 illustrates the approach used to process this information and knowledge as characteristics of the syntactic and semantic boundaries.

Of course, an interpretative approach (or organizational learning approach) that promotes an information processing approach or incremental improvements for executing internal procedures based on rules, efficient project management, or a business approach is also necessary in the basics of corporate activities. Innovation, however, tends to be generated among actors possessing different organizational rules or different specialties at organizational boundaries (Leonard-Barton, 1995), and it is not possible to sufficiently describe the innovation process at organizational boundaries just by using the information processing approach focused on information or knowledge processing efficiency or the information or knowledge context-based sharing approach.

On the other hand, various conflicts and contradictions occur at the pragmatic boundaries, which are also triggers of innovation. Pragmatic boundaries include context of the sort that denies the existing mental models and experiences of actors and provides a venue for various debates and battles. Important thinking and behavior that lead to innovation, however, consist of creative conflicts and constructive debates and behavior among the actors (Hagel III and Brown, 2005; Weiss and Hughes, 2005). Pragmatic boundaries that give birth to even greater innovation do not do so as a single entity but as multiple pragmatic boundaries, both within the company (among various divisions, businesses, and levels of management) and outside the company (among partners and customers), that actors must integrate. As the new business models under consideration grow in complexity, actors are increasingly required to form greater numbers of pragmatic boundaries and to network them.

Next, as the second point, this author would like to discuss the differences between SCs and existing traditional organizational theory as described by Duncan (1972, 1973) and Stein and Kanter (1980).

A number of pioneering studies have been made in the past concerning the forms of organizations that would be ideal for routine work (methods of mass production, for instance) focusing on creative innovation and efficiency. Two representative studies of particular importance were undertaken by Duncan (1972, 1973) who provided empirical evidence that creative and implementation aspects of innovation required two different unit structures and processes. Duncan argued that creativity in innovation required an open, organic unit structure and processes, while implementation was best achieved with a hierarchical, mechanistic unit structure and process. In addition, Stein and Kanter (1980) and Kanter (1983) developed the concept of the 'parallel organization' as a means of facilitating innovation. Their idea was that the traditional hierarchy would have problems innovating and that temporary organizations parallel to the traditional one should be set up as a means of facilitating innovation. The main task of the parallel organization was the continued re-examination of routines; the exploration of new options; and the development of new tools, procedures, and approaches. It sought to institutionalize change. As their utility was demonstrated, the new routines could be transferred to the bureaucratic organization for maintenance and integration.

On the other hand, the SC being newly proposed in this book is an informal organization that links and integrates a number of formal organizational members. Its major feature is that it integrates the business processes and strategic structures of disparate, contradictory organizations. We can describe the differences between the strategic communities and these two representative studies as follows.

Duncan's model does not depict the two organizational forms as antinomies but rather as alternative forms that can be used in succession during implementation, which is the strategy of temporal separation described in Van de Ven and Poole (1988). Ford and Bockoff (1988) describe four cells of diverse dualities of an organization from the viewpoint of time dualities (synchronic and diachronic) and orientational dualities (horizontal and vertical). In the context of this classification, Duncan's model corresponds to the diachronic yet horizontal duality, meaning that it vacillates between a mechanistic unit structure and an organic unit type structure. In other words, it corresponds to the paradox of a contingency theory. The strategic communities, however, correspond to the synchronic yet horizontal duality, which means that the two organizational forms (emergent communities and traditional communities) are clearly depicted as antimonies in the SCs. The SCs explicitly deal with how to effectively manage the paradox (Kodama, 2003).

In a low-uncertainty environment, Kanter's model executes routine operations in a bureaucratic organization. However, when it shifts to a high-uncertainty environment, it also depicts the organization's duality in which a parallel organization is built when executing solutions to problems. In other words, the simultaneous availability and operation of parallel and bureaucratic structures provide a basis for the efficient operation of each, since both are equally formal structures, able to carry out their specialized functions directly.

Although Kanter's model and the SCs both share the aspect of duality in their organizations, they are fundamentally different in two ways. The first concerns the method of securing the organization's knowledge and core competences. In other words, while the parallel organization takes on a temporary form, such as a task force or team-based organization within a bureaucratic traditional organization, their human resources, knowledge, and core competences are limited to those inside the company. The SC, however, is formed around community knowledge and community competences as a new SC representing the merging and integration of various different human resources, knowledge, and core competences derived not only from resources within the company but also from external partners and designated customers. The SCs, therefore, further expand Kanter's model to include external partners and customers, and is able to become an organization model that merges and integrates heterogeneous knowledge and competences in order to achieve radical change rather than incremental change. The second difference concerns the execution of paradoxical management. In other words, by allowing and at the same time innovatively merging and integrating the paradoxical elements (areas of conflict) in a number of SCs through the dialectical thinking and behavior of leadership-based strategic communities, the SCs are structured with the ability to create knowledge and competences of a higher quality.

The third and final point involves a comparison derived from studies on models of reformed corporations in international business. Until now, the 'Transnational Management' of Barlett and Ghoshal (2000) or the 'Integration and Responsiveness' of Prahalad and Doz (1987) and the 'Heterarchy Model' of Hedlund (1986) have been proposed as models of reformed corporations centered on multinational corporations aiming to flexibly respond to changes in global markets and competitive environments. These theories suggest that organizational boundaries occasionally become vague and the business activities of multinational corporations need a flexible corporate governance through such means as strategic alliances with partners or joint business ventures. In other words, they stress that it is important to build flexible network relationships within and outside the corporation. These authors' theories, however, are general and do not offer any details of the form or structure of the organizational networks or the networks' dynamics. They also do not offer any thoughts from the viewpoint of changes in organizational structures, the acquisition of organizational capabilities that emerge from these changes, or the creation of new businesses that result, through an analysis of individual organizational boundaries between corporations.

In this area involving the process of knowledge sharing and knowledge transfer, the SCs and networked SCs share common ground with knowledge networking organizations (e.g. Rosenkopf and Tushman, 1998, 1994) or strategic alliances (e.g. Gomes-Casseres, 1993; Doz and Hamel, 1998). In previous discussions on knowledge networking organizations or strategic alliances, however, the market was growing (or had already become established), changes in the external environment were relatively less severe, and networked relationships among companies were stable for several years. The analysis framework was also static, and there was no dynamic discussion that considered the dimension of time. The framework in this book, on the other hand, also covered a relatively short period of several months during which SCs and networked SCs formed collaborations and networks with partners as a means to cultivate unknown markets in a rapidly changing environment. This was a study on a process that was dynamic and considered the dimension of time.

Also, SCs and networked SCs are different from cross-functional teams (CFTs) in a certain respect. Generally, CFTs carry out New product development (NPD) in a project management style, with clearly defined resources and systems and following a predetermined schedule. However, SCs and networked SCs accept rearrangements in partners on the network level in response to fluctuations in the external environment. (This also means that internal and external resources, i.e. the arrangement of SCs or networked SCs, can change significantly according to conditions in time or space.)

There are also differences in the units of analysis under study. The units of analysis for previous studies on knowledge networking organizations, strategic alliances, or CFTs from the viewpoint of networking among units made up of corporations or organizations, while SCs or networked SCs discuss knowledge sharing or knowledge integration using a unit of analysis that is a community or a network of communities hidden behind the inter-corporate or inter-organizational layer. Normally, the observer (researcher) can easily find the relationship of network structures among corporations or organizations if they analyze NPD processes or organizational structures (through interviews, secondary sources and others) from outside the corporation. In the case used in this book, however, the author himself went inside the organization and collected detailed data from the viewpoint of the structure and networked arrangement of communities in order to analyze such topics as knowledge sharing or knowledge integration as an observer or practitioner (see 'Research Methodology' for details in the Appendix).

The networking of SCs that is proposed in this book refers to a practical method by which actors bridge and integrate multiple SCs, which are many of the pragmatic boundaries within and outside the corporation, how they form flexible, networked organizations, and how they create new business models.

Finally, from the viewpoint of strategic theory, such as the approach based on dynamic capability (Teece *et al.*, 1997), this author proposes that this approach can be interpreted as one that has integrated core knowledge at a variety of pragmatic boundaries, i.e. SCs, within and outside the corporation. In other words, rather than thinking of organizational capability in a corporation as an integration of resources (e.g. Barney, 1991), it is also possible see this as an amalgamation of core competences at various pragmatic boundaries (SCs).

In a business environment of high uncertainty and turbulent change, this author believes that a process by which corporations can dynamically form SCs (or rebuild SCs as needed) and create new knowledge (integrate or transform knowledge) by integrating (networking) these SCs to achieve a strategic goal (market position) is of primary importance to corporations. And from the viewpoint of strategic theory, the process of dynamic knowledge integration at pragmatic boundaries within and outside the corporation is also a dynamic view of strategy that is needed by corporations to acquire organizational capability with a competitive edge.

Knowledge-based view of corporate strategy

Dynamic view of strategy through networked SCs

Corporations naturally need to upgrade their capabilities in response to changes in their environment (market and technology). In the field of digital products for the consumer, such as large-screen LCD or plasma televisions, DVD recorders, digital cameras, Japanese corporations including Matsushita Electric, Canon, Sharp, and Sony have been upgrading their capabilities in the process of releasing new versions of products (two to three times a year on average) and expanding their product offerings. In recent years, these companies have been dominating the top three positions in global market share for this industry. These corporations have been able to maintain their competitive advantages in the digital products market due to the fact that they have been continually upgrading their technological capabilities (such as improving system Large scale integrated (LSI) development, and adopting cell production methods aimed at cutting costs and improving quality) and process capabilities (building supply chains for global marketing, production, and support systems) while customer needs for digital products have been growing more diverse (focusing on quality, price, functions, and others), technology has been evolving (bringing in particular greater functionality, lower power consumption, and greater miniaturization due to the development of system LSIs), and the competitive environment has been changing (caused in part by cost competition from Korean and Chinese companies such as Samsung and Haier).

In the field of third-generation (3G) mobile phone services as well, in the Japanese market, NTT DoCoMo, KDDI, and Vodafone have been continually upgrading their technological and process capabilities and introducing new mobile phones and services to the market in their efforts to respond to changes in customer needs and advances in technology. Responding to this sort of environment by constantly and dynamically changing their own capabilities is vital for high-tech companies in the digital consumer product and mobile phone markets. This is also the dynamic capability approach that these companies need (Teece *et al.*, 1997).

At the same time, these companies also possess capabilities to create an environment that spontaneously gives birth to new markets and technologies. Some examples of this are NTT DoCoMo's i-mode mobile Internet service, J-PHONE's (now Vodafone's) camera-equipped mobile phone, and the electronic money service for mobile phones that NTT DoCoMo and Sony started in spring 2004 through a strategic alliance. These developments did not occur so much as a result of responses to customer needs, technological advances or other changes in the external environment but as a deliberate effort of these companies to create new markets and technologies. Electronics manufacturers such as Matsushita Electric and Sharp in the fiercely competitive digital consumer products market mentioned above have each been crossing into other fields of technology and industries in a deliberate attempt to create new markets and technologies. Typical examples are the ubiquitous market that merges broadband and mobile multimedia, and the telematics market that merges electronics, IT, and automobile technologies.

An important issue facing corporations as they seek to achieve future innovation is not just to respond to changes in the environment but also to follow a process of creating an environment in which they can deliberately form a new market position. Particularly in the high-tech industry, where corporations must continue to introduce new products and services in the rapidly changing environment, corporations also need a dynamic view of strategy for creating their own changes in the environment as they respond to external environmental changes (Markides, 1997, 1999; Chakravarty, 1997).

The positioning-based view that had been the representative theory of strategy until now is a framework that identifies attractive positions through structural analyses of the market, including analyses of competition structures and transaction structures (Porter, 1985). On the other hand, there is also the approach of the resource-based view, which emphasizes that concepts explaining gaps in competitiveness and profitability among corporations are unique competences, resources, and capabilities possessed by the corporation (Barney,1991; Prahalad and Hamel, 1990). Given conditions in which markets and organizations can be analyzed, these theories represent a theoretical framework that can be sufficiently applied in situations where the corporate environment is relatively stable and market structures can be understood or predicted (D'Aveni, 1994, 1995; Chakravarty, 1997; Brown and Eisenhardt, 1998; Eisenhardt and Sull, 2001). Further, the dynamic capability approach representing a theoretical framework with a dynamic view of strategy is a concept that dynamically changes a company's own core capabilities in line with environmental changes (Teece *et al.*, 1997). In the dynamic capability approach, however, path dependency and market positioning are given conditions, and represent an in-out concept (from the organization viewpoint to the market viewpoint) whereby market position is strengthened after a company's own capabilities are rebuilt by the ideas and actions of a practitioner.

If one considers the framework of the company's strategic process from the business experience of the author himself, however, doesn't it seem that in its activities, the company is actually forming and executing strategies while dynamically and mutually complementing and reinforcing the company's own capabilities and market position the company should be aiming for? In other words, doesn't the essence of this strategy call for the company to take advantage of the view of strategy that dynamically synthesizes the internal (organization) and external (market) sides rather than allowing them to be in opposition to each other? Further, how should practitioners think and act in their efforts to cultivate new markets? What sort of strategy-making process is required of the company? These are the issues that this research addresses.

The strategy-making process that the company constantly uses to deliberately and spontaneously form new positioning (new products, new services, and new business models) beyond the company's own core capabilities especially under an environment of dramatic change and uncertainty is an issue of daily importance to practitioners. To that end, it is important for the company to continue working hard at creating the new capabilities it will need to establish a market position that will allow the company to deliberately create a new environment. Also important at the same time is a process that enables the company to establish a new competitive position as a goal through trial and error. In other words, a basic framework of dynamic ideas and action that simultaneously synthesizes the approach from the exterior (market viewpoint) to the interior (organization viewpoint) and the approach from the interior (organization viewpoint) to the exterior (market viewpoint) is important from the practical side.

As a research approach to the research questions mentioned above, the author believes that the knowledge of individuals, groups, and organizations within and outside the company, obtained from the author's business experience over the past 20 years (developing products and services, providing marketing and customer support, and launching new ventures in the fields of IT and info-communications), forms the basis of a framework for analyses aimed at dynamic strategy-making process.

Representative research results thus far, such as a knowledge-based view of the firm (Grant, 1996a, b), organizational knowledge creation (Nonaka, 1994), wellsprings of knowledge (Leonard-Barton, 1992, 1995). Intellectual capital (Stewart, 1997), working knowledge (Davenport and Prusak, 1998), knowledge workers (Fuller, 2001), and community of practice (Brown and Duguid, 1991), give us valuable insights into how companies can strategically create new knowledge and establish their target market position, from the viewpoint of corporate activities gained from the process of generating intangible assets known as knowledge.

The author believes that networked strategic communities, as a means of obtaining knowledge required by the company to quickly establish its own position as an environment encompassing newer markets and technologies, represents a process of integrating diverse core knowledge inside and outside the company and of obtaining new knowledge in the form of new products and services, and is a vital element of the dynamic view of strategy.

In Chapters 5 and 6, the author uses in-depth detailed case studies to describe the mechanism of networked strategic communities that enabled NTT Group firms and Matsushita Electric to simultaneously establish a new market position and achieve competitively advantageous capability in the hi-tech field of broadband service development and digital appliances by forming networked strategic communities.

Knowledge differences and a spiraling knowledge integrating approach

In using the dynamic view of strategy approach toward product and service development, it is important for actors first to deliberately establish new concepts concerning the new products and services as a new market position. Concepts in products and services refer not to technical architecture or component technologies but to how value is to be provided to customers. In product innovation incorporating completely new concepts, these concepts came not from facts underlying detailed marketing data but from the strong desire of actors to provide customers with value through certain new concepts for products and services that would foster an advanced information-oriented society for the future.[4] To achieve this, the organizations were required to transform existing mental models, abandon attachments to precedents, and to nurture radical ideas (also incorporating external knowledge) (Hamel, 1996, 2000; Markides, 1999). Actors for their part were required to set high goals for strategic market position and to cultivate a challenging new business while always bearing the risks of development capital. Particularly in the viewpoint of creating new markets, simply developing products from a path-dependent (Rosenberg, 1982; Hargadon and Sutton, 1997) technology base makes it easy to fall into competency traps (Levitt and March, 1988; Martines and Kambil, 1999), core rigidities (Leonard-Barton, 1992, 1995), and innovator's dilemmas (Christensen, 1997). This is another reason why product and service development from a concept base grounded in market creation and customer-oriented viewpoints is necessary.

Actors as marketers or engineers decide on concepts by bouncing their own ideas and beliefs off each other through constructive and creative dialog in the product planning and technology planning strategic communities. After the engineers decide on the product and service concepts, they devote themselves to tackling issues (realizing functions that give form to concepts: from the product's basic design to its detailed design, trial production, empirical tests, products, inspection, and so on), and the important viewpoint here is a new concept known as 'knowledge difference.'

Knowledge difference refers to one capability for recognizing three general categories for bringing new concepts to reality through thorough discussions among engineers: (1) the use of existing technologies, (2) improvements in existing technologies, and (3) elements for new development. An important point for engineers is the need for an ability to promptly and accurately obtain a clear picture of the extent elements to be newly developed (difficulty of development, scale of development, and others), and to decide on the development cost and time required for development.[5] Though the use and improvement of existing technology is strongly influenced by path dependency, i.e. technology accumulated thus far, path-dependent elements in new development are relatively weak and is a capability that engineers newly acquire. This capability is built from scratch within the company, or it can also be acquired from mutual learning through strategic links with other companies (both methods require considerable time and expense and are thus not practical in a case like high-tech business where speed is required). However, where the environment undergoes severe change and the need to merge complex technologies or develop new elements carries considerable weight, the knowledge integrating approach through the networked SCs, whereby capability is acquired by quickly accessing many core technologies of other companies while utilizing one's own company's core technology and then integrating them to realize new development, is more effective from the practical aspect. In this book, the author defines the knowledge integrating approach not only as knowledge integration for new product and service development but also as the integration of diverse knowledge required for building a series of business processes such as sales, promotion and advertising, and technical support, aimed at bringing new products to market.

This ability to recognize knowledge differences that accurately identify new development elements as innovation is related to the common knowledge (Star, 1989; Cramton, 2001; Carlile, 2002) shared by engineers. The existence of common knowledge is also necessary for enabling engineers to share and access domain-specific knowledge required by the new product development that they are targeting. In many product and service development cases, SCs are formed with a variety of partner companies, these individual SCs comprising various corporate engineers transcend the boundaries of their organizations, they together share and understand the context, and they then identify elements for new development based on their common knowledge (which includes technical terms and the past experiences and know-how of individual engineers in such fields as basic architecture for several technologies, which constitute both explicit and tacit knowledge that they can all understand). Engineers in the SC share dynamic context, asking a variety of questions such as 'What sort of architecture do we need to bring new product concepts to reality?' or 'What sorts of component technologies and communication protocols do we need to use?'

In this way, common knowledge and knowledge differences help engineers to efficiently and effectively promote knowledge sharing and knowledge integration processes as they work toward building a prototype that reflects the new product concepts and realizing concrete products and services. The product development process through which knowledge differences are recognized and desired product concepts are realized stimulate ideas and behavior among actors from external points of view (realizing new market position dictated by new product concepts) to internal points of view (acquiring new capability in the organization). (Figure 2.4)

To confirm whether or not the new product concepts as the goal for new product development are being realized, it is also important to conduct trial and error tests through experimentation of business models in the actual field (such as experimental services with specific customers or through consortiums and other means) and repeat various hypothetical tests (Hamel and Getz, 2004; Prahalad and Ramaswamy, 2004; Markides, 1999). The construction of a business process is another important issue for bringing new products and services to market in a commercially viable

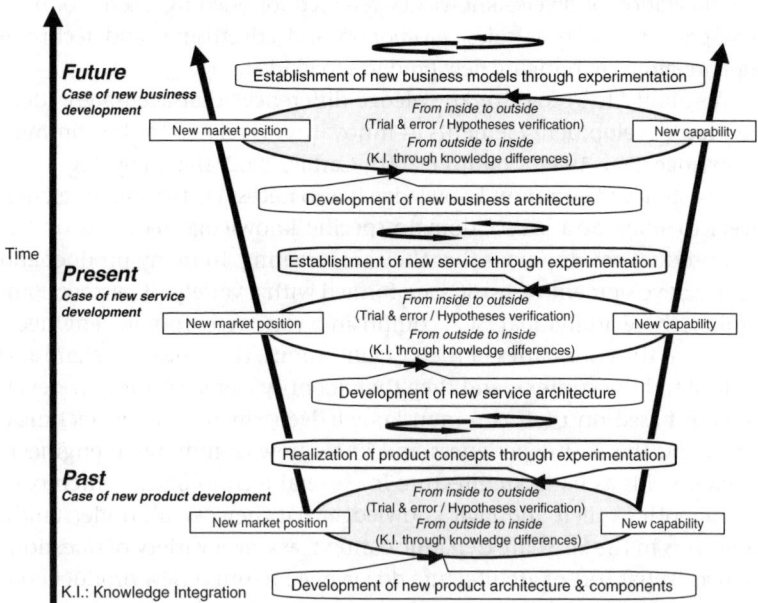

Figure 2.4   Interactive strategy dynamics

manner. Not only knowledge of product development and production but also different types of knowledge such as sales and support (establishing a sales structure and sales channels inside and outside the company, a structure for technical support and after-sale services, as well as employee training) is also required. To this end, the actors must understand and share the different contexts of their specialties, integrate their different knowledge extending across development, production, sales, and support through their networked SCs, and build a solid value chain by establishing a business model that can reliably bring the new products to market. The actors must direct their ideas and behavior from the internal point of view (of acquiring new capability in the organization) to the external point of view (realizing new market position by bringing new products and services to market). (Figure 2.4)

Executing the knowledge integrating approach through the ideas and behavior of actors from the external (market) to the internal (organization) and from the internal (organization) to the external (market) is a vital element in the dynamic view of strategy. Then in their aim to establish their goal of new market position, the actors recognize their knowledge differences, integrate internal and external knowledge through the networked SCs in order to acquire the new organization capabilities that they need, and synthesize the new capabilities with the new market position.

By executing the series of processes in the knowledge integrating approach, the actors must share and integrate the various internal and external knowledge required not only in product development but also in the various business process through the networked SCs that they form. The actors then accumulate new knowledge assets required for bringing the new products and services to market, and build a value chain. As a result, acquisition of new market position and new capabilities can be achieved simultaneously. By spiraling this knowledge integrating approach at each stage along the time axis (spanning past, present, and future), the actors in product development cases are able to realize a dynamic strategy-making process in which they can deliberately acquire market position and new capabilities. (The dynamic view of strategy using the spiraling knowledge integrating approach corresponding to Figure 2.4 is illustrated in Figure 2.5.)

In Chapter 5, the author aims to identify, from longitudinal qualitative research into the IT and multimedia business in Japan over the past 11 years, a theoretical framework of a dynamic strategy-making process that enables the corporation to establish an ongoing advantageous position in a rapidly changing environment.

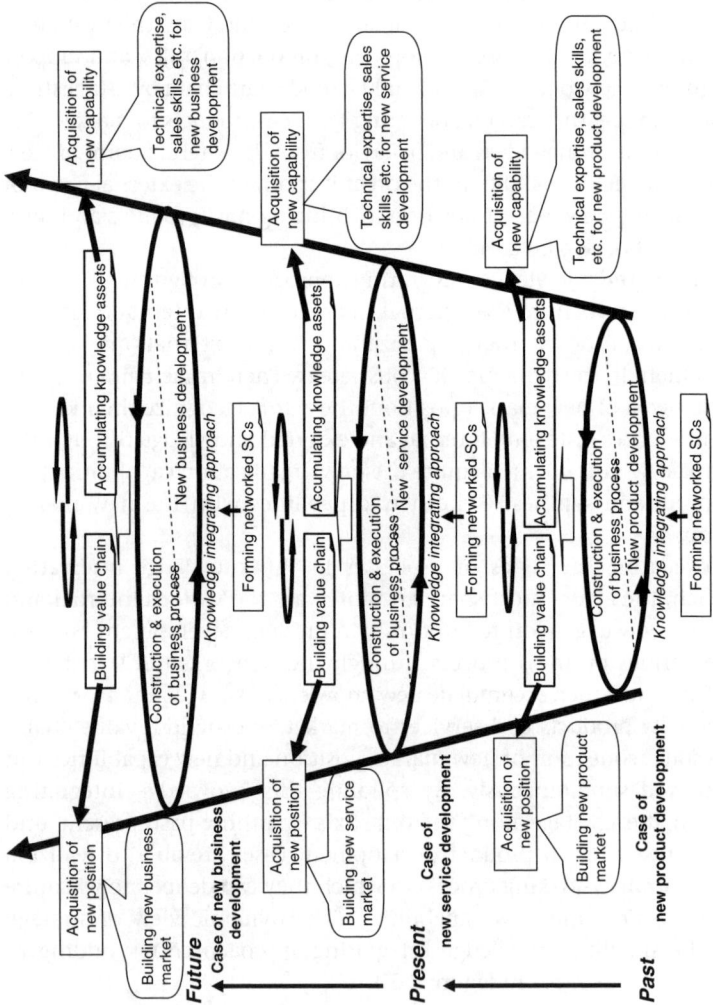

Figure 2.5 Dynamic view of strategy through spiraling knowledge integrating approach

Integrative competences in a SC-based firm

Managing paradox through the creation of SCs

Companies in businesses such as IT, multimedia and communications, which expect to face a complex and uncertain future, need to find new directions in the 21st century in order to dominate the competition. They need to oversee a radical transformation of the basic framework that was used in the past, including existing strategies, structures, cultures, competencies and business processes.

Amid rapid technological change, those businesses seeking competitive advantage in the global market need to expand certain characteristics that are apparently in conflict with one another. Organizations must be flexible enough to promptly cope with the threat of competition from others on one hand, yet they must ensure stable operation on the other hand so that they can continue to grow based on the advantages they enjoy. In other words, each organization is now obliged to face an agility paradox that is brought about by the need for such promptness. Along this line, managers are asked to ensure higher efficiency, foster creativity with innovative management, and think globally while acting locally.

Generally, paradoxical phenomena can be seen internally at every level of the organization. Various paradoxes exist not only in the entire company but also in elements of business units such as divisions and teams. Specifically, we can mention the 'management paradox' (Thompson, 1967) of flexibility and certainty, the 'organizational culture paradox' (Pascale, 1985, 1990) of autonomy of organization members and socialization, and the 'strategic paradox' of deliberate and emergent strategies (Minzberg and Walters, 1985, Mintzberg, 1987).

Paradox is the simultaneous existence of the two inconsistent states mentioned above. Rather than compromising between these two states, vibrant organizations, groups, and individuals change by simultaneously holding both. This duality of coexisting tensions creates an edge of chaos, not a bland halfway point between one extreme and the other. The management of this duality hinges on exploring the tension in a creative way that captures both extremes, thereby capitalizing on the inherent pluralism within the duality.

Lewis (2000) discussed the most central concept of 'paradox.' Paradox is neither a compromise nor a split between competing tensions but is, rather, an awareness of both. Change and pluralism are spurred by these paradoxical tensions and reinforcing cycles. Managing paradox emerges as an opportunity to explore the tensions at the boundary that reveal themselves in terms of mixed messages and contradictions. As a result, managers counteract their tendency to over-rationalize and over-synthesize by simultaneously holding and even exploring opposing views.

If such paradoxes are to provide corporations with the chance for radical transformation, the content and quality of radical transformations must greatly be influenced by the nature of the paradox conditions. Therefore, it may become increasingly important to adopt the point of view that the paradox phenomenon is constructively and positively understood as being the driving force for the radical transformation of corporations (Quinn and Cameron, 1988).

Addressing the need for an integrative framework in the strategy-making process in an attempt to resolve the issue of how business can strike a balance in managing the paradox through surveys of strategic typology by a number of debaters, Hart (1992) proposed an 'integrated strategic theory' as one of the issues to be studied further, arguing that 'the more strength the business has to build multiple strategy-making modes, the better its performance.' The first question of primary importance here is whether it is possible for a business to permit the coexistence of strategy-making modes that are heterogeneous and often contradictory with each other. To be more specific, it is a paradoxical perspective on organizational effectiveness that requires balancing and simultaneous mastery of seemingly contradictory or paradoxical organizational capabilities including decisiveness and reflectivity, broad vision and attention to detail, bold moves and incremental adjustment, and the combination of rational-analytical techniques with intuition. The second point of importance concerns what sort of organization must be built to realize the coexistence of these contradictory strategy-making modes. This is because there is a kind of antimony between strategy and creativeness: the former requires a tightly-coupled organization, whereas the latter is enabled through a loosely-coupled organization.

This section provides an overview of a framework for building integrative competences in a SC-based firm, and analyzes the type of mechanism that the SC-based firm uses to integrate the heterogeneous core competences and strategy formation modes of the traditional organization and the emergent organization possessing paradoxical characteristics through dialectical management.

Innovative corporations of the 21st century require a strategic organization in which a number of SCs possessing several heterogeneous characteristics has been integrated. In other words, innovative corporations merge and integrate in a careful balance the functions of the infrastructure of traditional communities possessing track records extending over many years with the infrastructure of emergent communities possessing new intellectual assets of different qualities (Figure 2.6).

Feature	Emergent Organization	Leadership-based Strategic Community	Traditional Organization
Strategic thinking and behavior	Imagination/Speed/Risk		Discipline/Stability/Certainty
Strategy formation	– Emergent strategy – Entrepreneurial strategy		Deliberate strategy
Leadership	Mainly autonomous/decentralized		Mainly integrated/centralized
Organization structure	– Networked organization – Semi-structured organization		Hierarchical, but Community of Practice also exists
Management method	Strategic community management		– Business process management – Knowledge management
Strategic community formation	Mainly external partners and customers		Mainly outsourcing partners
Community competences	Creation and renewal of new core competences		Upgrading and improvement of existing core competences
Value chain	Concept making – Marketing – Training -Incubation		Commercialization – Manufacturing – Sales – Distribution – After-sale Support

Innovation

Integrative Competences

Company

Emergent Organization

Traditional Organization

Leadership-based Strategic Community

Group of Emergent Communities

Group of Traditional Communities

– Strategic business partners
– Innovative customers, etc.

– Strategic outsourcing partners, etc.

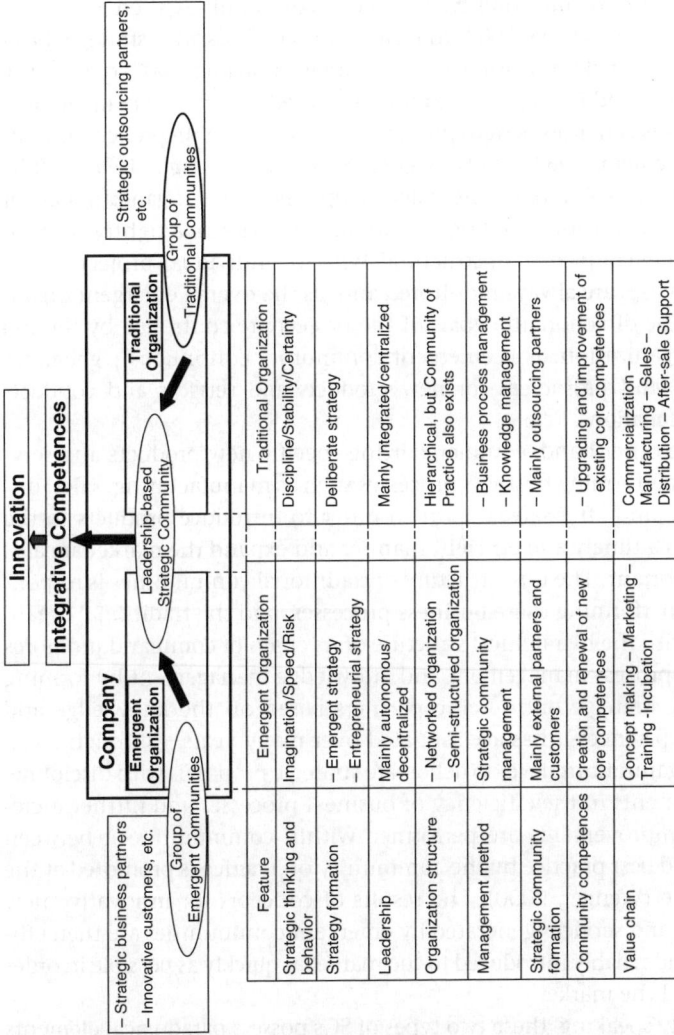

Figure 2.6 Integrative competences of strategic community-based firm
Source: Kodama (2004).

Emergent communities are constantly able to create the sort of new community knowledge and community competences capable of generating concepts for new business models (new products, services, and business frameworks) based on imagination and creativity for innovation in environments of uncertainty. Emergent communities then utilize SC management (Kodama, 2003) to form a cluster of SCs with strategic business partners including innovative customers (Kodama, 2002) outside the corporation and incorporate external knowledge and core competences in a high-risk environment to promote an emergent, entrepreneurial strategy (Burgelman, 1983; Mintzberg, 1978; Mintzberg *et al.*, 1998). While emergent organizations internally adopt network organizational or autonomous decentralized organizational behavior of a tightly coupled and loosely-coupled semi-structural type for individual projects, business activities are always monitored and, as the overall emergent organization, the direction and goals of the project are controlled by the top of the organization. This emergent community continuously generates concepts and prototypes for new products and services and conducts many incubations.

On the other hand, commercializing specific new products and services and performing business processes such as manufacturing, sales, distribution, and after-sale support in order to introduce products to the market in a timely and efficient manner and expand the market are also very important. The infrastructure of traditional communities is responsible for performing these business processes, and the traditional organization with the hierarchical structure of its chain of command promotes business process management and knowledge management by forming SCs with strategic outsourcing partners based on the knowledge and core competences it has accumulated over many years. Although traditional organizations develop deliberate strategic proposals with discipline, improvements in the efficiency of business processes and further incremental improvements are performed within communities or between them, and best practice by the community of practice is promoted at the workplace (Wenger, 2000). The results of concepts for innovative new products and services generated by emergent communities are then efficiently and reliably introduced to the market as quickly as possible in order to expand the market.

Roughly speaking, these two types of SCs possess paradoxical elements that pursue creativity and autonomy on the one hand and efficiency and control on the other, causing struggles and conflicts to constantly occur between both organizations within the corporation. These elements become obstacles to the merging and integration of community knowledge and community competences of both communities. However, this integration is promoted by the LSC discussed above.

The LSC is formed by the community leaders Chief Executive Officer ([CEO], directors, department and division managers, project leaders, and others) of all layers (top management of emergent and traditional organizations, middle management, and the management teams, cross-functional teams, and task forces included in these organizations) of the corporation. The role of the LSC is to merge and integrate the community knowledge and community competences in the emergent community and traditional community and then to produce an integrative competences for the corporation overall. To realize this integrative competences, the LSC adopts integrative strategies founded on disciplined imagination (Weick, 1989). In other words, integration is effected by balancing and integrating paradoxical strategies that are creative and emergent while being also planned and deliberate.

In the LSC, problems and issues are thoroughly understood through dialog and discussions among community leaders, and through mutual communication and collaboration, each community leader becomes aware of the roles and value of each other's work. As a result, community leaders are able to transform the various conflicts occurring between them into constructive conflicts.[6] In this process, to draw closer to the mission they are aiming for, each community leader must think about the sort of strategies or tactics they themselves would adopt and the specific actions they would take within those strategies as well as what they themselves could contribute toward innovation in the company. On the other hand, it is important for the CEO which heads the LSC and is the final decision maker to apply top-down leadership in certain cases while actively creating a forum for dialog and discussion within the LSC in order to strengthen links for interactive collaboration among the CEO and community leaders and to maximize the coherence of leadership that each community leader possesses. Then, with the aim to achieve the business goals of innovation, the LSC encourages sympathy and resonation of the values of all community leaders including the CEO (Kodama, 2001), forms a value chain of a solid new business with the integrated synergetic effects of the leadership possessed by each community leader, and is then able to create new customer values.

In this way, the SC-based firm takes advantage of its integrative competences, and sources capable of realizing innovation result from building a platform of resonating values and continuously raising the level of new knowledge creation and core competence through dialectical management

in the internal community centered on the LSC. We will look into the
dynamic process of this SC-based theory of firm later in Chapters 3 and 4.

SC-based firms

The author wish to emphasize that leading companies of the 21st century must be SC-based firms. In other words, the author believes it is important for leading companies to continually produce innovations through the business activities of strategic communities founded on a social vision and corporate value (Figure 2.7). Knowledge, the only significant management resource in society, is created by strategic communities, and the many types of knowledge and core competences inside and outside the company, including customers and strategic partners, are then merged and integrated to produce the integrative competences that become new sources of competitive advantage.

It is important for the leaders (top and middle management) of the corporations that form the SCs to single out new values for innovation with the leaders and customers of strategic partners inside and outside

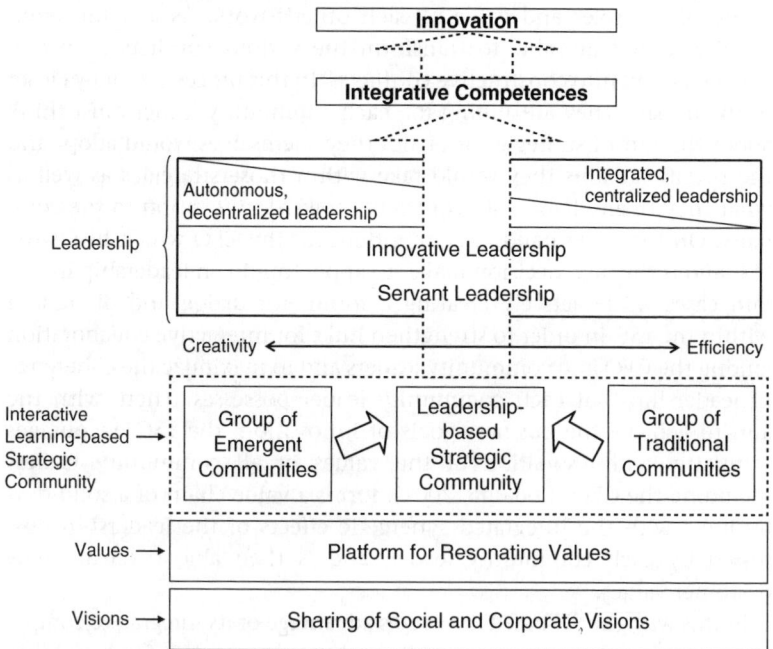

Figure 2.7   Strategic community-based firm
Source: Kodama (2004).

the corporation that would lead to a social vision and a vision or mission that the corporation should aim for. This newly created value is then shared, sympathized, and resonated among all community members through constructive dialog and discussion within the community. To reach this value, the ideas and philosophy of an interactive learning-based SC, in which members study together and learn from each other, are important.

Along with promoting the resonance of values within the community, the community leader must also not only exercise innovative leadership as a leader, coach or even monitor to produce reforms and efficiency in innovative and creative business concepts and business processes, but in turn assume the role of 'servant leadership' (Greanleaf, 1979; Spears, 1995) as well, becoming a listener and recipient, providing continuous support to community members, and working hard to raise the motivation of all members. Community members are thus able to participate in decision making themselves within the community and to deepen their ties within the community through mutual understanding and their noble positions. In this respect, SC-based firms become models not of a leadership supported by rigid old hierarchies but of a new leadership that aims to achieve innovation. This model for leadership at the same time aims to foster growth not only in individuals but also in the groups and organizations that are communities.

The features of the leadership in the aspect of management in the two types of communities can be identified as follows. In order to produce creative business concepts, 'autonomous, decentralized leadership' is mainly required of all community leaders in emergent communities. Concerning multiple groups of autonomous, decentralized communities in general, however, the top leaders of emergent organizations that organically integrate groups of emergent communities must also possess elements of 'integrated, centralized leadership' in order to appropriately steer the community in the direction that the corporation should be aiming for. On the other hand, while 'integrated, centralized leadership' is mainly required of the leaders of traditional communities in order to improve the efficiency of business processes, the top leaders of traditional organizations that organically integrate groups of traditional communities must also possess elements of 'autonomous, decentralized leadership' in order to promote best practice by the community of practice through knowledge management within and among traditional communities.

Members of the LSC consist of members of the top management team including the CEO and the top management in emergent organizations and traditional organizations. In order to pursue imaginative powers, community leaders of the emergent organization discard the hierarchy of experience and place priority on the hierarchy of imaginative power (Hamel, 1996). They tap their imagination to produce diverse creative SCs within and outside the company through autonomous, decentralized leadership, and thereby quickly and continuously give birth to new businesses (new products and services, new strategic alliances, etc.). While imaginative power and related concepts of foresight, creativity, and intuition, however, are extremely important in the area of devising strategies, there also is the strong possibility that excessive imagination resulting from autonomous, decentralized leadership may lead to chaos, a lack of realism, or an underestimation of past track records. The community leaders of emergent organizations must therefore understand appropriate discipline, and community leaders of the autonomous, decentralized leadership type who are equipped with these abilities are required as structural members of the LSC.

The community leaders of traditional organizations, on the other hand, thoroughly pursue efficiency and productivity through an integrated, centralized leadership that emphasizes discipline and process, and actively promote internal process reforms and efficient outsourcing. There is a high possibility, however, that the excessive discipline that results from integrated, centralized leadership may crush the wealth of ideas and buds of invention. Community leaders of the integrated, centralized leadership type capable of understanding and tolerating imagination, creativity, and flexibility are therefore also required as structural members of the LSC.

The LSC comprising community leaders possessing the thinking and behavioral patterns born from these two types of leadership execute a management and decision-making process that focus on disciplined imagination. The CEO and members of top management engage in constructive dialog with community leaders to learn from each other and resolve a variety of opposing views and conflicts. By further analyzing the problem areas and actively resolving the issues, the CEO and top management consciously execute dialectical management aimed at creating higher levels of knowledge and competence. Based on Hegelian philosophy, dialectical management is a method of resolving opposing views and conflicts both inside and outside the organization in a practical manner. In other words, it is a dynamic methodology whereby the new thinking and behavioral patterns of community leaders, incorporating the opposing viewpoints of both sides (such as ideas based on imagination and creativity or realistic understandings based on discipline and efficiency), merge and integrate the paradoxical elements and enable innovation.

This dialectical management merges and integrates the paradoxical leadership elements of autonomous, decentralized leadership and integrated, centralized leadership in a skillful balance, enabling the birth of a new leadership that adheres to disciplined imagination.

The role of the CEO in the LSC is to act as a catalyst for transforming conflicts with the community leaders of emergent organizations and the community leaders of traditional organizations into constructive conflicts and make final decisions on important matters. To this end, the CEO himself or herself engaged in repeated dialog with the community leaders of middle management and actively promoted the sharing, sympathizing, and resonance of values toward the mission that company should be aiming for. The CEO also performed specific actions soliciting the cooperation and assistance of the community leaders of traditional organizations when the community leaders of emergent organizations clashed over problems in individual issues, becoming engaged in the building and ongoing maintenance of the LSC.

As seen above, the elements of autonomous, decentralized leadership and integrated, centralized leadership are well balanced in an LSC that is positioned in the higher ranks of management in a corporation. The CEO and many community leaders exercise a coherent leadership (that is dialectical leadership mentioned above) toward obtaining the integrative competences of the corporation that targets both creativity and efficiency in business. By merging and integrating the community competences and strategy formation mode of multiple groups of communities, they also generate new community competences that become the source of innovation, enabling them to form new business models founded on new value chains.

3
Dialectical Management in a Large Corporation: The Case of Innovation at NTT DoCoMo

This chapter describes SC management that can be implemented by large established companies through the creation of a variety of strategic business communities. The author focuses in particular on the case of NTT DoCoMo, Inc., Japan's largest mobile telecommunications carrier, which has utilized SC management principles in their efforts to cultivate and expand the mobile Internet market in Japan over roughly the past seven years.

This chapter also deals with the development of an emerging mobile internet and multimedia market spawned by the creation of SCs supported by SCs consisting of informal in-house organizations and diverse strategic heterogeneous alliances with outside firms including customers, and elucidates SC management as an effective methodology aimed at strategic innovation conducted by major enterprises.

Current condition of mobile communication services in Japan and DoCoMo's radical change

The first generation of car and mobile phone services to appear in Japan was the analog car phone service that was introduced in 1979. The second generation was the digital services commercialized in 1993. Since then, the introduction of terminal sales (rather than rentals), lower charges and other measures resulted in an extremely rapid increase in the number of mobile phone subscribers (Figure 3.1). In March 2000, this number surpassed the number of fixed line subscribers. The rapid growth of the mobile communications market centered mainly on voice communications. However, since population places limits on the penetration of voice communications, DoCoMo not only further strengthened its existing

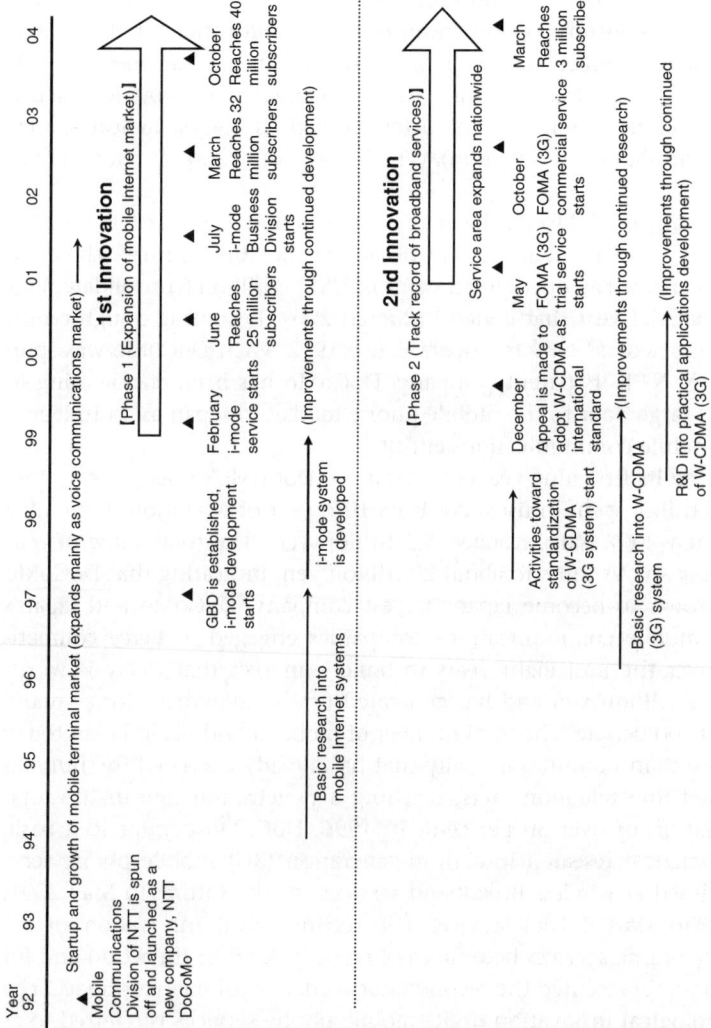

Startup and growth of mobile terminal market (expands mainly as voice communications market) →

1st Innovation

[Phase 1 (Expansion of mobile Internet market)]

Year												
92	93	94	95	96	97	98	99	00	01	02	03	04

Mobile Communications Division of NTT is spun off and launched as a new company, NTT DoCoMo

GBD is established, i-mode development starts

February i-mode service starts

June Reaches 25 million subscribers

July i-mode Business Division starts

March Reaches 32 million subscribers

October Reaches 40 million subscribers

Basic research into mobile Internet systems

i-mode system is developed

(Improvements through continued development)

2nd Innovation

[Phase 2 (Track record of broadband services)]

Service area expands nationwide

December Appeal is made to adopt W-CDMA as international standard

May FOMA (3G) trial service starts

October FOMA (3G) commercial service starts

March Reaches 3 million subscribers

Activities toward standardization of W-CDMA (3G system) start

(Improvements through continued research)

Basic research into W-CDMA (3G) system

R&D into practical applications development of W-CDMA (3G)

(Improvements through continued applications development)

Figure 3.1 Transition in innovation at DoCoMo

voice communications services but also launched a basic strategy for cultivating a second area of growth by expanding traffic in the area of non-voice communications. The i-mode service, which merges mobile phone and Internet services, represents the first step in this direction. By December 2003, the number of subscribers surpassed the 40 million mark, contributing significantly to the cultivation of the mobile multimedia market. This explosive growth in the Japanese mobile Internet market resulting from the development and provision of this i-mode service has for DoCoMo represented its biggest radical change (discontinuous transformation). (The i-mode innovation is referred to as Phase 1.)

In Japan, DoCoMo has been evaluated as one of the fastest growing businesses to emerge in the last decade of the 20th century. The company registered an operating income of US$7.3 billion (consolidated) for the financial year that ended in March 2001, becoming a high-return company second only to Toyota. Since 1992 when DoCoMo was spun off from NTT, its parent company, DoCoMo has been endeavoring to open a large door to the mobile phone market in Japan as an independent mobile communications entity.

During its first nine years of operation, DoCoMo's sales grew 12 fold to 4.6 trillion yen. In fiscal 2001, its 10th year of operation that ended in March 2002, sales reached 5.2 trillion yen. The total value of outstanding shares came to about 20 trillion yen, indicating that DoCoMo had grown to become Japans largest company. DoCoMo and Japan's other mobile communications companies engaged in fierce competition over the past eight years to build a market that today is worth about 7 trillion yen and has generated new employment for as many as 800,000 people. The total number of mobile handsets in Japan today is more than 60 million, a tally that has already exceeded the number of fixed line telephone sets, reaching a penetration rate in the total population of over 50 per cent. In 1996, DoCoMo commenced basic and practical research into third-generation (3G) mobile phone services aimed at wireless broadband services for the future. In May 2001, DoCoMo started trial service. The technological innovation of 3G mobile phone services became the first of its kind in the world and for DoCoMo represented the second radical change following i-mode. (The technological innovation of 3G mobile phone services is referred to as Phase 2.)

In this case study, the author shall next analyze in detail the mechanisms of radical change involved in Phases 1 and 2 from the perspective of DoCoMo's strategies, organizational structure, processes and other aspects.

i-mode Revolution: creation of a mobile Internet market in Japan (Phase 1)

Creating a new mobile market

Data communication over mobile phones has contributed to major progress in the feasibility and availability of mobile computing. The Internet access technology implemented over mobile phones represented by DoCoMo's i-mode service has stimulated an evolution from today's mobile phones into portable terminals. Japan reportedly outperforms America and European countries in the use of mobile Internet technology by two to three years. American journalists also suggested that the wireless Internet service that has become so popular among the Japanese would certainly spread around the world (*Business Week*, 2000).

Mr Oboshi, who was CEO of the company in 1997, predicted that the growth curve reflecting the increase in the number of subscribers of mobile phones in terms of voice communications would become saturated in the near future. As a result, he felt a sense of impending crisis over the returns and growth of DoCoMo. Focus was placed on the data communications market that would eventually take over the voice communications market.

Formation of a new organization directed by top management

To cultivate a market for this service, Mr Oboshi led the team that would build a new organization for planning new services. In January 1997, Mr Enoki, who was serving as Corporate Business Director at the time (currently senior vice president, senior manager of the Gateway Business Department), was appointed by Mr Oboshi to develop non-voice communication services over mobile phones targeting general users. Mr. Oboshi then assigned Mr Enoki to the task of building a new organization by means of recruiting human resources within or outside the company, and empowered him (with personnel and financial management) to start up the new service.

With diverse and talented human resources recruited from both within and outside the company, Mr Enoki started a new project (responsible for the Gateway Business) staffed by some 10 persons, a unit that by August 1997 had evolved into the Gateway Business Department (GBD) staffed by 70 employees. The GBD was then at working developing a new service dubbed 'i-mode.'

Strategies at the GBD, an emergent organization

GBD's tasks and actions aimed at implementing i-mode service

Positive feedback of the elements through which IPs would continuously provide useful content to end-users of i-mode-compliant mobile phones was urgently needed for the business model that was planned for successful i-mode service.[1] This model was designed to expand the number of end users as well as enhance the content provided by IPs.

One of the tasks aimed at implementing this business model was to develop easy-to-use i-mode-compliant mobile phones and to develop the network system (i-mode servers and other hardware) that would deliver content (*NTT DoCoMo Technical Journal*, 1999). The second task was a software-based effort to obtain IPs with content that would attract end users.

To solve those two hardware and software tasks and implement the new service, Mr Enoki felt that it was essential to integrate knowledge and core competences that could generate new business models based on the new concepts and viewpoints of the diverse human resources of the GBD, its years of experience with existing organizations within DoCoMo other than the GBD, and the intellectual assets inherent in the IPs which were external customers of DoCoMo. It was then apparent that the integrative competences, i.e. the heterogeneous knowledge and core competences of these emergent organizations and traditional organizations, would become important elements capable of building a new business model for i-mode services.

Consequently, Mr Enoki endeavored to form a strategic business community with the business division managers, department managers, project leaders and others in DoCoMo's traditional organizations centered around the GBD and to form a SC with IPs who were customers of DoCoMo. As a result, DoCoMo overcame the hardware and software problems through the integration of new knowledge and competence born out of the formation of these communities, and created the business model for i-mode service capable of establishing positive feedback of such successful elements.

GBD's promotion of SC management (Figure 3.2)

Mr Enoki and Mr Natsuno, who led the business strategy, felt that a number of measures had to be implemented so that end users could enjoy the advantage of subscribing to i-mode to its maximum extent in order to trigger an explosive growth of the i-mode service.

The biggest issue facing the GBD leading up to the start of the i-mode service was how to find and establish ties with IPs that could provide useful content. This was an issue to be tackled by the GBD Content Planning Project. The strategy elaborated by Ms Matsunaga and Mr Natsuno, who both led the Project, was to establish win-win relationships between DoCoMo and the IPs (Natsuno, 2000).

An important factor in the establishment of win–win relationships was the idea that both IPs and DoCoMo would think and behave in a manner of equal partnership, sharing the risks and profits, instead of the behavior of DoCoMo simply purchasing content from certain IPs or charging IPs with tenant fees when providing a lineup of i-mode content. As a solution, DoCoMo encouraged IPs to create their own content and provided them with the platform used in establishing a 'content service charge collection agency system[2]' to allow users to earn profits from providing their own services.

Ms Matsunaga and Mr Natsuno explained the concept of a win–win relationship to many IP personnel, successfully obtained their understanding, and aroused sympathy for the concept. As a result, the value systems of both DoCoMo and the IPs were unified, and a community aiming to start a new business was formed. The common questions in this community concerned the content that would be attractive to end users and the service fees they could charge. Quick delivery, accuracy, and continuity of content and end user satisfaction were discussed, and content that was considered to be consistently attractive to end users was created.

The GBD Content Planning Project working around Ms Matsunaga and Mr Natsuno developed a concept for the i-mode business model that would win the satisfaction of many IPs and signed up many leading businesses (engaged in mobile banking, credit cards, airlines, hotels, news sources, magazines and so on) in quick succession. At the start of the service in February 1999, 67 IPs had been signed up as i-mode service providers.

Following the start of service, the Project's focus turned to three strategies aimed at promoting the i-mode service. The first was the 'portal strategy' for developing new, useful content for the i-mode service. The second was the 'terminal strategy' with the aim to develop new i-mode mobile phone terminals including add-on features. And the third was the 'platform strategy' to break ground for i-mode users using platforms other than mobile terminals. Furthermore, these three business strategies were interactive with each other, thus capable of triggering a major synergy depending on the strategy concerned. In order to promote these business strategies, an important task was to proceed with the strategic alliance with many outside partners so as to yield practicable results.

After the i-mode service was launched in February 1999, the GBD formed the communities in succession through strategic alliances with outside partners in order to sign up end users in the early stage of the project. The first step was to form a 'portal community' to act as the core of the portal strategy and enhance the details of the i-mode portal operated by DoCoMo through which diverse risks and interests would be shared with IPs while enhancing the value of the content so as to provide new values for the end user. In addition, the advertisement delivery service was promoted on the i-mode portal, and a top-flight financial service was also implemented at the birth of the net-based banking business. This strategy was recognized as an important positioning of services prior to the launch of i-mode sales.

The second step was to form a 'technical community' linked with terminal manufacturers that would form the core of the terminal strategy. This strategy was intended to trigger new demand for end-user terminals and to motivate users to replace their terminals by periodically adding new features to i-mode mobile phones. For IPs, the development of new mobile phones (such as JAVA-compliant phones) opened the possibility that content could be developed under new applications with the advantage of attracting new end users. DoCoMo could also enjoy an increase of new revenue from increased communications traffic due to a greater penetration of mobile phones equipped with new features.

The third step was to form a 'platform community' to serve as the core of the platform strategy in order to expand the scope of i-mode availability. Combining i-mode mobile phones with game machines, car navigation systems and other platforms would further expand i-mode availability.

Thanks to the emergent strategy which continuously put forward three strategies on an individual organization basis, the GBD continued to acquire new end users and IPs as customers in quick succession. Figure 3.2 shows the practicable measures arranged in time series regarding the three business strategies proposed by the GBD.

Each project team in the GBD that was working to promote strategic tie-ups with outside partners continued to proceed with their business through prompt decision-making and expeditious activities as though they were small venture businesses themselves. The relationship between and within project teams and projects was therefore flexible and autonomous, with the project team itself being loose-coupling in nature.

On the other hand, each project team leader continued to fulfill new concepts, strategies and tactics adopted by strategic concepts and the innovative leadership of Mr Enoki, the top leader of the GBD. At the same time, new strategies and tactics that emerged from the close tie-ups with project leaders were also implemented. Meanwhile, Mr Enoki and all GBD members shared the vision and value systems that aimed to achieve the primary mission of promoting the i-mode service.

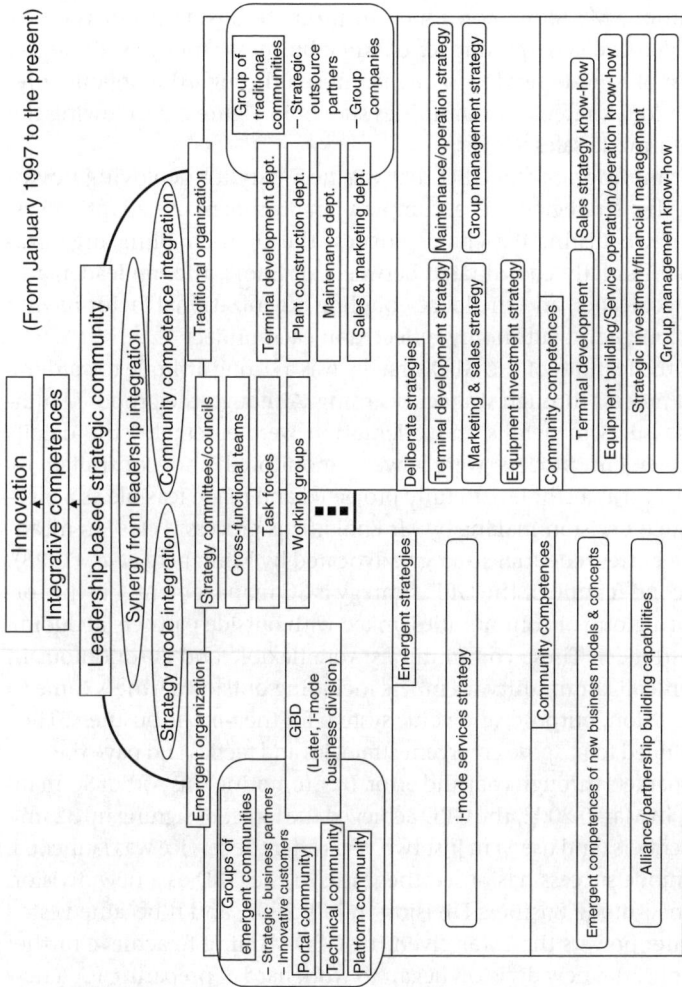

Figure 3.2 DoCoMo integrative competences in FOMA service (Phase 1)
Source: Kodama (2004).

Although the GBD had, as a whole, strong emergent factors on a strategic basis, the intentional and deliberate strategic factors of each project leader, and the tight-coupling factors linking each project leader under Mr Enoki, eventually allowed the i-mode business model to be combined with practical businesses in an intentional and feasible manner.

In addition, Mr Enoki continued to promote businesses of the sort that enabled the synergy impact of three business strategies aiming at expansion of i-mode service to be maximized through the organic integration of four strategic communities shown in Figure 3.2 following the launch of i-mode sales.

The organization of the GBD that was necessary for deploying novice and complex strategies was a complex, environmentally adaptive system with two distinctive characteristics: the tight-coupling organizational factor strictly coordinated between Mr Enoki, the top leader, and each project leader, and the loose-coupling organizational factor having both flexibility and autonomy reflected in each project.

One of the features of the GBD strategy was a strong attitude toward the emergent process through strategic learning. Although the proposed individual measures in details and orientation were emergent, the details of the emergent process were always monitored and controlled by Mr Enoki, and as a whole, carefully projected and made feasible as a business through decision-making by Mr Enoki. This process is close in meaning to the entrepreneurial strategy advocated by Mintzberg *et al.* (1998).

The second feature of the GBD strategy is SC management, i.e. the formation of a group of communities linked with outside partners including IPs as customers. These communities were flexible and autonomous in nature, and all community members including outside partners came to share the vision, purpose, and value system for the i-mode business. They also continued to propose emergent strategies and tactics and pave the way for new markets through trial and error. By promoting this sort of SC management, in March 2002, the GBD achieved the target of signing up 32 million subscribers (end users) in just two years after the service was launched.

This i-mode success has raised the status of the GBD as a new division named the i-mode Business Division in July 2001, and it became vested with greater powers than was given the GBD. Aiming to achieve further innovations, the new division began to work hard at preparing for a new i-mode service known as IMT-2000, a 3G mobile service that would be marketed under the FOMA (Freedom Of Mobile multimedia Access) Service brand name, DoCoMo's 3G mobile communications service. Among the services being planned, high-speed data transmission as a trial i-mode service was launched in March 2001, and the world's first moving picture clipping service for mobile phones was slated to start in November 2001.

It is not imaginable, however, that an explosive diffusion of the i-mode service shown in Figure 3.2 could be triggered only with the action carried out by no more than 70 members of the GBD organization alone. The reason behind the success was that the GBD, including the CEO, and the leaders of the traditional organizations (hereafter referred to as 'community leaders') formed an LSC and initiated a deliberate strategy aimed at diffusing the i-mode by virtue of the traditional organizations. With these two different strategies integrated by two different organizations, a radical and discontinuous transformation was fulfilled throughout the entire GBD organization.

Building integrative competences at DoCoMo via LSCs

Eliminating conflicts through mutual learning within LSCs

Coordination among the community leaders of the development and technical departments of traditional organizations was required in order to realize i-mode service business models and develop i-mode-compliant mobile phones and network systems. At the outset, conflicts arose out of differences of concept or opinions between the GBD and other departments, or voices within the company expressed objections to the service. To overcome the various conflicts arising between the GBD and the traditional organizations, with the support of Mr Oboshi, the CEO, Mr Enoki led the team at the forefront of coordination and consensus building efforts through persistent dialog and collaboration with the departments concerned. Mr Enoki strove to leverage such conflicts as a catalyst for constructive and productive dialog and discussions. The strong motivation of professionals assembled at the GBD, staking their pride on the success of the i-mode service, and the innovative leadership of Mr Enoki to orchestrate the operation of GBD members was the motivating force that led the traditional organizations.

The i-mode development structure within DoCoMo used a pattern that was completely different from DoCoMo's conventional development structure. The SCs made up of the GBD and traditional organizations in Figure 3.2 formed multilayered, hierarchically networked SCs as shown in Figure 3.3. Though the existing development structure that was used for service development (incremental technology development for improving existing services) prior to the i-mode service was sufficient, it was difficult to use the development structure of existing traditional organizations to develop services with service concepts and

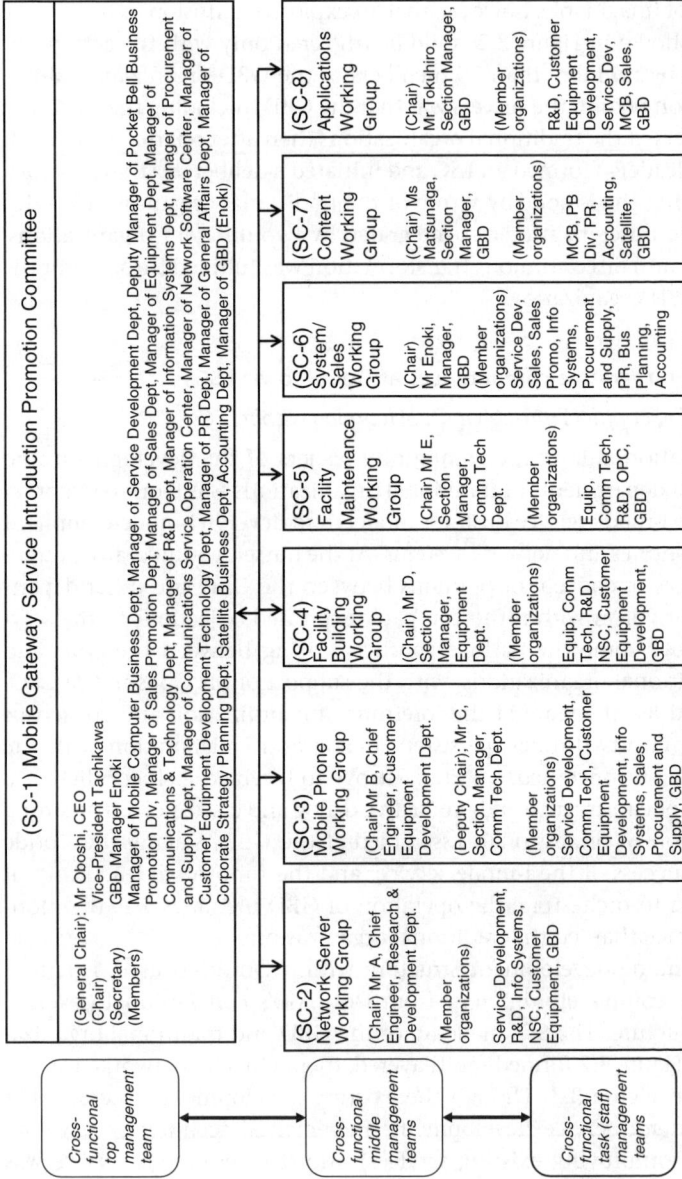

	(SC-1) Mobile Gateway Service Introduction Promotion Committee						
	(General Chair): Mr Oboshi, CEO (Chair) Vice-President Tachikawa (Secretary) GBD Manager Enoki (Members) Manager of Mobile Computer Business Dept, Manager of Service Development Dept, Deputy Manager of Pocket Bell Business Promotion Div, Manager of Sales Promotion Dept, Manager of Sales Dept, Manager of Equipment Dept, Manager of Communications & Technology Dept, Manager of R&D Dept, Manager of Information Systems Dept, Manager of Procurement and Supply Dept, Manager of Communications Service Operation Center, Manager of Network Software Center, Manager of Customer Equipment Development Technology Dept, Manager of PR Dept, Manager of General Affairs Dept, Manager of Corporate Strategy Planning Dept, Satellite Business Dept, Accounting Dept, Manager of GBD (Enoki)						

(SC-2) Network Server Working Group	(SC-3) Mobile Phone Working Group	(SC-4) Facility Building Working Group	(SC-5) Facility Maintenance Working Group	(SC-6) System/ Sales Working Group	(SC-7) Content Working Group	(SC-8) Applications Working Group
(Chair) Mr A, Chief Engineer, Research & Development Dept.	(Chair)Mr B, Chief Engineer, Customer Equipment Development Dept. (Deputy Chair) Mr C, Section Manager, Comm Tech Dept.	(Chair) Mr D, Section Manager, Equipment Dept.	(Chair) Mr E, Section Manager, Comm Tech Dept.	(Chair) Mr Enoki, Manager, GBD	(Chair) Ms Matsunaga, Section Manager, GBD	(Chair) Mr Tokuhiro, Section Manager, GBD
(Member organizations) Service Development, R&D, Info Systems, NSC, Customer Equipment, GBD	(Member organizations) Service Development, Comm Tech, Customer Equipment Development, Info Systems, Sales, Procurement and Supply, GBD	(Member organizations) Equip, Comm Tech, R&D, NSC, Customer Equipment Development, GBD	(Member organizations) Equip, Comm Tech, R&D, OPC, GBD	(Member organizations) Service Dev, Sales, Sales Promo, Info Systems, Procurement and Supply, PR, Bus Planning, Accounting	(Member organizations) MCB, PB Div, PR, Accounting, Satellite, GBD	(Member organizations) R&D, Customer Equipment Development, Service Dev, MCB, Sales, GBD

Cross-functional top management team

Cross-functional middle management teams

Cross-functional task (staff) management teams

Note: This chart was generated based on interviews.

Figure 3.3 Multilayered, hierarchically networked SCs within DoCoMo

technology architectures like i-mode that were completely different from conventional mobile phone services.

The reason for the above was that, while the internal structures of development organizations reflected the technology structures or the services that built these structures, when basic technology was being transferred (such as when radical innovation accompanied dramatic changes in the business model or the product and service architecture), the response of the corporation was protected by the existing organizational structure (Henderson and Clark, 1990). In other words, DoCoMo needed new internal coordination. While existing organizations facing major challenges suffered from major limitations in achieving their goals, by forming a network of flexible, organic pragmatic boundaries within the company, DoCoMo was able to take on the challenge of new development that i-mode presented.

The multilayered, hierarchically networked SCs within DoCoMo, illustrated in Figure 3.3, were formed as follows. The cross-functional decision-making team, known as the Mobile Gateway Service Introduction Promotion Committee (SC-1) made up of top management from all divisions, was formed in order to engage in discussions that led to decisions on such matters as the final service architecture for i-mode, development investment, capital investment, development schedule, human resources, selection of development partners, and important strategic alliances with external entities.

A number of SCs was also formed under this final decision-making team (SC-1): the Network Server Working Group (SC-2), Mobile Phone Working Group (SC-3), Facility Building Working Group (SC-4), Facility Maintenance Working Group (SC-5), System/Sales Working Group (SC-6), Content Working Group (SC-7), and the Applications Working Group (SC-8). These SCs were formed as hierarchical structures consisting of middle management and task management teams. They were also organically linked, they shared and integrated the context and knowledge they needed for service development, and as a result, they were able to create knowledge that represented the fruit of new development which was i-mode. (The Introduction Promotion Liaison Meeting is held about once every two months, Working Groups meet regularly or irregularly as issues require, and Working Group leaders meet whenever required.)

Enhancing the motivation of all organizations and employees for the diffusion and growth of i-mode

While the community leaders of all management layers, including the CEO, in the GBD and the traditional organizations sympathized and resonated

the visions and values that would fulfill the mission and bring the
i-mode service to success, the LSC needed to have all employees (community members) involved with the i-mode service understand the mission and values of the LSC activities.

Various strategic communities (concerned with development, technology, facilities, marketing, and content) that were operated by task
forces organized within the company prior to the startup of i-mode sales
were continuously maintained and vitalized. A diverse range of information and knowledge about the reaction of end users, ongoing sales of
mobile phones and services, as well as usability and troubleshooting,
were shared among the personnel involved. Members of the top management themselves strove to enhance the motivation of many employees within individual organizations for the company-wide challenge to
propagate the growth of i-mode service throughout Japan and to stimulate a revolution in the awareness of employees.

As one of the commitments addressed by the LSC, the community that
links the GBD and the content team of the nationwide traditional organizations allowed information and knowledge about the IP acquisition
strategy, tactics and guidelines to be shared among the community members, and the motivation for the inducement of IPs was increasingly
strengthened. For steady and explosive growth of the i-mode service,
imminently required was a nationwide inducement campaign aimed at IPs
that could provide useful content. To cope with the impending need, the
GBD periodically held editorial meetings attended by personnel scattered
across the country in charge of content. The GBD instructed these personnel responsible for content to interpret the common content editing standard proposed by the GBD for i-mode and enabled the same information
and knowledge to be shared among all community members, thus allowing the members involved to proceed with the IP inducement strategy. The
understanding of the i-mode service concept by the personnel concerned
plus the sharing of the value system was subsequently concentrated on the
motivational power of the positive cycle of increasing returns that evolved
from the increase of attractive IPs to the increase of end users, and further to increase the number of IPs offering more attractive content.

Promoting the deliberate strategy and business process management of the traditional organization

In response to the emergent strategy and SC management proposed by
the GBD, the traditional organization steadily promoted sales activities,
equipment building and maintenance systems for the growing number
of i-mode users as business process management and a deliberate strategy.

On the other hand, DoCoMo also actively formed a SC with strategic outsourcing partners and group companies as a means of implementing this promotion.

First, the content teams of the traditional organizations steadily continued to acquire more IPs based on the IP strategy proposed by the GBD with a view to conducting a nationwide IP inducement campaign. Secondly, with the upgrades of i-mode mobile phones and the release of new products, the terminal development departments of the traditional organizations gradually determined the terminal specifications against the functional requirements requested by the GBD, and carried out the guidance and coordination for the terminal manufacturers as strategic outsourcing partners in accordance with the schedule for the sale of terminals. Thirdly, the sales departments of the traditional organizations, including the terminal sales branches at the forefront of marketing, identified sales objectives to cope with the move of nationwide sales drive for i-mode mobile phones and, with the SC with Group companies and external sales outlets, were committed to sales activity.

Finally, to cope with the increasing number of end users associated with various network facilities typically represented by the i-mode server, the facility and maintenance departments of the traditional organizations and the SC with Group companies fulfilled prompt and precise measures taken for failures and troubles arising in connection with subscribers' equipment. In particular, in the event of faults in the i-mode service (due to errors in software built in the i-mode center facility) in March and April 2000, the traditional organization promptly increased capacity for the subscribers to the i-mode center, launched the i-mode Service Stability Project, and continued to enhance the reliability of the service on an organizational basis. Further progress toward the thorough introduction of IT in internal corporate operations, improving efficiency in business processes in such areas as sales management systems, maintenance systems, and network operation systems and so on, has improved all business processes. In particular, total services of added value such as the prompt provision of services (that can be used immediately following application), timely version upgrade information, prompt response in the event of breakdowns, and courteous customer service, are being provided to end users in order to continually raise the value of i-mode services.

With the traditional organization promoting a deliberate strategy and business process management in this manner, the formation of a SC with strategic outsourcing partners and Group companies led to organizational and efficiency improvements, as well as consolidation of the business process involving IP acquisition, terminal development, sales, equipment and maintenance, in order to move toward the steady implementation of the strategies and tactics created by the emergent strategy and SC management of the GBD as daily tasks. In addition, knowledge management based on the community of practice is promoted in the traditional organization, and cases of improvements based on best practice, such as greater thoroughness in the sharing of information and organizational horizontal development, were also actively promoted.

Although such organizational behavior entails incremental changes, it constituted a major contribution, together with the strategies and tactics continuously put forward by the GBD, to the impressive growth of the i-mode market. Under a scenario in which a certain result was to be achieved within a certain period of time from the startup to the diffusion of the i-mode service, the LSC including the CEO felt that the time constraints and the results were of equally important positioning. The community leaders of the LSC also consciously continued to follow the methodology of integrating the emergent strategy of their own organization with the deliberate strategy of the traditional organization.

The integration of the strategic modes of these two paradoxical SCs with the community competences enabled DoCoMo to acquire their solid leading edge in the emergent market called the mobile Internet market and fulfill a major discontinuous transformation.

The GBD created a new core competence through the formation of diverse outside SCs amid the challenging organizational culture, and continuously put forward the emergent and creative measures targeted at long-term innovation. In the traditional organizations, on the other hand, by improvement and modification of the core competence built over years of performance, the GBD continued to carry out the planned measures aimed at short-term efficiency with emphasis on stability and control maintained through the traditional and consistent organizational culture. The LSC at DoCoMo consciously caused internally inconsistent paradoxical organizations, strategies, culture, and competence to be indwelled within the company, and let these different systems become concurrently activated and integrated at a time so as to allow the company-wide integrated competences to be enhanced.

3G Revolution (Phase 2): creation of broadband mobile services in Japan

Strategic positioning of FOMA service

On 30 May 2001, DoCoMo became the first mobile phone carrier in the world to launch trial services for 3G mobile communications, the

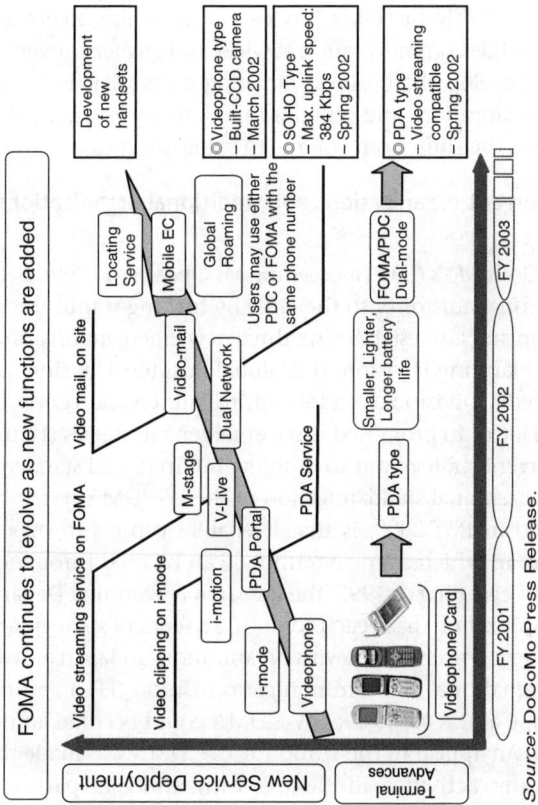

Figure 3.4 New mobile multimedia services by FOMA
Source: DoCoMo Press Release.

IMT-2000 (International Mobile Telecommunications – 2000), being marketed under the name FOMA Service (Figure 3.4). The FOMA Service, which maximizes high-speed, high-capacity data transfer, has been positioned to play a central role aimed at dramatically expanding the international mobile multimedia market. The various services, such as more advanced i-mode service, videophone service, video distribution, music distribution, global roaming and mobile commerce that the FOMA Service will provide to business, government, and consumers, will greatly expand the mobile multimedia service. With the FOMA Service, DoCoMo aims to bring higher added value to mobile communication services and greater convenience to customers, and develop the business targeting users that demand high-speed data communications and superior functionality. Indeed, FOMA is a service that makes the shift 'from volume to value' practical.

Integrating emergent organizations and traditional organizations via the LSC

Mr Tachikawa, DoCoMo's CEO (succeeding Mr Oboshi in 1999), delegated more organizational authority to the GBD by turning it into the i-mode Business Division and also establishing three new emergent organizations: the Research & Planning Division, the Global Business Division, and the Mobile Multimedia Division. In addition, to launch the FOMA Service from nothing, DoCoMo promoted three emergent strategies (Figure 3.5).

The first emergent strategy was to promote international standards. The merit of the international standardization of the W-CDMA system, one of the systems used in IMT-2000, is that it enables carriers to offer global roaming services in which a single terminal can be used throughout the world. Since the beginning of 1997, the Research & Planning Department, an emergent organization, has been promoting a series of strategic alliances by forming strategic communities with organizations in Japan and abroad, such as the International Telecommunication Union (ITU) and telecom carriers in Europe and Asia, so that W-CDMA could become an international standard. An appeal to the world for W-CDMA was made through consensus-forming activities in tie-ups with strategic partners, and W-CDMA was ultimately recommended as a technical standard at the ITU in December 1999. At the same time, joint research, joint trial development, joint experiments and other basic research aimed at making W-CDMA practical were actively conducted by forming a strategic community with partners (Ericsson, Nokia, Motorola, Lucent Technologies, NEC, Fujitsu, Matsushita Communication Industrial, Mitsubishi Electric, and others) engaged in R&D to standardize the system. On the other hand, the Practical Development Department and the Procurement and Supply

Department, which are also emergent organizations, established detailed technical specifications aimed at developing high-quality, low-cost commercial devices and procuring strategic materials for these devices, as required in making the FOMA Service a reality, based on the results of joint research (basic research know-how such as standardized communications infrastructure equipment or mobile handsets) conducted by the emergent organizations. These Divisions also deliberately used competitive bidding (conducting comprehensive assessments in such areas as technology, quality, price, and long-term maintenance structure) to select strategic vendors. And concerning the business processes of manufacturing commercial products, building equipment, and maintenance, a W-CDMA infrastructure was steadily built by forming a SC with strategic outsourcing partners.

The second emergent strategy was to promote international business. This strategy was designed to actively develop the i-mode and FOMA Service business overseas. Specifically, this strategy aimed to stimulate new communications demand by expanding global roaming and the licensing business developed from DoCoMo's service know-how into overseas markets. To this end, the Global Business Division, another emergent organization, has been investing capital and establishing a series of alliances since the beginning of 1999 aimed at forming SCs with overseas carriers (such as KPN Mobile, Hutchinson 3G UK, AT&T Wireless, and KG Telecom). In sync with this global tie-up strategy, the Finance Department, a traditional organization, produced a long-term deliberate funds procurement strategy. One of the steps in this strategy was to list the company on the London Stock Exchange and the New York Stock Exchange so that funds procured on overseas capital markets could support the development of the emergent organizations' global strategies. In another step, the Practical Development Department, another traditional organization, promoted the formation of SCs with strategic equipment vendors to conduct technical studies into various customization schemes aimed at the overseas introduction of communications infrastructures and mobile handsets in order to develop the technical merits of i-mode and the FOMA Service in overseas markets. In the first results of these efforts, KPN Mobile, KPN Orange, and E-Plus launched i-mode service initially in Germany, the Netherlands, and Belgium in spring 2002, and W-CDMA service is being launched as the next step. AT&T Wireless launched 'm-mode,' a version of i-mode, in 2003.

The third emergent strategy was to promote new mobile multimedia services. In this strategy, the i-mode Business Division and the Mobile Multimedia Division generated a series of new service concepts such as the High-speed i-mode Service, Videophone Service, Multi Call Service, Video Distribution Service, Music Distribution Service, PDA Portal Service, Position and ITS Service, and Mobile e-commerce. In this emergent strategy, completely new markets are created through the formation of SCs with content providers who are customers, innovative customers, and strategic partners (Figure 3.4). Market viability of the new services is confirmed by the emergent organizations through a process of concept making, marketing, trial development, and incubation, and the traditional organizations (the Practical Development Department, Plant Department, Maintenance Department, Marketing Department, and others) commercialize these services in a timely manner. The traditional organizations promoted a series of efficient business management cycles by establishing efficient and highly accurate equipment investment plans to meet new service demand forecasts, introducing network operation systems to maintain high-quality service, and establishing nationwide sales, maintenance, and after-sale support systems.

Innovations resulting from integrative competences generated by the LSC for DoCoMo

The LSC, on the other hand, through task forces, working groups, various types of counsels and strategic committees and other bodies for each task including marketing, research, practical development, sales, equipment, investment, and maintenance services (Figure 3.5), held discussions and made decisions on these three emergent strategies including when and what sort of strategies, tactics, groups, and resources should be used for the deliberate strategies that support these emergent strategies. There were also measures that were rejected by final decisions within this LSC, strategies and tactics with real potential to become buds of innovation were selected in thorough dialogs and discussions among community leaders, and they were then put into specific action through the initiative of all the community leaders.

At the same time, while the leadership of the top management promotes the activities of the LSC made up of the group of emergent organizations and the group of traditional organizations, empowerment aimed at promoting LSC activities was also granted to middle management which consisted of people with practical business experience. An understanding of mutual tasks and values was sympathized and resonated among community leaders in the LSC with the aim of achieving the mission, and a relativity of mutual instruction and learning was built.

Top management promptly made final decisions on vital matters after conducting dialogs and discussions through groups such as the anagement

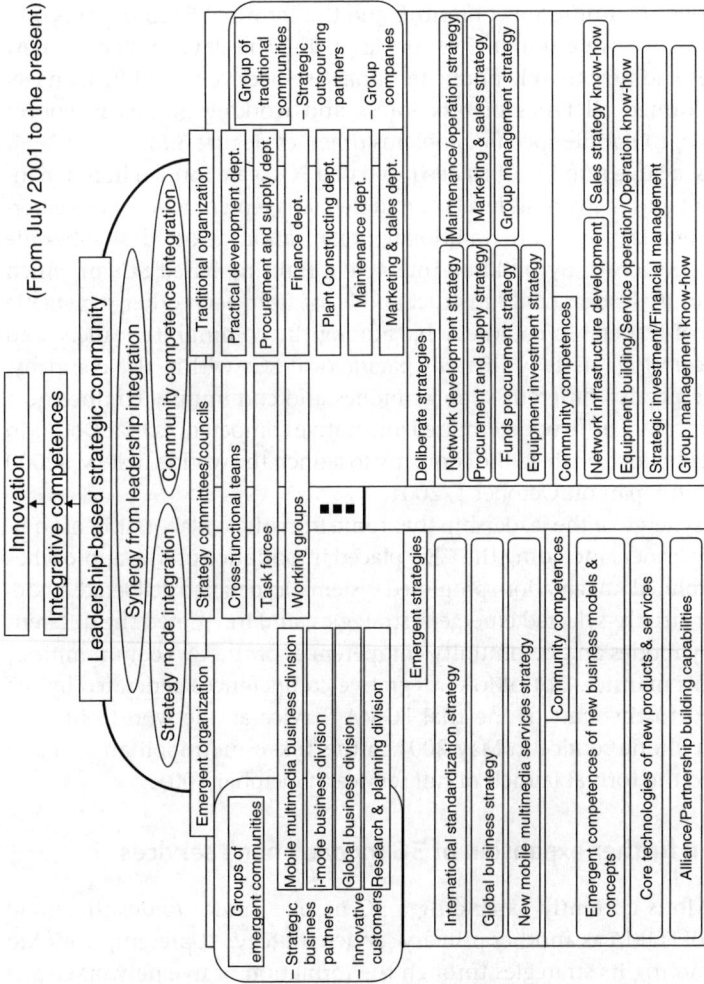

Figure 3.5 DoCoMo's integrative competences in FOMA service (Phase 2)

Strategies Committee and the Basic Issues Liaison Committee responsible for management strategies and business operations, the R&D Strategies Committee concerning new services and R&D, and the Sales Information Liaison Committee related to company-wide sales strategies. Middle management, on the other hand, was actively engaged in the operation of the Service Planning Subcommittee and the Terminal Planning Subcommittee which were responsible for discussing the development of new services and new mobile phone terminals, respectively. Middle management formed all types of task forces and working groups whenever required, to handle specific problems or issues (Figure 3.5).

Thus, a large number of leadership-based SCs were formed in top management and the various levels of middle management where both emergent organizations and traditional organizations existed side-by-side within DoCoMo. By building interactive learning-based SCs in which community leaders could instruct and learn from each other, synergetic effects of leadership could emerge among the community leaders, and by integrating the two different paradoxical SCs within the company, their respective different strategy modes and community competences could merge. The new, determined integrative competences that DoCoMo overall obtained enabled the company to launch the world's first IMT-2000 service in Japan on October 1, 2001.

The synergy of the leadership that came from the collaboration of community leaders including the CEO placed importance on the approaches of disciplined imagination, promoted systematic, detailed deliberate strategies for strictly-selected emergent strategies, and integrated the different strategy modes and community competences of the two communities.

In this manner, DoCoMo's integrative competences generated by the LSC led to the start of the trial FOMA Service as the world's first 3G mobile phone service in May 2001 in the Tokyo metropolitan area and enabled the formal launch of full service in October 2001.

Toward further expansion of 3G mobile phone services

DoCoMo is currently expanding a 3G mobile service under the brand name of FOMA as another primary service strategy. At present, DoCoMo is promoting its strategies through the formation of five networked SCs (Figure 3.6).

The first strategy was to build networked SCs for a platform strategy. This was to form a network of pragmatic boundaries aimed at developing attractive services that would stimulate the expansion of 3G, and one of these services to be developed was a mobile e-commerce service.

This effort involved forming strategic alliances with partners such as Sony, JR (Japan's largest railway company), and the Mitsui Sumitomo Bank (a large financial institution in Japan) in order to jointly develop a mobile e-cash service and a mobile e-credit service. The mobile e-cash service was already started in October 2004. The SCs (pragmatic boundaries) with influential partners were linked in a strong network with SCs (also pragmatic boundaries) within DoCoMo through which they deeply shared context and knowledge, worked on solving problems, and made important decisions at the top management level.

Though DoCoMo is also currently forming SCs with other financial institutions and credit card companies and is searching for advantages together with these partners, they are not leading to important decisions made at top management through strong links with SCs within DoCoMo. Rather, it is at the stage where information or knowledge is shared at the lower management level (task level) or the middle management level. In other words, DoCoMo is maintaining flexible relationships, or weak links, with potential partners. However, when discussions develop and lead to a concrete business opportunity (a decision made at top management), the weak links between SCs change to strong links.

The second strategy involves building networked SCs for the purpose of joint product development concerning a terminal strategy for new mobile phones. As in the networked SCs for the platform strategy mentioned above, this network format has both strong and weak links between SCs. Strongly networked SCs are being formed with strategic partners, such as NEC, Fujitsu, Panasonic, Mitsubishi, and Sharp, while weakly networked SCs are being formed with potential partners, such as Sanyo, Motorola, Nokia, LG, and Samsung, as new avenues of development. In addition, DoCoMo has also decided to enter into joint development relationships with the chipset maker Texas Instruments (TI) and RENESAS (a semiconductor-related joint venture between Hitachi and Mitsubishi) to develop processors for FOMA handsets. DoCoMo has built strongly networked SCs with these semiconductor manufacturers.

The third strategy concerning content, the fourth strategy concerning solutions, and the fifth strategy concerning overseas expansion are each also networked SCs like those for the platform and terminal strategies, comprising both strong and weak links between SCs.

As seen above, DoCoMo balances paradoxical relationships between SCs that are strongly linked or weakly linked on a network through which it promotes current businesses through the strong links, and searches for new potential businesses through the weak links. Each of the networked SCs in these five strategies is dynamically rebuilt and new knowledge is created in an ongoing process. The number of subscribers to DoCoMo's FOMA service reached 10 million in February 2005 and is forecast to exceed 25 million by the end of March 2006.

Creation and development of the LSC

In 1992 when NTT DoCoMo was spun off from NTT, its huge parent, it was a small-scale organization of only about 2,000 people. At the time, top management, including the CEO, and middle management shared a social and corporate vision of launching the mobile telephone market in Japan at an early date. This new mobile communications environment would enable anyone in Japan to make a phone call at any time wherever they were. In order to quickly expand the new mobile phone market on the foundation of their corporate vision and work toward constructing a mobile communications infrastructure and developing new services and telephone handsets, top and middle management actively promoted the sharing of information and knowledge and rapid decision-making through-out the company among all levels of management.

The LSC concept first emerged when DoCoMo was started, and the driving force behind the LSC was the creation of new values based on the social and corporate vision that was shared and resonated among all levels of DoCoMo management. DoCoMo's LSC, which was still a small-scale organization at the time DoCoMo was started, comprised the top management team, including the CEO, and members of middle management at all the main organizations.

In July 1998, when DoCoMo's mobile phone market was expanding and the company was growing (through improved profits and larger size), the LSC divided into two parts, one centered on top management and the other on middle management. To strengthen the linkage between the LSC of top management and the LSC of middle management, decisions that the LSC of middle management made on important issues were discussed by the LSC of top management (including main members of middle management involved in the discussion) who quickly and accurately made final decisions.

The basic concept of the LSC and the source of its members' activities are rooted in the platform for resonating value which in turn is based on the sharing of DoCoMo's social and corporate visions and their new value. At the time DoCoMo was established, the new company constructed a concept tree of social and corporate visions.[3] The concept presented mobile communications as a tool that empowered people to communicate wherever and whenever they liked, freeing them from the constraints of time

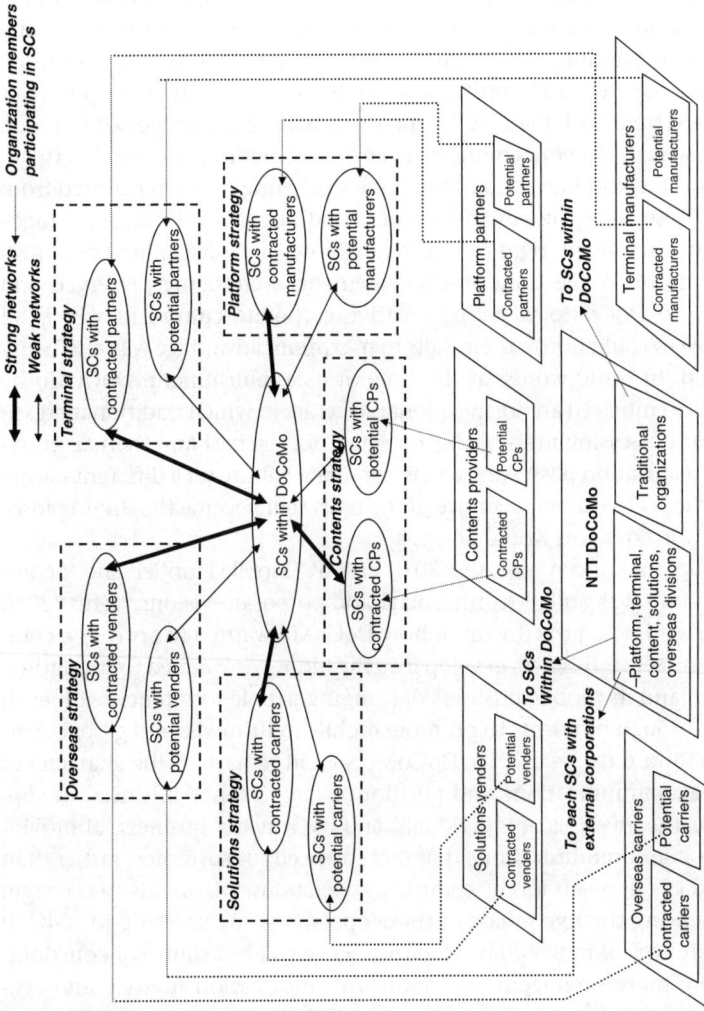

Figure 3.6 Characteristics of networked strategic communities (3G service development)

and space. Mobile communications would mark the advent of a completely new culture of communication in both business and personal lifestyles. In other words, mobile communication services would trigger the growth of a new type of knowledge-oriented society. DoCoMo played are large role toward achieving this aim of enabling people to contact anyone from anywhere, assiduously addressing such issues as improving services, expanding service areas, developing higher-quality and more detailed services, and setting affordable charges. With the spinoff of DoCoMo from NTT, many NTT employees with considerable skills in such areas as R&D, network engineering and construction, advanced network operation technology, and nationwide marketing, were transferred from NTT. These were the advantages of a traditional organization, a high-quality, disciplined, rigid business system within a disciplined organization culture. While these positive elements were being preserved and shifted to DoCoMo, a young creative corporate culture in which all employees could utilize their skills to maximum advantage was also being fostered. In other words, at the time of its establishment, DoCoMo by necessity embraced an organizational structure in which traditional organizations possessing invisible NTT assets from the past and then an emergent organization possessing a new corporate culture (of a different nature from the NTT corporate culture of the past) that became the driving force for new innovation would co-exist.

Besides the concept tree, the '2010 Vision' ('Mobile Frontier' and 'Action Principles') was added to the social and corporate visions.[4] This '2010 Vision' embodied the dream of how DoCoMo wanted to grow as a company and see its business develop into the future. As it aimed to strengthen and expand its mobile business of bringing people into touch with each other through its efforts to promote mobile multimedia and global operations toward the year 2010, DoCoMo sought to harness the character of mobile communications and positioned its 'personal' business, of supporting the lifestyles of individuals, and its 'wireless' business, of providing mobile communications that met the needs of customers rather than individuals, as pillars for the company's operations. 'MAGIC' is an acronym representing the five pillars of these operations. By bringing MAGIC to fruition, DoCoMo would be able to achieve its ideal stance of contributing to a more intelligent and abundant information lifestyle and economic society for individuals. And the 'DREAM' is the component that replaces the action that each employee needs to take as a corporate body in order to bring MAGIC to fruition. In its aim to realize the Concept Tree and the 2010 Vision, the LSC promoted the creation and resonance of new values (building a platform of resonating values), and the innovation that became the new mobile Internet market known as the i-mode service was achieved.

Integration of strategies: linkage between the radical change loop and the incremental change loop

What we need to do in parallel with a revolution in employee consciousness is to integrate the paradoxical strategies in the two organizations. Figure 3.7 shows the integration of this strategy. The new emergent organization with a different nature and entrepreneurial spirit pursues the feasibility of future business through creative and innovative-oriented experimentation and incubation based on new core competences using internal and external core skills and technologies.

As exploratory activities, the emergent organizations continuously promoted an emergent strategy and drew the interests of many customers, thus rousing a new mobile communications market such as i-mode and FOMA. Furthermore, as additional inducement, the emergent organizations looked for and created new business concepts and ideas, and spiraled a change loop of emergent strategy. (Here, this emergent organization's strategy process is called a radical change loop.)

At the same time, however, the emergent organizations and traditional organizations formed an LSC to promote knowledge management (interactive learning and collaboration process) and set up an arena to convey the will of the company to all employees, based on the vision and values shared by the top management team.

Based on accumulated core competences, the traditional organizations with an occupation ability-based, tight-coupling structure execute their current business using deliberate strategies that are well planned in terms of efficiency and certainty. The deliberate strategy using organizational manpower on a nationwide scale was fully activated. Stimulated by emergent strategies, the new mobile communications market underwent considerable growth. In line with the incremental change processes as exploitative activities that were part of this deliberate strategy, plans were continually adjusted and corrected. (The traditional organization's strategy process is called an incremental change loop.) By linking and integrating each loop of the two strategies, DoCoMo created new mobile communication services markets, obtained an advantageous leading position, and achieved great discontinuous transformation.

The emergent organizations formed various internal and external SCs in its challenging organizational culture, created new core competences, and continuously hammered out emergent and creative measures aimed

68

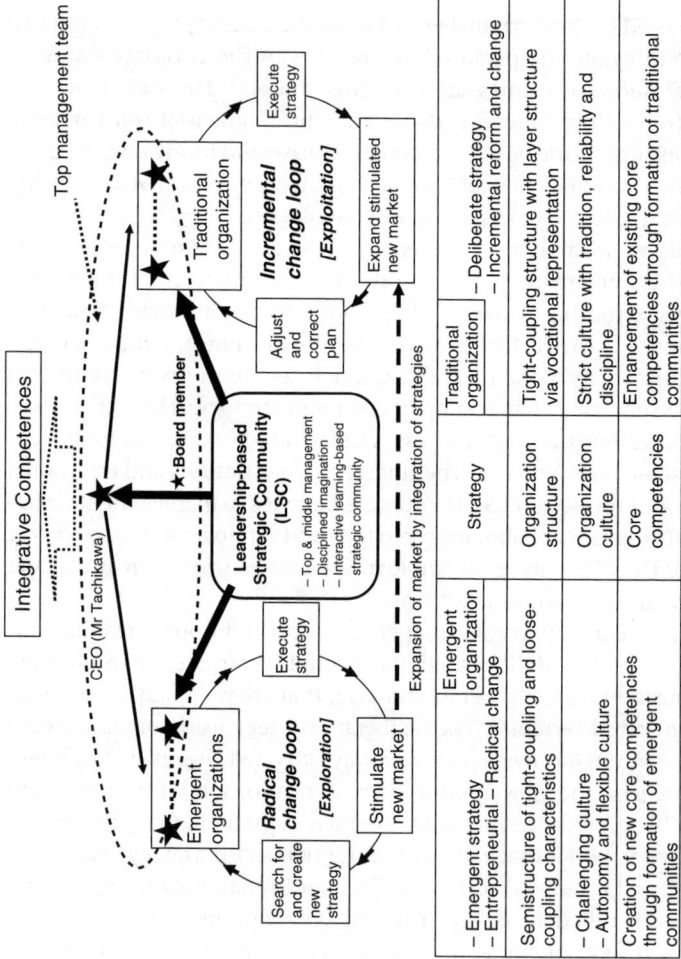

	Emergent organization	Traditional organization
Strategy	– Emergent strategy – Entrepreneurial – Radical change	– Deliberate strategy – Incremental reform and change
Organization structure	Semistructure of tight-coupling and loose-coupling characteristics	Tight-coupling structure with layer structure via vocational representation
Organization culture	– Challenging culture – Autonomy and flexible culture	Strict culture with tradition, reliability and discipline
Core competencies	Creation of new core competencies through formation of emergent communities	Enhancement of existing core competencies through formation of traditional communities

Figure 3.7 Linkage between emergent change loop and incremental change loop
Source: Kodama (2003).

at long-term innovation. On the contrary, the traditional organization executed planned measures aimed at short-term efficiencies in which importance was placed on stability and control through a traditional and reliable organizational culture that was cultivated by reform and improvement of core competences acquired by the long process of accumulating achievements. For companies like DoCoMo to maintain competitive advantage on an ongoing basis, it is important for them to promote exploitative and explorative activities at the same time. DoCoMo's top team intentionally maintained paradoxical organizations, strategies, cultures and competences inside the company, activated and integrated these different systems simultaneously, and enhanced the output of the entire company.

4
Managing Paradox in a Large Corporation: Challenging a Vision for New-generation Optics

This chapter presents a case study of how a large, traditional corporation simultaneously created new service markets and established a dominant position in the competitive fields of digital communications in Japan. The corporation accepted a new organizational body imbued with an entrepreneurial spirit supported by different types of personnel and then continuously promoted entrepreneurial strategies based on time pacing. At the same time, with the aim to implement strategic innovation, the company integrated the above strategies with deliberate strategies based on event-based pacing practiced by the existing organizational bodies. This chapter uses a case study to discuss factors for success and the problems encountered in the course of achieving strategic innovation in the communications field, specifically in the creation of new markets, through the deliberate and strategic maintenance and subsequent integration of paradoxical organizations and strategies under a single corporate umbrella.

Changing from a telephone company to a multimedia company

On New Year's Day, 1994, then president Kojima declared that NTT would change from a telephone company to a multimedia company. At the time, NTT was facing a period of significant transition from an engagement of approximately 40 years as an analog telephone company to a future of creating new businesses utilizing multimedia technologies.

Following privatization in 1985, NTT implemented incremental changes by spinning off group companies (the data communications section in 1988 and the mobile communications section in 1992), entering new business fields, introducing voluntary retirement, and adopting other in-house streamlining policies. As a result, by the beginning of 1994 the company had reduced the number of its employees from around 300,000 to 180,000. Regarding its business operations, income from analog telephone sales, the company's core business, entered a gradual decline due to the liberalization of the telecommunications market in 1985 which allowed new common carriers to enter the market and forced telecommunication fees to be reduced.

On the other hand, the demand for non-voice services such as data communications was gradually increasing, primarily from corporate users. At that time, however, it was an unknown field for telecommunications carriers in terms of what strategies should be used to create what kind of services for the Internet which had begun to spread, primarily in the US. by 1994.

Corporate reorganization by top management

The two persons who felt the greatest sense of crisis regarding NTT's future were then-president Mr Kojima, who made the 'Multimedia Declaration' in 1994, and then-vice president and person responsible for technology Mr Miyazu, who took up the president's post in 1996. They searched for a future structure for the business and radically changed NTT's constitution which included the company's culture and business style. They concluded that they had to construct a new department in the head office to introduce multimedia strategies for the future. The person who was assigned this responsibility was then-board member and director Mr Ikeda, who became managing director of NTT in 1996. This department was named the Multimedia Business Department (MBD) and was launched in June 1994 with about 50 staff members. Two years later, the department's staff had grown to about 850. Top management members Mr Kojima, Mr Miyazu and Mr Ikeda shared a common value system, a future vision, and a firm belief and will to dismantle NTT's traditional culture and create a new multimedia business market drawn from information and communication technologies.

MBD entrepreneurial strategy

The grand design of the multimedia service promoted by the MBD as a means to change NTT from a telephone company to a multimedia company was a hop-step-jump scenario, moving from analog telephones to ISDN service (Kodama, 1999) to the era of optical fiber (Figure 4.1). Of these three, the broadband network known as fiber-to-the-home (FTTH) was a process that corresponded to the ultimate multimedia service in

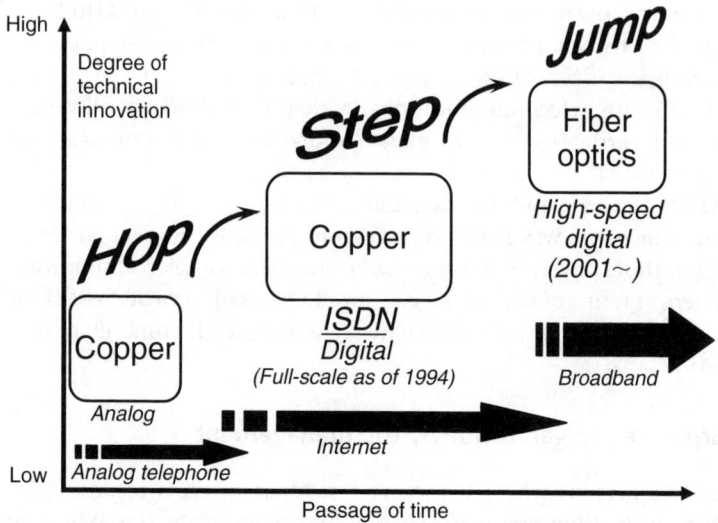

Figure 4.1   Scenario for digital network service
Source: Kodama (2003).

the 21st century. In 1994, the mass marketing of optical fiber was not considered to be realistic due to insurmountable hurdles of demand, technology and cost. The basic policy of the MBD was therefore first to provide multimedia services to customers using currently available network technologies. The MBD's vision was 'multimedia that can start today' (Now-ISDN),[1] which meant using the ISDN communications system as a platform to provide a variety of services to customers.

Around the beginning of 1996, the number of ISDN subscriptions increased sharply, reaching a total of approximately 20 million channels by December 2000 as a result of an intensive promotion campaign for ISDN (Figure 4.2). The penetration of ISDN in Japan quickly surpassed that of Germany (Deutsche Telecom) which had been the world leader in ISDN promotion and deployment until then.

Characteristics of MBD business strategies and organizational structure

Mr Ikeda was thinking about the need for measures designed so that customers really felt compelled to subscribe to ISDN services. The first measure consisted of ISDN terminal strategies, including low-priced terminals, and the development of various new terminals. The second measure

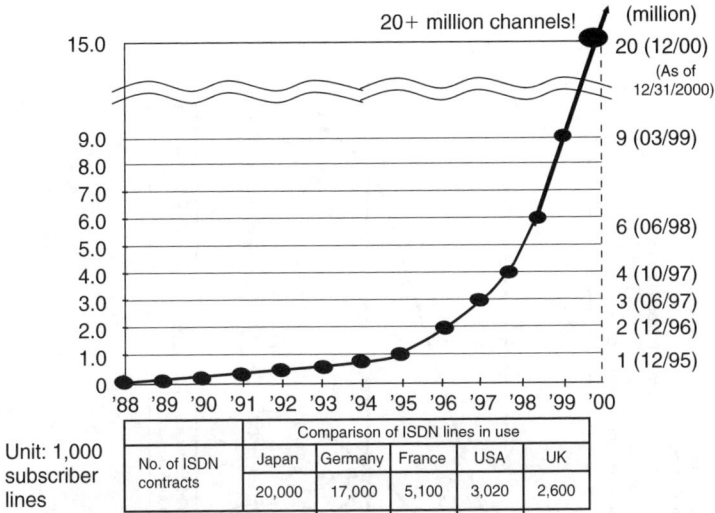

Figure 4.2 ISDN channels in use in Japan
Source: Kodama (2003).

involved network strategies aimed at the development of new and attractive network services that used ISDN. The third measure consisted of content strategies aimed at the development of content that would be distributed to customer terminals (PCs and other devices) via the ISDN network. These three business strategies were mutually related and could induce a significant synergy depending on the content of the strategies.

The key in promoting these business strategies was to obtain specific results through joint development or ventures via strategic tie-ups with various partners outside NTT as well as the active promotion of incubation through joint experimentation with specific customers.

In the MBD, about 20 projects related to video, electronic commerce, joint ventures and the like were established. Each project formed multiple strategic business community groups through strategic tie-ups with outside companies or partnerships with specific customers based on the above three business strategies (Figure 4.3), and project leaders comprehensively managed and promoted more than one strategic business community. Each project team consisted of 30 to 40 employees. In virtual communities with outside partners or specific customers in each project, the Internet and videoconferencing were freely utilized for project management

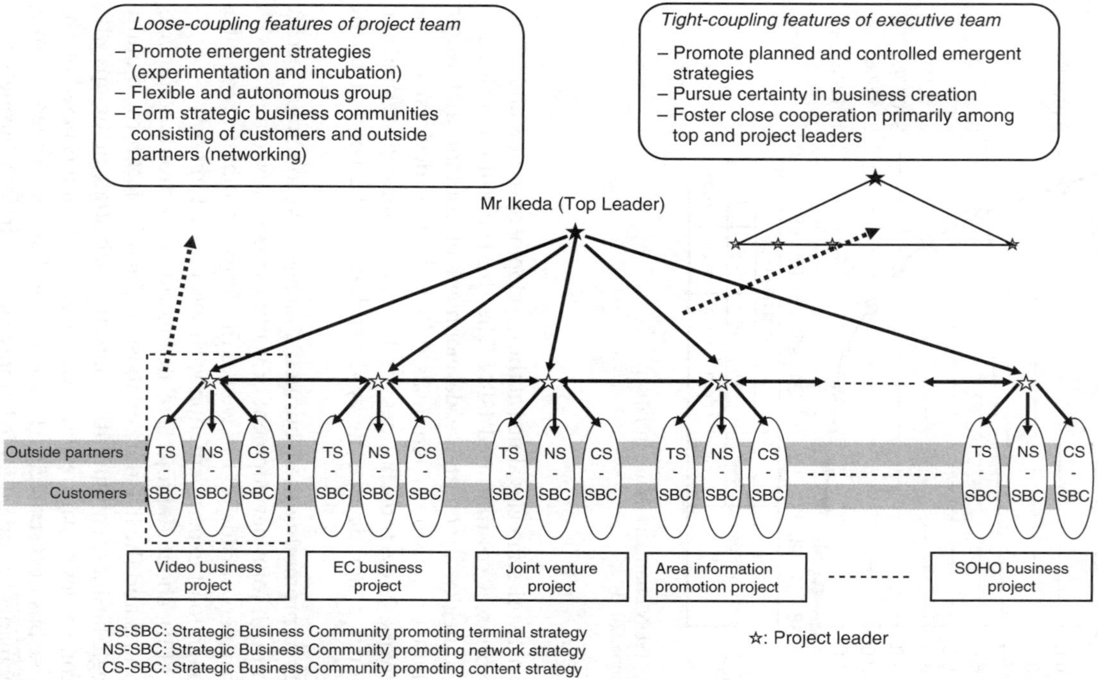

Tight-coupling features of executive team

- Promote planned and controlled emergent strategies
- Pursue certainty in business creation
- Foster close cooperation primarily among top and project leaders

Loose-coupling features of project team

- Promote emergent strategies (experimentation and incubation)
- Flexible and autonomous group
- Form strategic business communities consisting of customers and outside partners (networking)

Mr Ikeda (Top Leader)

☆: Project leader

Video business project

EC business project

Joint venture project

Area information promotion project

SOHO business project

Outside partners

Customers

TS-SBC: Strategic Business Community promoting terminal strategy
NS-SBC: Strategic Business Community promoting network strategy
CS-SBC: Strategic Business Community promoting content strategy

Figure 4.3 Characteristics of MBD organizational structure
Source: Kodama (2003).

in joint development or as a means of sharing information or knowledge related to joint incubations with customers. Project leaders actively
configured an adhocracy organization that was deliberately networked
(Nohria and Ghoshal, 1997). These projects promoted businesses that were
based on quick decision-making and action, as if they were small venture companies.

On the other hand, project leaders implemented both the strategic
thoughts of Mr Ikeda, leader of the MBD, and the concepts, strategies
and tactics that were promoted by the MBD's innovative leadership. At
the same time, MBD leadership worked closely with other project leaders to realize new strategies and tactics. The executive team in the MBD,
which consisted of 20 employees including Mr Ikeda and the project team
leaders, shared a vision and value system for the larger mission of promoting ISDN. This promotion was being collectively referred to then as
'Now-ISDN.' Although strategically the MBD had a strong emergent aspect
as a whole, the deliberate, planned strategic factors identified by the executive team and the tight-coupled organization that resulted from close
cooperation between the project leaders under Mr Ikeda made it possible to channel the results of experimentation or incubation into the formation of actual businesses.

The organizational structure of MBD necessary to develop such original and complicated strategies was a system designed to handle a complex environment characterized by both tight-coupled and loose-coupled
organizational elements, i.e. strict control among executive team members while at the same time granting flexibility and autonomy to each
project (Figure 4.3).

Entrepreneurial, time pacing, strategic community management

Specific measures with respect to the three business strategies promoted
by MBD projects are shown in Figure 4.4 in time series.[2] With the terminal business strategies, new products (including product upgrades) were
put on the market continuously through joint development with various outside strategic tie-up partners, primarily US companies. With network business strategies, new network services were also worked out
through joint ventures, primarily with the US. Furthermore, with the
content business strategy, new services were developed one after
another through experimentation or incubation jointly carried out with
various content providers, specific customers (universities, hospitals,
local governing bodies) and government and municipal offices.

Strategy \ Time	1994	1995	1996	1997	1998
Terminal Strategy	• Tie-up with Microsoft (CD-ROM decryption key technology) • Tie-up with Silicon Graphics (interactive multimedia technology)	• Tie-up with PictureTel (joint development of videoconferencing) • Started selling very low priced ISDN MN128 TA (a best-seller in Japan) • Reduced ISDN-DSU price (reduced by 1/3) • Started selling simple ISDN installation kit	• Started selling 'Phoenix' videoconferencing system created through tie-up with PictureTel • Started selling new version of MN128 • Started selling WINE kit through tie-up with Microsoft (SOHO kit)	• Started selling 'Phoenix WIDE' through tie-up with PictureTel • Started selling very low priced 'Phoenix mini' video phone through tie-up with Mitsubishi Electric • Started selling new version of MN128	• Started selling new version of 'Phoenix series' equipment • Started selling 'Debut mini (ISDN router)' through tie-up with Whistle Communications Inc. in the US • Started selling new version of MN128
Network Strategy	• Tie-up with General Magic Inc. (Magic Cap technology) • Tie-up with Microsoft (fax network technology)	• Established GrR Home Net Inc. (joint venture with Sony, etc.: Started ISP business) • Tie-up with Microsoft (began offering Micro-soft Network Service) • Started high-speed videoconferencing experiment with first Virtual Corp. in the US	• Established 'One Number Service, Inc.' joint venture with AT&T, Access line technology • Started audio conferencing service • Started 'avex network service' music distribution service	• Established Phoenicom, Inc. joint venture with PictureTel – Started creation of world's largest multi-point video-conferencing connectivity service • Started video streaming service (tie-up with VDO Net Corp. in the US)	• GrR Home Net Inc. (started EC mall service) • Phoenicom Inc. (started Multipoint videoconferencing service using high-speed ISDN) • Started CTI service
Content Strategy	• Tie-up with content holders of various types and in various fields	• Established NTT Virtual Young Company • Started 'World Nature Network (WNN)' content service • Started 'Hello Net Japan' content service	• Community creation through nationwide inter-school multimedia network (started Konet Plan) • Created new virtual services: virtual education, medical care, medical services • Started virtual home language study experiment	• Started EC mall service (G-square) • Developed 'Goo' search engine (tie-up with INKTOMI Corp. in the US) • Started VOD service via videoconferencing	• Started area information promotion policy (multimedia) village business, etc.) • Started multimedia housing • Started virtual sign language support and interpretation service

Figure 4.4 Main activities in three main MBD business strategies
Source: Kodama (2003).

One of the characteristics of the MBD's strategies was that there was a strong tendency toward emergent processes through experimentation or incubation (Minzberg *et al.*, 1998). Although the intention for each measure that the MBD worked out was emergent, the emergent processes were always monitored and controlled by the MBD executive team. As a whole, they were carefully planned and specifically developed to grow into a business through decisions made by the MBD executive team. This is similar to the entrepreneurial strategy presented by Minzberg and Walters (1985).

The second characteristic was a time pacing strategy (Eisenhardt and Brown, 1998). In order for the MBD to continuously promote creative measures and induce continuous change, improvisation was required throughout the entire organization, and there was always tension among MBD members. Specifically, targets were set each month for the number of ISDN sales channels and for sales of commercial terminals and achievements with regard to established joint venture companies. Each project used these targets as guides to promote individual target businesses.

The third characteristic was the formation of strategic business communities with outside partners including customers. These strategic business communities themselves were flexible and autonomous. IT or multimedia technologies were used as needed to create networks so that the business vision, purpose and value system were shared by community members. Emergent strategies and tactics were promoted to target new business creation through trial and error.[3]

It is hard to believe, however, that the explosive growth of ISDN shown in Figure 4.2 could be brought about solely by an MBD organization comprised of 850 people. As a prelude to this growth, the MBD and the traditional organization formed in-house virtual communities, and deliberate full-scale ISDN promotional strategies were launched by the traditional organization.

MBD's project leaders recognized that it was difficult to achieve innovative radical discontinuous transformation of ISDN simply through market pump-priming. How to reform NTT's old corporate culture and rapidly achieve innovation was thus a major issue for MBD's project leaders.

Promoting knowledge management through in-house communities

A large number of employees including the top management of traditional organizations was strongly opposed to the development of measures brought about by the string of new strategies and tactics that the MBD was developing through large-scale business investments. To solve such problems, MBD project leaders tenaciously and actively promoted dialog and collaboration with these employees. Both sides engaged in productive and constructive discussions that led to a resolution of the conflicts that occurred between them.[4]

Specifically, the two sides promoted a number of large-scale, company-wide knowledge management policies. President Miyazu, leader of the 'J Project,' a computer communication demand creation project; 'Multi Net I.I.I.' (Nikkei Sangyo Shimbun, 1996), and the 'Meeting of 100,000 People' (Nikkei Sangyo Shimbun, 1996), which comprised the top management team that included company-wide knowledge management, promoted this knowledge management[5] to all headquarters-related organizations and across organizations centered on middle management at the sales and equipment divisions at 200 branches nationwide.[6]

A series of MBD measures to promote knowledge management in this in-house virtual community stimulated creativity and innovation among employees in the traditional organization and aroused interest in multimedia. Knowledge management provided the means to deal with problems that NTT faced at the time and to ease tensions. This fostered an environment in which employees could evaluate themselves and improve. As a result, conflicts became constructive and productive, and the danger that NTT would yield to the old traditional culture of the organization was alleviated (Janis, 1982).

In terms of conflict management in such a large and complex organization, solely issuing orders from the top of the company could not on its own bring about a complete reversal in the consciousness of some 180,000 employees. In this case, two conflict management models had to be considered. One was the internal conflict model in which a large company was simply understood as a single system, and the top management team led by the president assumed an important role in a high-order system. The other model was one between two systems with different organizational cultures, namely the MBD and the traditional organization (Tracy, 1989). For that reason, it was necessary to practice inter-system control by knowledge management using 'Yarima SHOW Multi Creation' and internal conflict control by the top management team through knowledge management via the 'J Project' and 'Multi Net I.I.I.' The resulting controlled constructive and productive conflicts fully activated the deliberate strategy of the traditional organization with regard to Now-ISDN.

Integration of two strategies by the MBD and the traditional organization

At the same time, while progress was being made within the entire company and the revolution in employee consciousness was underway, various measures promoted by the MBD bore fruit and, at the beginning of 1996, the number of ISDN subscribers began to grow. To handle this significant change in the ISDN market, the overhead section of the traditional organization urgently needed to create strategic plans for sales, facilities, customer service and maintenance service that were sufficiently robust to handle a full-fledged expansion of Now-ISDN.

These plans were rapidly implemented to smoothly provide ISDN to customers. First, all frontline sales and technology employees received training to acquire knowledge and skills with respect to ISDN service. Second, an efficient service order processing system (from application to installation and connection of the line) was created by introducing a new information system so that customers could begin using the service as soon as possible following the submission of an application for services. Third, switching system software was developed so that customers could retain their original phone number after changing from an analog system to ISDN. Fourth, investments in switching system facilities were implemented earlier than originally planned to handle the rapid increase in demand for ISDN. Fifth, the frontline service structure was enhanced to handle the vast increases in customer inquiries.

In terms of the behavior of the traditional organization, such actions were unthinkable. Incremental change combined with measures continuously promoted by the MBD greatly contributed to dramatic growth in the ISDN market.

Linkage between time pacing strategy and event-based pacing strategy

The basic strategy of the traditional organization was to respond promptly to sales and service orders from customers for ISDN, and to plan the implementation of facility requirements (expansion of switches and circuit installation) to improve the quality of customer service. It was therefore necessary to accurately predict ISDN demand. To do so, it was necessary to precisely monitor the time pacing strategy promoted by the MBD. The event-based pacing strategy thus became important in terms of responding in a timely manner to customer demand for ISDN (Gersick, 1994).

The advantage of event-based pacing, which is one of the formal management strategies, is the wide range of environmental adaptation measures that are available, and that selected measures can be pursued without change until the expected event becomes successful. Event-based pacing thus enables the establishment of the same stability that the traditional organization enjoyed, and it is also effective in implementing incremental change for disciplined top-down-type organizations. On the other hand, since actions are taken in response to a phenomenon, it could become an unstable strategy due to the possibility that good opportunities can be missed (Eisenhardt and Brown, 1998). However, by linking event-based pacing with the MBD's time pacing strategy, in terms of the entire company it became possible to continuously monitor market trends and take quick actions in response as conditions warranted.

Van de Ven and Poole (1995) pointed out that there is significant conflict between managers and investors in the realistic scheduling of product development and the securing of expected profits. For the manager, smoothly developing products is more important than securing profit, while the investors' sole interests are in securing profits.

In this case, the finance section of the head office and overhead section of the traditional organization were critical and skeptical about these investments which were accompanied by the continuous implementation of various measures performed by the MBD. However, the MBD placed importance on both time restrictions and the fruits of the investment collected. The time restrictions required that a certain result must be achieved within a certain period of time. The MBD consciously followed the methodology in which they integrated their own time pacing strategy with the event-based pacing strategy of the traditional organization.

Specifically, the MBD's time pacing strategy that involved the placement of monthly advertisements in national newspapers and periodic ads in specific magazines led to an increase in orders for ISDN service, especially from ordinary people. The traditional organization was thus able to achieve their sales targets and facility plans using relatively accurate predictions for ISDN demand obtained from records of past demand and the MBD's future publicity and advertising plans. Based on the expected demand, frontline sales, facilities and customer service became more efficient, and event-based pacing was successfully executed.

Linkage between the continuous change loop and the incremental change loop

Figure 4.5 shows the integration of this strategy. The MBD continuously promoted an emergent and time pacing entrepreneurial strategy which

81

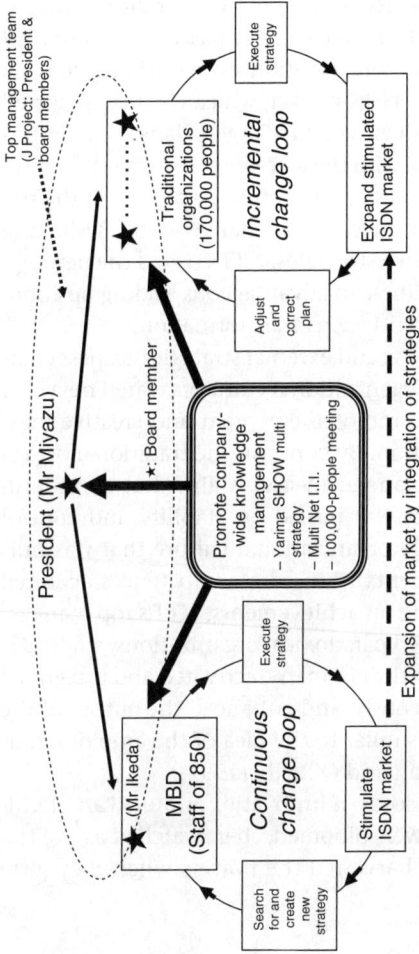

Figure 4.5 Linkage between continuous change loop and incremental change loop
Source: Kodama (2003).

attracted the interest of many customers and aroused a sleeping ISDN market. Furthermore, as additional inducement, the MBD looked for and created new business ideas and spiraled a change loop of entrepreneurial strategy. (Here, this strategy process of the MBD is called a continuous change loop.)

At the same time, the consciousness of the employees of the traditional organization was changed and a deliberate strategy based on event-based pacing using the manpower of an organization on a nationwide scale was fully activated. This caused the ISDN market, which was being spurred on by entrepreneurial strategies, to grow much larger. Plans were continually adjusted and corrected in line with the incremental change processes that were part of this deliberate strategy. (The strategy process of the traditional organization is called an incremental change loop.) By linking and integrating each loop of the two strategies, NTT created the new digital network services market, obtained an advantageous leading position, and achieved a considerable discontinuous transformation.

The MBD formed various in-house and external strategic business communities within its challenging organizational culture, created new core competences, and continuously promoted emergent and creative measures aimed at long-term innovation. By contrast, the traditional organization implemented carefully planned measures aimed at short-term efficiencies in which importance was placed on stability and control through a traditional and reliable organizational culture that was nurtured by reforms and improvements from core competences acquired through a long process of building on achievements. NTT's top management team deliberately maintained paradoxical organizations, strategies, cultures and competences within the company, activated and integrated these different systems simultaneously, and enhanced the output of the entire company. This concept is similar to the idea of the ambidextrous organization reported by Tushman and O'Reilly (1997).

The MBD continuously sowed seeds of innovation, watered and fertilized them to ensure that the flowers bloomed, then watched as the traditional organization efficiently harvested the flowers when they were in full bloom.

Changes in the communications market and the age of broadband

Since NTT announced its management strategy known as the 'Basic Multimedia Concept' (NTT's basic concept and details of current engagement toward the age of multimedia) in 1994, the explosive growth of the Internet along with the spread of ISDN, which is the STEP process shown in Figure 4.1, prompted NTT management to ensure that all employees undergo a reform in awareness based on the vision that NTT was transforming itself from a telephone company to a multimedia company. All employees of NTT Group companies continued to fully devote themselves to the corporate awareness vision (challenging the JUMP process in Figure 5.1) in various areas through R&D, business, and other activities even after NTT was split (into an NTT holding company, NTT East, NTT West, and NTT Communications) in July 1999.

The explosive spread of the Internet in recent years has brought about rapid changes in the information communications market. Over six years, the number of subscriber telephones dropped from 61 million units in March 1997 to 59.57 million units. On the other hand, the number of contracted mobile phones, including PHS terminals, hit 79 million in December 2002, surpassing the total number of analog and ISDN fixed line telephone subscribers in November 2000. One noteworthy point in the area of user networks is the rapid rise in the number of subscribers to i-mode and other mobile phone Internet connection services, and the rapid expansion of broadband access to the Internet using DSL and optical-fiber lines. Japan has become one of the major broadband countries of the world.

More recently, in August 2001, NTT East and NTT West started their full-scale optical-fiber access service known as 'B Flet's' in response to the growing shift toward broadband, and in November 2001, NTT Resonant launched their broadband distribution and video communication services. In these and other ways, NTT has been embarking on new endeavors that symbolize the new 'light' of optical-fiber communications for broadband in the 21st century.

Challenging the JUNP step: formulating and implementing the new-generation vision of 'light'

In November 2002, NTT unveiled a 5-year broadband vision dubbed 'The new-generation vision of "light": toward a world of resonant communications in broadband.' This represented the start of a new engagement toward the JUNP step in Figure 4.1. Resonant communications denotes the natural communications environment for high-quality video that was not possible with ISDN and other narrow bands in Figure 4.1 while the Internet was undergoing a transition from narrowband to broadband. 'Resonant' expresses the meaning of 'resonating' or 'reverberating,' and 'resonant communications' refers to a new-generation optical-fiber

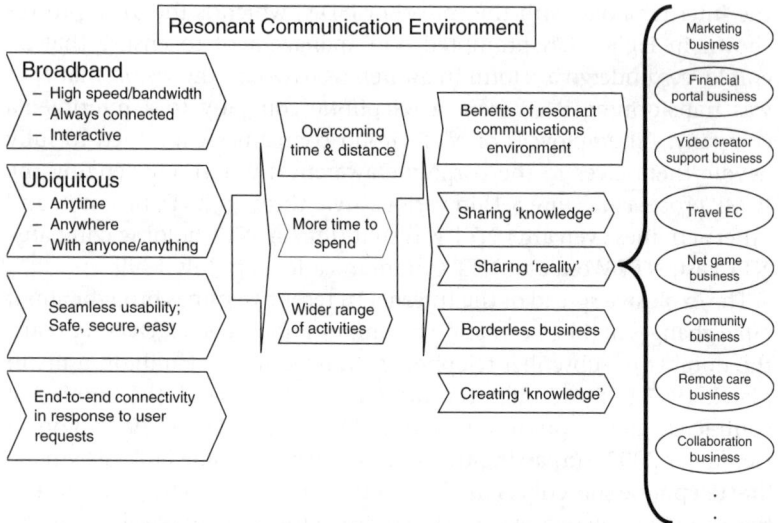

Figure 4.6   Resonant communication and new business creation
Source: Prepared by author based on NTT media releases.

communications environment of superior safety, reliability, and ease of use in which people, businesses and other entities are linked ubiquitously in virtual networks where they can communicate interactively with anyone, anywhere, and at any time over broadband and whose growth is fostered through resonation among its various entities. This vision also serves to clarify the value of NTT presence in how it is involved in the manner in which society, lifestyles, and businesses change.

The resonant communications environment makes possible real, natural communications for high-quality video that was not possible with narrowband, and realizes the original function of networks, which was to overcome time and distance. By overcoming time, people will have more time at their disposal, and by overcoming distance, people and companies will enjoy a dramatic boost in the range of their activities. In addition, rich video communication resulting from a fusion of real and virtual technologies will transcend people, organizations, corporations, regions, countries and other entities in real-world activities, and share and create tacit and explicit knowledge as people and organizations share the realities they possess. This will then lead to new innovation in business and social activities (Figure 4.6).

The realization of this new platform known as the resonant communication environment facilitates the creation of various new knowledge in the social and corporate activities of individuals and supports new business models. On the business side, specifically, this environment makes it possible for corporations to contribute to improvements in efficiency and corporate creativity such as strengthening internal and external collaboration (in development, design, manufacturing processes and so on) and communications, along with sales, marketing, and personnel training, through creation with customers, and then to create new business models. On the other hand, this environment also contributes economic development and resolving social problems such as (a) the aging demographics of society, (b) problems associated with energy and the natural environment, (c) safety and security, and (d) education and regional disparities.

NTT group strategies and organization

By proposing their next-generation vision for new 'light' in optical-fiber communications, the NTT management team is promoting the sharing and creation of global knowledge, and along with using these results to resolve a number of issues facing Japan, such as aging demographics and the environment, and realize a society with a lifestyle of abundance, a vital mission of NTT is to strengthen creativity, efficiency and competitiveness and to become deeply aware that this vision also gives meaning to NTT's existence. Building the resonant communication environment, the new broadband platform that is to support innovation among individuals in society and the corporate world in the age of ubiquitous communications and broadband that is expected to become a genuine reality in the future, is a major strategic goal for NTT as it heads toward its new-generation vision of 'light.' The NTT Group (NTT East, NTT West, NTT Communications, NTT DoCoMo, NTT Data and others) shares the concepts of this big new-generation vision of 'light' in their respective businesses, and has been devoting all their energies to dynamically sharing and utilizing the Group's intellectual capital while balancing market needs and technological seeds in order to create new knowledge.

At present, the NTT Group is promoting the formation of various multi-layered SCs and networked SCs including external partners and customers. With the aim to develop future businesses, the emergent organizations in the respective Group member companies are implementing entrepreneurial strategies aimed at launching emergent strategies or internal corporate ventures. In addition, the emergent organizations of the various member companies, among whom SCs have been formed, are pursuing synergistic effects within the Group aimed at developing new businesses. (One example of this sort of new business involves the fixed and mobile convergence [FMC] service that merges fixed-line and mobile communications.) On the other hand, the traditional organizations at the respective member companies are steadily implementing deliberate strategies aimed at promoting their current mainstream businesses. SCs are formed among these traditional organizations with the aim to share management strategies or build efficient network equipment, and they pursue synergistic effects within the Group for service strategies and other areas. In addition, with respect to important strategic items related to the NTT Group as a whole, leadership-based strategic communities (LSCs) – which are cross-functional teams of top management and senior middle management across the emergent and traditional organizations in the various member companies – are formed in multiple layers at the management level to generate integrative competences that would be ideal for the overall corporate strategy (Figure 4.7).

Mr Junichiro Miyazu, the previous president of NTT, spoke as follows as he looked back on the history of transformation at the NTT Group such as the digital revolution, the growth of multimedia, reorganizations within the Group, the Group's structural reforms, and the optical vision:

> The various members of the Group have a different awareness of the problems and different details they are involved with. In the undercurrent of the various corporate activities, however, is a common recognition that could be called the corporate culture. Since NTT was once a single entity (before it was split into different entities), it was a matter of course that it embraced common ways of thinking, and the important point here is how these ways of thinking have been changing during this period of reforms. While the common recognition has been changing as a whole, it hasn't been changing in completely independent ways at the various companies in the Group, but rather it is perhaps more accurate to say it has been changing as a whole in a uniform direction. Seen in that sense, the fact that everyone has been acting on the same awareness indicates that this awareness represents the moving spirit of the NTT Group (Miyazu, 2003).

In other words, 'common awareness' refers to the vision for optical-fiber and the 'realization of the resonant communication environment' that is the strategic goal aimed at embodying this vision. While individual Group companies adopt autonomous, decentralized leadership and behavior toward the vision and strategic goals, in its 'common awareness,' NTT as a whole utilizes integrated, centralized leadership and behavior to maximize the synergy of knowledge creation activities at individual NTT Group companies. This is the dialectical leadership at SC-based

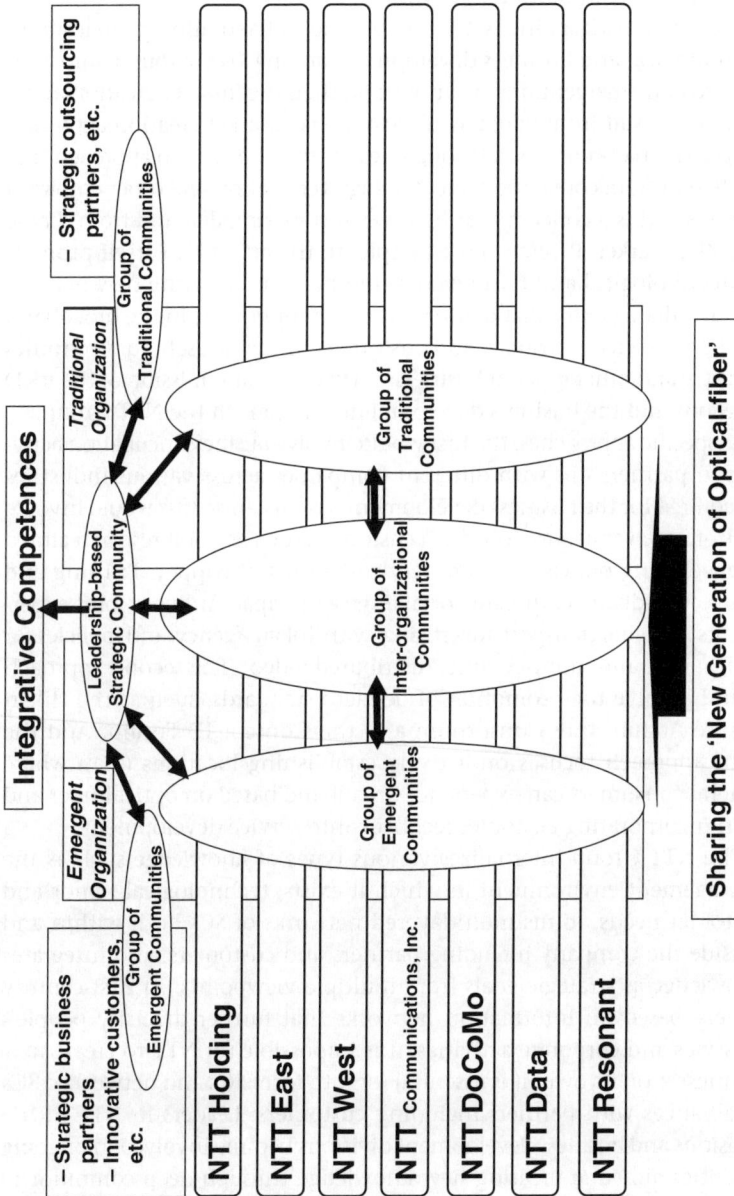

Figure 4.7 Integrative competences of NTT group firms

firms mentioned in Chapter 2 which gives birth to integrative competences for the corporation as a whole.

A characteristic point is the dialog and collaboration that leads to technological and business development among NTT Group companies centered on emergent organizations and then the 'market creation activities' that result from dialog with customers. 'Market creation activities' refers to market cultivation through 'real business' and is an approach that is different from conventional technology verification and other empirical field tests. It is a concept that involves stimulating demand from dialog with the market. It refers, for example, to the act of NTT itself promoting technological and business development and creating new markets through dialog and collaboration with content holders in the broadband business, service providers, and customers in the household electronics industry and other types of businesses. This is a major mission of the R&D divisions and the business development divisions in the NTT Group.

As specific approaches, the first would involve business incubation activities in partnerships with different companies across various industries as required for the business development. For instance, this would involve multi-faceted collaborations with customers such as 'joint research aimed at developing optical software services' with Dai Nippon Printing and Sharp, 'broadband corporate portal tests' with Japan Airlines, 'joint experiments in digital transport advertising' with Tokyu Agency, and 'policies for multi-angle and multi-channel distributed video.' The second approach would involve the promotion of de facto standards, such as the Hikari Service Architecture Consortium and the Content ID Forum. And the third approach focuses on actively establishing locations ('Ba') where general consumers can experience broadband based on optical-fiber and then incorporating customer feedback into service development.

The NTT Group internalizes various types of knowledge such as the management environment in which it exists, technological trends and customer needs, forms multi-layered networks of SCs both within and outside the company including partners and customers, and integrates knowledge as strategic goals from multiple viewpoints. In 21st-century society based on information networks that further diversify people's lifestyles and corporate activities, it is impossible for NTT to create new businesses on its own; it is essential for it to form SCs and networked SCs in alliances with partners including customers. Leaders in NTT's R&D divisions and business development divisions became involved in ongoing activities aimed at creating new knowledge through deep communication and collaboration in SCs and networked SCs with partners.

Broadband businesses utilizing optical-fiber are continuing to be launched in Japan. The road map in Figure 4.1 that NTT drafted around

1994 entered the final stage. When NTT launched its optical-fiber vision, it was heavily criticized by many journalists, the media, and competitors. In reality, the industry was moving toward the vision that NTT had drafted. Mr John T. Chambers, President and CEO of Cisco Systems in the United States, commented as follows:

> Japan has surprisingly progressed in a short time to become one of the world's most advanced network-based societies. Japan's broadband communications is 30 times faster than the speed in America and at one thirtieth the cost. The world was skeptical when NTT started devoting its energies to optical-fiber communications, but now most people say that this was the right thing to do. It is rare for the majority of people to provide support for the first move when the market undergoes a major change. But companies need to have the courage to bear the required risk. Whether a company can or not will determine its future. (*Nikkei Business*, 2005)

Looking back on the history of the past 20 years with privatization, digitalization, concepts of multimedia, reorganizations, transitions to optical-fiber, and structural reforms at NTT, in this management environment that changes at blinding speeds, NTT Group member companies have truly undergone enormous change. At the same time, all employees embrace a sense of crisis in their ways of thinking, becoming imbued with the awareness that their company is in transition from being a telephone company to becoming a multimedia company and that they are fostering an entrepreneurial spirit. Mr Junichiro Miyazu, a former president of NTT, used to emphasize the following in his dialogs with people in management positions including top managers and employees out in the field:

> At every critical juncture from the digital revolution to the age of multimedia and to reorganizations, I gathered employees out in the field and had been having good talks with them. Since the structural reforms (NTT Group companies), however, were directly related to the lives of individuals, I was more nervous than ever when talking with them. They gave me various opinions. Many of them said they understood my thoughts about reforms, but they wanted to know why we had to do them now. All I could ask in reply to them was who, other than us, would be able to work so hard for the future of NTT? But that was enough. While everyone understood my basic ideas, I think they needed some reassurance that they were the ones who were going to do it (Miyazu, 2003).

This 'reassurance' that Miyazu spoke about served to establish for these employees including top management an awareness of their existence that would trigger a major reform in themselves and a new value that would become the driving force for a new recognition that would lead them into the future.

Implications

This chapter has discussed a new, practical viewpoint exhibited during the process of radical change within NTT. Future research themes include whether or not the practical aspect of discontinuous transformation of the case can be applied to other large corporations. It goes without saying that the actual discontinuous transformation method used by a specific large corporation depends on the environment, business type or form and the existing organizational culture, as well as the value systems exhibited by top management, the leadership style, and so on.

Based on the new perspectives obtained from this in-depth case study, the following points are noteworthy in terms of the impact of innovation in other large-scale companies as well:

The creation of a trigger for innovation: creating a new organization imbued with an entrepreneurial spirit

Paradoxical elements inside the company are essential for a large corporation to continue growing. Its business needs a stable section characterized by incremental growth juxtaposed against another section of emergent, even radical thinkers who 'think outside the box' in terms of identifying possible new avenues for business development and further expansion. To this end, top management must form and grant significant operational latitude to a new organization within the organization that is made up of personnel whose entrepreneurial spirit is understood to be an important asset for the development and creation of future opportunities for further business growth. Following this step, it is important that this new organization (emergent organization) be charged with planning the overarching strategic design for future business creation and also understand the need to quickly execute the specific actions detailed within that grand plan.

The creation of a foundation for innovation: creating new core competences

Leaders of the new entrepreneurial spirit-driven emergent organization should not be biased by existing conceptions and structures but should instead, while embracing this new point of view, take into consideration the future environment that the company may face; actively absorb knowledge generated through its partnerships outside the organization, including customers; create new core competences that will serve as the foundation for new business opportunities (products or services); and understand and act on the need to continually build on the foundation for innovation.

The acceleration of innovation: promoting overall company knowledge management

To ensure that the new business opportunities created by the new organization are given the chance to blossom into full-fledged businesses and business opportunities, it is imperative for both the traditional and new elements of the organization that knowledge management be promoted to the extent that the value system and success that accompanies innovation inherently resonates throughout the collective consciousness among employees (Kodama, 2001). This promotion of knowledge management by and across the entire organization serves as the impetus for business growth and expansion, and also accelerates the pace of innovation itself.

Strong leadership from the top management team

It is highly likely that there will be conflicts between the new and traditional organizations with regard to the promotion of knowledge management by and across the entire organization. Knowing this, however, in providing strong leadership, the top management team must understand the need to create a mechanism based on close inter-employee communication that serves as a platform by which the entire organization and its employees can convert conflict into constructive dialog and action. By acting as the steward overseeing both paradoxical strategies and paradoxical organizations within the company, the top management team encourages the growth and development of innovation.

In this chapter, the introduction of paradoxes was constructively understood to be the driving force behind organizational change, indicating one practical method for discontinuous transformation that uses paradoxes. Here, members of the top management intentionally introduced paradoxes within the corporation in terms of strategies, organization, culture, and competences and the like, and achieved strategic innovation through the use of knowledge management across the entire organization to control these paradoxes.

5
Dynamic View of Strategy in a Large Corporation: Challenges Toward Next-Generation Video Communications

NTT, Japan's largest telecommunications carrier, is currently facing a major period of transformation. As in other regions of the world, an optical-fiber infrastructure for broadband is being constructed at a rapid pace in Japan, and new products and services need to be created to generate customer value in this environment. NTT urgently needs to create new services that can compensate for the declining income from telephone services, once its largest source of profits, due to the growing penetration of IP telephone services. Meanwhile, in 2003, NTT Group member NTT DoCoMo and others introduced a flat-rate data communications service as part of their 3G mobile phone service, as developing new services that could differentiate themselves from competitors (KDDI's au and Vodafone) became an issue as urgent as broadband was on fixed communication networks.

This chapter will focus on NTT's video multimedia strategy, one of the fields of leading-edge technology that was included in the many business strategies that the company developed over the past 11 years. This chapter will describe in three general phases how NTT deliberately and strategically formed their video multimedia strategy as a new technology and market within a rapidly changing technology and market environment. Phase 1 covers new products and service development aimed at creating a new technology and market (1999–2002), Phase 2 covers the creation of new innovative services aimed at connecting PC-based videophone and mobile videophone (2002–2003), and Phase 3 covers the creation of new integrated services (visual fixed and mobile convergence services) for broadband and mobile multimedia (2004–present).

Phase 1: development of new products and services aimed at creating new technologies and markets (1999–2002)

In June 2000, the Multimedia Business Division of NTT started marketing a videoconferencing system for fixed telecommunication networks that also supports the 3G mobile videophone services that were launched in the spring of 2001. Videoconferencing systems using fixed networks have already become well established around the world as an IT tool for enhancing management efficiency (supporting decision-making via remote conferences and the like) at corporations. In the future, however, when technological advances allow videoconferences to be held over mobile networks, it will be possible for workers to videoconference with their office while they are out.

This new IT tool holds great promise for corporations to conduct business activities 'at any time, anywhere, and with anyone' on a level that was not possible before. The marketing and development teams of the Multimedia Business Division have formed an SC (SC-a in Figure 5.1) with the marketing and development teams of the Telecom Division of Mitsubishi Electric Corp. to conduct marketing surveys of mainly corporate users and to analyze the specifications that potential customers would require, including customers' usage scenarios and desired functions.

When this new videoconferencing system appears, not only will Mitsubishi Electric be able to sell the systems but it is expected that NTT will be able to benefit from an increase in new traffic resulting from video communications between fixed and mobile networks. From the results of marketing research conducted among users of existing videoconferencing systems, SC-a community members were able to identify sufficient potential demand for new fixed network videoconferencing systems that could be connected to 3G mobile videoconferencing systems.

A major hurdle toward the development of new videoconferencing systems has been the development of new system LSIs (Large Scale Integrated Circuits) to support the new multimedia applications handled by 3G mobile videoconferencing systems. The marketing and development teams of the Telecom Division formed an internal SC (SC-b) with the Information & Communication Laboratory in charge of internal R&D, and launched basic investigations aimed at developing system LSIs.

In addition, in order to absorb new digital video technologies that represent the core technologies of 3G mobile videoconferencing systems, the marketing and development teams of the Multimedia Business Division at NTT and the marketing and development teams and Information & Communication Laboratory at Mitsubishi formed an SC (SC-c) with the

R&D Laboratory and the video development team in the Mobile Multimedia Division at NTT DoCoMo, and started technical investigations into the details of communication interfaces and other areas of new fixed network videoconferencing systems that can be connected to 3G mobile videoconferencing systems.

A major advantage for DoCoMo was that the appearance of new fixed network videoconferencing systems that could be connected to 3G mobile videoconferencing systems would generate new, video-based traffic in addition to the existing voice and mobile Internet traffic over mobile phone networks. Though these technical issues for DoCoMo were only informal, the company devoted significant resources in the form of capable engineers and other resources.

In their new product development efforts, SC-a, SC-b, and SC-c created a network among themselves through which they could integrate the new knowledge they each generated and thereby determine technical specifications for the product based on customer needs and investigate system LSI architecture, design details, and other issues concerning the product. In this way, the networked SCs created new knowledge.

Approximately one year later, they completed a system LSI that formed the core technology of the new product. This was the first system LSI in the world to offer the dual functions of 3G mobile videoconferencing and fixed network videoconferencing, and it also succeeded in making the new product smaller (completed in December 2001).

The development of this product made peer-to-peer connection between fixed and mobile videoconferencing equipment possible. The next challenge for the video development team at the Mobile Multimedia Division of NTT DoCoMo was to develop a fixed teleconference device to which multiple mobile videoconferencing terminals could be simultaneously connected, allowing multiple people (or locations) to videoconference with one another.

At first, six employees in the video development team in the Mobile Multimedia Division, including a team leader, set to work drafting a plan for establishing a market for 3G-based mobile videoconferencing applications. Their vision was to construct a new, video communication-based video culture in Japan out of the country's telephone and text-based mobile communications of the past.

A team leader combined with other leaders outside the company (including customers) to create various SCs. He managed these several SCs simultaneously, then created networked SCs and worked to promote the mobile videoconferencing business. As a first step, in December 2000 DoCoMo agreed to form a strategic partnership with Mitsubishi which had capabilities in the core multimedia technology of videoconferencing. The partnership's purpose was to jointly develop a multipoint mobile videoconferencing system. An SC between DoCoMo and Mitsubishi was therefore created immediately (SC-d).

For DoCoMo, the objective of the SC with Mitsubishi was to ignite the Japanese mobile videoconferencing market in a single stroke, and at the same time launch the new wireless videoconferencing service to promote the 3G mobile market. Further, the multipoint mobile videoconferencing system for engineering, operation and customer support was performed through the creation of an SC (SC-e) with DoCoMo Systems, Inc., a DoCoMo Group company.

Along with developing the multipoint mobile videoconferencing platform, in March 2002 DoCoMo formed SCs with customers (SC-f) in order to set up the Multipoint Connection Experiment Consortium with the assistance and participation of companies in a variety of industries.[1] The main aims of the Consortium were to 1. verify the experimental platform for multipoint videoconferencing, 2. use empirical tests to evaluate marketability, and 3. work toward the development of applications that support services. Along with founding the Consortium, in May 2002, through the creation of networked SCs (SC-d to SC-f), DoCoMo also started conducting field tests of mobile videoconferencing to 3G mobile phones within corporations or at specific consumers.

DoCoMo was conducting a trial through the Consortium to study and verify the applications by each company based on actual usage. As part of the trial, DoCoMo conducted interviews and surveys concerning additional functions aimed at improving convenience and practical usage time. Engineers on both sides needed to have common specialized technical knowledge and a common language in order to address the issues they faced and make these efforts at joint product development a success. The issue of what portion of existing intellectual capital could be harnessed by this common specialized knowledge to bring reality to architecture or components or whether they could be utilized in version updates, or what portion of components or subsystems to be newly developed should be used to realize new architecture, was one of the important elements that enabled specialized engineers themselves to generally discriminate between differences.

The SC-d and SC-e networked task teams produced a prototype aimed at realizing development of the new service and conducted experiments aimed at verifying the desired functions and checking the service concept by having specific customers use the service. Through this trial and error process, the task teams were able to raise the level of perfection of the service that was to fulfill its positioning in the new market. The task teams were also able to accumulate knowledge assets in the form of new technical capability in the area of new service development. This process aimed to integrate competences (the organization's knowledge assets) and the target market position (service concept).

To establish market position, however, the developed product and service must be marketed through firm sales channels, and sufficient customer services must be provided. It is thus an urgent issue for NTT and NTT DoCoMo to establish a single business process of development, production, distribution, sales, and support. In parallel with the product and service development process, NTT and NTT DoCoMo development teams also formed an internal leading-edge sales organization (including other NTT Group firms and external sales outlets) and a technical support organization (also including other NTT Group firms and external sales outlets), as well as an informal task team (in the context of sales and technical support) aimed at establishing sales and after-sale support systems for bringing the new products to market. Through daily training in sales and support for bringing the new products to market, new capabilities in the form of sales skills and technical skills were also accumulated within the organization along with product and service development know-how.

The individual SCs in Figure 5.1 have different contexts. By having the same person participate in different SCs, however, they collectively understand and share the different contexts and knowledge above and beyond the borders of the SCs (pragmatic boundaries), and these different SCs thus form a virtual network. The roles of the leaders in the organizations (the SC leaders) are particularly important, as they are committed to more than one SC and they need to understand and share the constantly changing dynamic context with the members of each SC. Understanding and sharing dynamic context is not just a product and service development process but it also integrates the individual knowledge assets required by various business processes, such as sales and support or publicity and advertising, and allows new products to be brought to market. Organization leaders understand and share issues that emerge on a daily basis, such as 'How much progress has each SC made for the project?' or 'What are the current issues?' or 'Who will be the key person responsible for finding solutions?' The leaders extemporaneously find solutions to these issues.

In this way, not only was it possible for the sharing and integration of understanding and knowledge in the different contexts of the networked SC to turn new product development into reality, it was also possible for it to integrate the series of knowledge – from marketing, product development, and technical planning, to product development and manufacturing, and on to sales and support – required for bringing the new products to market, and to build and execute new business processes. As a result, the building of a new value chain and the accumulation of new knowledge assets were promoted simultaneously, the goal of being a world-first new product and service to be introduced from Japan was achieved, and a new market position and new capabilities were acquired at the same time (Figure 5.1).

Following the Multipoint Connection Experiment Consortium, as a second step, DoCoMo created networked SCs aimed at launching a commercial multipoint mobile videoconferencing service called 'M-Stage Visual Net' beginning October, 2002.[2] M-stage Visual Net provides a communications platform that enables numerous people to participate simultaneously in mobile videoconferencing via 3G video-enabled phones. Three different videoconferencing methods are possible. First, if a videoconference involves four people or less, the phone screen can be split into four windows to show each person simultaneously. Second, the phone can be set for full-screen display of each person (up to eight participants) as they speak. Third, all participants (up to seven participants) receive the same image from a single videophone.

Following the commercial service, as a third step, starting March 24,[3] 2003, DoCoMo expanded its M-stage Visual Net service to include the Personal Handyphone System (PHS) and wired videophones mentioned above using an ISDN network that had videoconferencing capabilities. With the service expansion, users of PHS video handsets and wired ISDN-based videophones were also able to participate in mobile videoconferences. The enhanced service further allows users to register up to five videoconferences at once. Previously, users could only register one videoconference. Moreover, a short comment on the meeting agenda and details, for example, could be included in the registration confirmation e-mail sent to participants together with log-in details citing the specific time of the conference and the designated access number.

Phase 2: the creation of innovative new services aimed at connecting PC-based videophones and mobile videophones (2002–2003)

Next, the author analyzes and discusses the case of the NTT Group's recent concrete efforts to realize the resonant communications environment through optical-fiber that form the core of NTT's Next-generation Vision of Optics that was mentioned in Chapter 5. On January 26, 2003, a consortium of companies centered on NTT, NTT Resonant, and NTT DoCoMo,

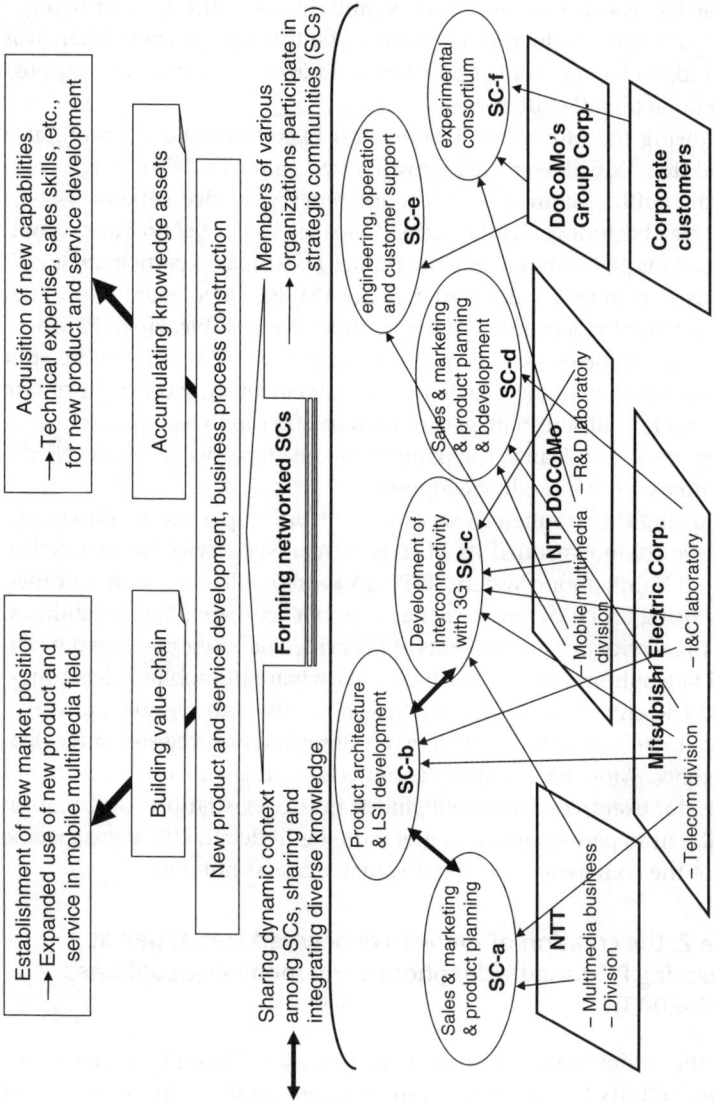

Figure 5.1 Acquisition of new position and capabilities (Phase 1)

three members of the NTT Group, developed a brand new video communications platform that utilizes a PC and 3G mobile phone (FOMA).

The videophone, a representative function of FOMA, creates a brand new style of communication that allows anyone to communicate anywhere, anytime. As of February 2005, the number of FOMA subscribers has topped 10 million, camera-equipped mobile phones with the ability to send emails with attached still photos have become a hit, and a future 3G-based communication style centered on email with moving pictures and on to videophones is stimulating the creation of a new culture based on video compared to existing 2nd-generation mobile phones.

At present, however, FOMA-based videophones can only communicate with other videophones connected either to FOMA or to an ISDN-based narrow-band videophone system. NTT therefore launched efforts to develop a platform with a resonant communications environment where a broadband PC-based video phone system and FOMA can engage in seamless mutual communication. Mr Hasegawa of the NTT Broadband Promotion Office at the center of NTT's broadband strategy commented:

'The lack of killer content even for broadband had been continuing for some time. We were especially aware that there were no examples of success in video-related content. We therefore wanted to establish a new platform that suited the age of optical communications. Video communications using videophones is already possible between FOMA mobile phones. However, a video communications environment where both fixed-line phones and mobile phones can freely communicate with each other as it has been possible with voice communications does not exist. Our wish is to come up with a practical platform that will realize a world where people can easily enjoy communicating with one another anywhere and at any time.' (NTT Technical Journal, 2003) NTT has embraced the conviction and belief that it will take even one step toward the strategic goal of realizing resonant communications.

Mr Sakuda of NTT Resonant, provider of the BROBA service that is already distributing a large volume of video content, has expressed strong interest in video communication services: 'A major theme of the broadband world is not just content but also communications. I feel there is tremendous potential in video communications focused on FOMA. A large number of BROBA members has expressed a desire for video communications with FOMA' (*NTT Technical Journal*, 2003).

The development of this platform started with the formation of SCs among NTT Group companies and various dialogs and discussions.

The NTT Broadband Promotion Office and the NTT Cyber Space Lab (NTT-SP Research) were looking into the development of new, seamless video communication services utilizing FOMA-based broadband, designed for NTT DoCoMo's FOMA service that was started in October 2001 in Japan ahead of any comparable introduction elsewhere in the world.

The success of this development, however, required the merging and integration of largely three different technologies. The first of them was broadband network technology, the second was operation technology, and the third was multimedia conversion technology. It was utterly impossible for NTT to pursue this development and realize a practical system on its own. It was therefore necessary for NTT to give birth to new knowledge in the form of compound technology by merging and integrating various element technologies such as broadband network technology and multimedia processing technology in the possession of the R&D Division in NTT's own organization and broadband operation technology in the possession of the development team at NTT Resonant.

To this end, the NTT Group immediately formed a cross-functional 'Ba' (SC-a in Figure 5.2) that transcends the boundaries between Group member companies. In addition, the sales division that possessed marketing and sales functions also participated in SC-a, and dialog and collaboration aimed at the target development was begun in this Ba. One of the core focuses of this development was the instant messenger (IM) functions newly developed by NTT-SP Research. NTT-SP Research developed a function capable of confirming whether a user was online or not and an IM function that could also be used from a FOMA mobile phone, though this function was not unusual between PCs.

According to Mr. Jozawa of NTT-SP Research, 'We were aware that IM could become a new tool for communication in the age of broadband, so this time we developed an IM function that used a FOMA i-appli. When this allowed users to confirm from their FOMA terminal that a PC user was online, they could then contact them by videophone' (*NTT Technical Journal*, 2003).

The development teams from NTT and NTT Resonant then formed an SC (SC-b) with the video business planning and development team in the Mobile Multimedia Division at NTT DoCoMo at an early stage of the development. They also engaged in thorough dialog and collaboration aimed at studying technologies for interface conditions such as the technical communications network configuration of the 3G mobile phone network and interoperability for 3G mobile phones and multimedia communications. At the same time, they actively collected information on customer needs that would be useful in this development. At this stage, linkage between SC-a and SC-b and the various Ba was realized. Then to clear a number of technical issues that occurred as the technologies were being studied in detail, NTT DoCoMo pursued collaboration with the world's best partners.

In developing protocol conversion (Gateway System), the NTT DoCoMo development team formed strategic ties and promoted joint development with company A, a best partner in Japan for IT system integration, and RADVISION whose headquarters are in Tel Aviv, Israel (SC-c). RADVISION is a global leader in the development, sales and marketing of products for multimedia communications that integrate sound, video and data in videoconferencing and video communications and on IP networks. Mr. Elie Dlon, Chief Technical Officer (CTO) of RADVISION, has been a stronger believer that demand for seamless video communications on broadband would certainly emerge if 3G mobile phones penetrated global markets in the future.

'DoCoMo has been a pioneer in 3G wireless since the standard's initial inception and rollout and, by delivering gateway functionality for real time multimedia between its users over its 3G network and users of IP based video clients, it will further solidify this leadership position,' said Gadi Tamari, president and CEO of RADVISION.

A second point following IM development and also a core development issue was to establish conversion technology for a communications protocol with different video and sound encryption systems. The main video and sound encryption system on broadband at the time was H.263/G71X, whereas FOMA used MPEG4/AMR, a different international standard. In addition, the communication protocol on broadband was H.323, whereas with FOMA it was 3G 324M. There was a need for technology that could convert in real time and in both directions these systems that were as different as oil and water. The three SCs from SC-a to SC-c were networked at this stage (Figure 5.2), and the development of a variety of new element technologies, including multimedia conversion processing and communication conversion, were thoroughly discussed in order to achieve live, interactive video communication end-to-end between a PC on broadband at one end and a FOMA terminal at the other.

At the end of this stage, platform development was completed in January 2003, and a three-month trial service for corporate customers was launched in March 2003. The development of this platform represented the first time in the world that international knowledge (in Japan and Israel) was merged and integrated to create new knowledge. Besides the realization of videophone communications between a PC and a FOMA

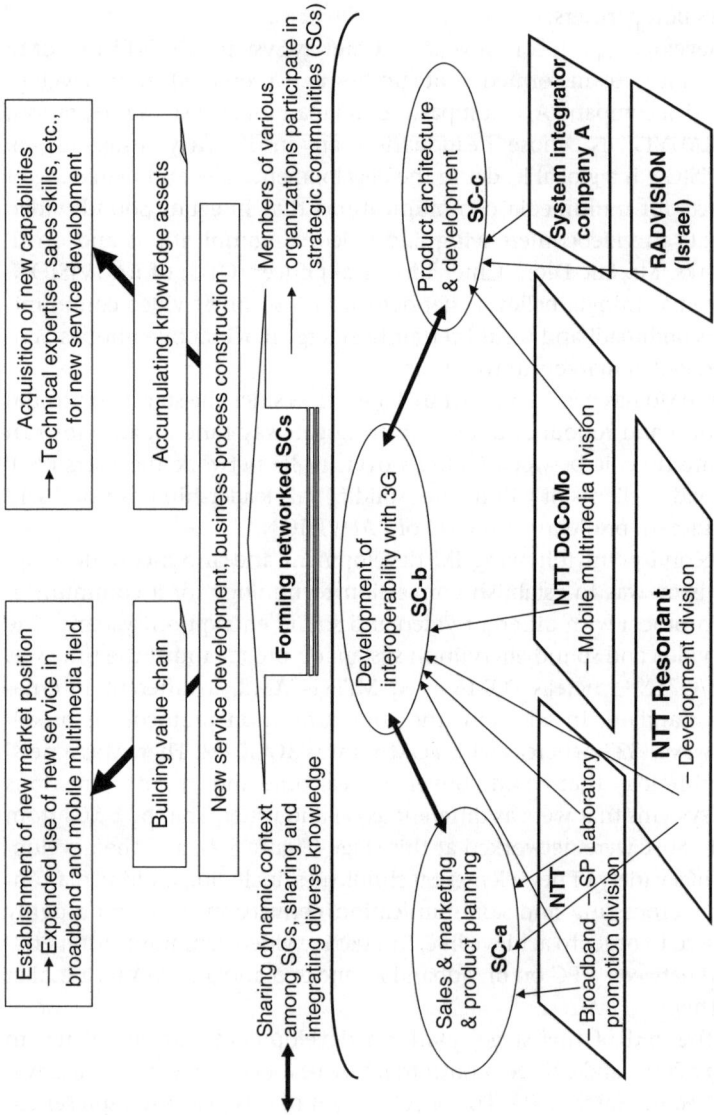

Figure 5.2   Acquisition of new position and capabilities (Phase 2)

device, this trial service also featured more advanced interactive communication thanks to the addition of the IM function. In videophone communications, it is possible not only to converse with someone but also to visually check their situation and respond accordingly. The development of this new platform promises to bring about a revolution in ubiquitous video communications, allow many people and businesses to overcome the limitations of time and distance and create new knowledge through real-time communications, and to become a tool for revitalizing community life and business life.

In this way, while NTT Group firms were establishing the new trial service in Japan and securing new market position, they were also accumulating new knowledge assets in the form of technical skills and sales skills in the areas of service development, sales, and technical support, as well as acquiring new capabilities (Figure 5.2).

Phase 3: the creation of new integrated services (visual fixed and mobile convergence service) for broadband and mobile multimedia (2004–present)

By verifying marketability and technical features in Phase 1 and 2 thus far, the NTT Group became engaged in the development of a new, full-fledged visual fixed and mobile convergence service. France, on the other hand, was pursuing the development of a similar service centered around France Telecom, Alcatel, Siemens, Lucent Technologies and others. At this same time, 3G mobile phone service was launched in Europe and video telephony was making news. The NTT Group had already led the world in introducing 3G mobile phone service and was aiming for its goal of being the first in the world to realize a full-scale service merging fixed-line broadband video service and 3G videophone service that would start in Japan.

As a first step, NTT, NTT Communications, NTT DoCoMo, and NTT Resonant formed an SC (SC-a) among themselves to look into marketing and technology strategies. To give form to these strategies, NTT, NTT Resonant, and Company B, a large domestic manufacturer of communications equipment, formed an SC (SC-b) to pursue joint development. SC-a and SC-b were then networked (Figure 5.2) in order to promote knowledge integration aimed at developing a service that would lead to a trial service in Phase 2 for the full-scale commercial service. About a year and a half later, in July 2005, it became possible to realize a videophone connection service between a PC-based IP videophone and FOMA (Figure 5.3).

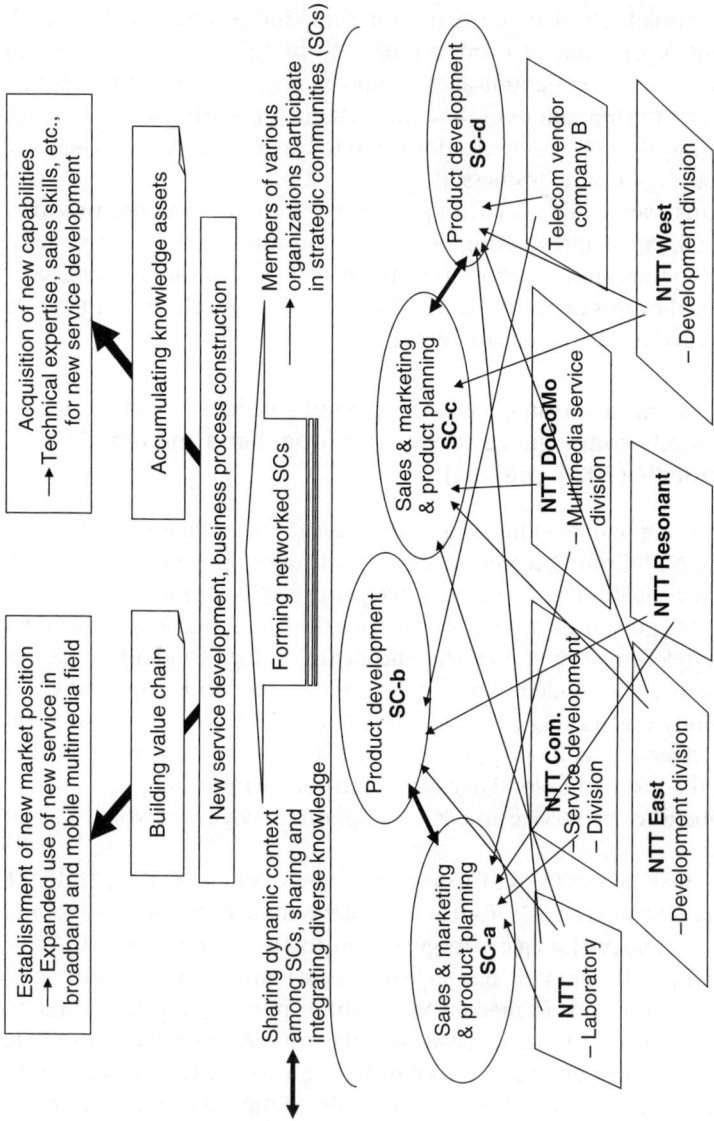

Figure 5.3 Acquisition of new position and capabilities (Phase 3)

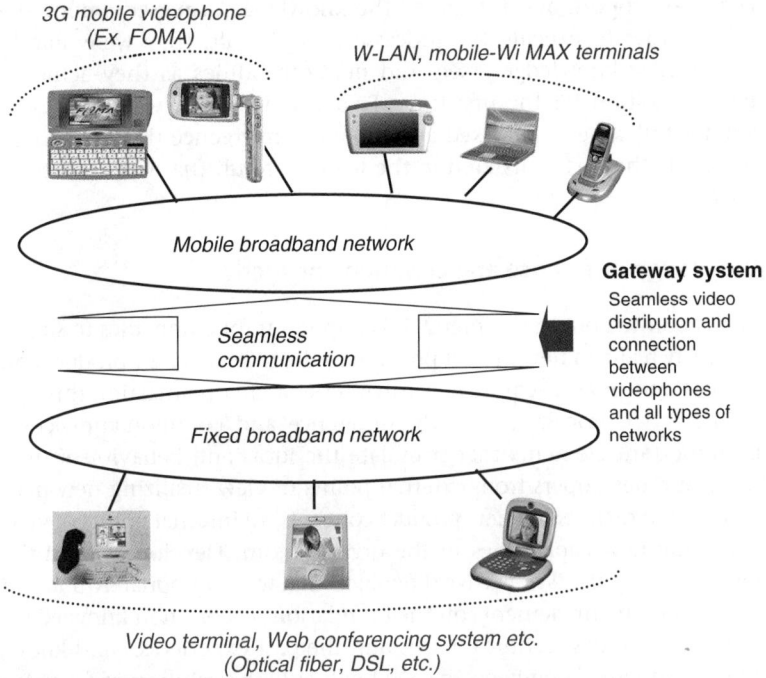

Figure 5.4 Integrated video transmission systems developed

Meanwhile, NTT East and NTT West, NTT's regional telephone companies, developed the FLET's Videophone, a single-unit device that represented an extension of the conventional analog phone and was different from the PC-based IP videophone. NTT East, NTT West, and NTT DoCoMo then formed an SC (SC-c) centered around NTT's research laboratories to look into marketing and technology strategies. To then give shape to these strategies, NTT research laboratories, NTT East, NTT West, and Company B, a large domestic manufacturer of communications equipment, formed an SC (SC-d) among themselves to pursue joint development. With the aim to start full-scale commercial service, SC-c and SC-d were networked (Figure 5.3) to promote knowledge integration, and about a year and a half later, in November 2005, a videophone connection service for FLET's Videophone and FOMA became possible (Figure 5.4).

The above three focuses in new commercial service development became the first of their kind in the world. Many members of the networked SCs shared dynamic context. Not only did they develop services but they also built a variety of business processes that led to sales and technical support, and integrated the knowledge dispersed among the SCs in order to execute the processes. As a result, they were able to acquire new knowledge assets and new capabilities as they achieved market position for the first time (Figure 5.3). This service in Phase 3 denotes full-scale visual fixed and mobile convergence (FMC) and also represents the first of its kind in the world, a result that was realized in Japan.

Knowledge difference and common knowledge

As was pointed out in Chapter 2, it is important for companies to simultaneously realize a new market position in the form of a new product and service concept and acquire new capabilities as an organization through an interactive process. 'Knowledge difference' and 'common knowledge' are important elements that stimulate the ideas and behavior of marketers and developers from external points of view (realizing new market position dictated by new product concepts) to internal points of view (acquiring new capabilities in the organization). Developers need the ability to recognize 'knowledge difference' that will appropriately uncover new development elements on the foundation of 'common knowledge.' This case includes technical terms and the past experiences and know-how of individual engineers in such fields as basic architecture for video communications technology, moving picture and sound compression technology, communications technology, Internet technology, and computer technology, which constitute both explicit and tacit knowledge that they can all understand. This represents 'common knowledge,' while 'knowledge difference' is represented, for instance, by new video compression element technology (or codec), new video transmission switching architecture, information management system architecture on mobile phones, and new LSI architecture, which are the new development elements identified among the developers.

On the other hand, in their aim to give shape to new products and services and establish business models, it is important for actors to reflect on ideas and behavior from the internal point of view (of acquiring new capability in the organization) to the external point of view (realizing new market position by bringing new products and services to market) through experimentation based on trial and error and a process of verifying hypotheses (a method of ideas and practice using abduction that is neither deductive nor inductive).

Executing the knowledge integrating approach through the ideas and behavior of actors from the external (market) to the internal (organization) and from the internal (organization) to the external (market) is a vital element in the dynamic view of strategy. Then in their aim to establish their goal of new market position, the actors recognize their knowledge differences, integrate internal and external knowledge through the networked SCs in order to acquire the new organization capabilities that they need, and synthesize the new capabilities with the new market position.

Tightly coupled networks and loosely coupled networks

According to lessons learned from the results of past research, systems integrators (such as the automotive industry or the hard disk drive industry) that independently execute R&D, design, architecture, assembly and other aspects of product development build loosely-coupled networks with many parts suppliers, facilitating efficient product development. On the other hand, since communication manufacturing companies that develop mobile phone systems need to respond to dramatic changes in the environment, it would be better for them to build tightly-coupled networks in vertical integration with parts developers and manufacturers (Busoni *et al.*, 2001; Busoni, 2001). These results can be considered a theoretically appropriate conclusion if the network structure is taken from the aspect of coordination via systems integration or coordination via vertical integration. On the other hand, however, a different interpretation is possible if taken from the aspect of the environment that companies face (the growing diversity of customer needs and rapid advances in technology in particular), the technological context (in the fields of technology and products), and how much knowledge is shared among partners.

If, for example, the author's experience as a developer in the field of IT and info-communications is compared with the details obtained from discussions with developers at electronics manufacturers, in reality, there are numerous scenarios in which consistency in architecture and components among parts manufacturers and systems integrators, a number of delicate adjustments in hardware and software to be developed, and in-depth discussions and exchanges among engineers with tacit knowledge are necessary. In a case like this, for instance, once a decision has been made to form ties with vendors and detailed task-based collaboration has started among engineers, in the aspect of the extent to which information and knowledge is shared, loose relationships change to tight relationships as sharing at a deeper level is required.

Though communication carriers like NTT Group firms and communications equipment manufacturers like NEC, Fujitsu, Hitachi, and Mitsubishi also rely on target development products, handsets that change dramatically with customer needs or technology, multimedia products, software and other products are very different from communications equipment related to infrastructure (such as switching and transmission equipment), and there are many cases (especially in the mobile field) in which not only tight relationships need to be maintained but also partners must be frequently recombined while monitoring many candidate partners.

NTT Group firms as knowledge integrators in this case formed a number of flexible loosely-coupled networks (Weick, 1976; Morgan, 1981; Orton and Weick, 1990) with various internal and external vendors in the process of forming new strategies at each stage, and monitored a variety of internal and external information and knowledge (Weick, 1982). (NTT Group firms were in charge of the overall system except R&D, product concepts, device design, product functions, architecture, and others.) NTT Group firms then selected what they felt was the best vendor, and when they formed a strategic alliance with the vendor, the SC that was in a flexible relationship changed to a tightly-coupled network aimed at an integration in which context and knowledge was shared at a deeper level for the sake of product development. To build a solid business process, NTT Group firms established strong links between the SC with the vendor and other internal and external SCs such as the sales and support divisions, fostered the sharing and understanding of different contexts, and promoted the process of sharing and integrating the different knowledge.

The SCs that were in a tightly-coupled network with the vendor, however, were not continually maintained, and the SCs were rebuilt in response to the company's own desires and changes in the environment. The linked relationships were reviewed according to changes in customer needs and technology, an SC was formed with another partner, and the SC that had the character of a tightly-coupled network changed to a loosely-coupled network or a decoupled network. In reality, the relationships between NTT Group firms and external vendors in Figures 5.1 through 5.3 were never fixed network relationships. NTT Group firms used tightly coupled networks to promote current development, and in their aim to develop subsequent businesses at the same time, they together sensed and monitored information and knowledge in loosely coupled networks with various vendors at home and abroad. These sorts of network relationships between firms provide different perspectives than would occur in the Keiretsu (mutual share-holding) relationships of Toyota and other automobile manufacturers that maintain long-term business transaction relationships by building relationships of trust. In other words, in industries where markets and technologies such as broadband, multimedia, and mobile communications undergo considerable change, stable long-term business transaction relationships are conversely like leg-irons.

One observation that can be made from these phenomena is that the character of the relationships with the partners, from the viewpoint of sharing and integrating knowledge, constantly changed on the time axis between a tightly-coupled network and a loosely-coupled network. A second observation is that companies build tightly-coupled networks with the best partners timed with decisions made concerning strategic ties while loosely-coupled network relationships are maintained at the same time with other vendors to search for new businesses. A practical benefit of paradoxical management[4] concerning networks among organizations that synthesize different modes of SC formation on both the time axis and space axis could be that it is an effective way for these companies to avoid falling into core rigidities or competency traps caused by path dependence. In other words, project leaders in charge of development promote product and service development currently in progress through tightly-coupled networks while they search at the same time for future business opportunities through loosely-coupled networks (Figure 5.5). These companies' use of the bipolar mode with loosely-coupled networks and tightly-coupled networks can be seen as being similar to the research results of Pettgrew noted below (Pettgrew, 2000).

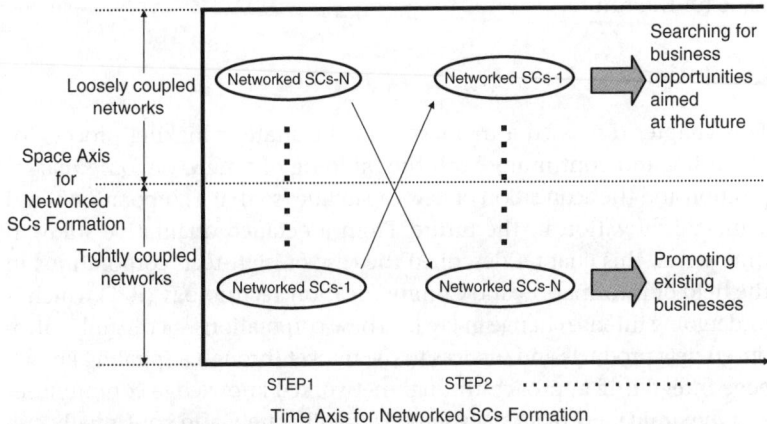

Explanatory note: Loosely coupled network and tightly coupled network SCs (SC-1 to SC-*N*) co-exist at each step of strategy execution. These network relationships change dynamically along the time axis according to environmental changes or deliberate corporate strategies.

Figure 5.5 Dynamics of paradoxical SC formation

There is a long tradition in management and organization theory of using bipolar modes of thinking and action. The bipolar concepts are variously explained and used as paradoxes and dualities. Pettgrew reported nine key dualities that innovative firms use to simultaneously build hierarchies and networks, seek greater performance accountability upward and greater horizontal integration sideways, empower and hold the ring, maintain the discipline to identify knowledge and the good citizenship to share knowledge, and attempt to centralize strategy and decentralize operations, and so on. This survey also showed that some firms were innovating simultaneously in many of the elements of the three areas of structures, processes and boundaries, and that many of the innovative firms were exposing themselves to a range of dualities.

An important point here is Pettgrew's assertion that the bipolar mode comprising tightly-coupled networks as vertical integration within the corporate hierarchy and flexible network relationships among various companies is one factor that produces innovation. The SCs in the tightly coupled network of this case are joined in a tightly coupled network as vertical integration with SCs within the company, while the SCs in the loosely coupled network with external partners can be interpreted to be the flexible network described by Pettgrew. Though this sort of paradoxical management in networks among companies can be thought to be dependent on the environment around the company, the type of industry, or the character of the product to be developed, a detailed study will be an issue for the future.

Conclusion

This chapter discussed a framework of the strategy-making process for executing and continuing both the building of a new, ongoing market position and the acquisition of new capabilities so that a corporation could achieve innovation in the future. From a detailed qualitative study in time series, this chapter described the case of high-tech corporations in the field of Information and Communication Technology (ICT) which is undergoing intense change in Japan. These corporations successfully introduced new products and services to the market through a spiraling knowledge integrating approach through networked knowledge communities as a dynamic view of strategy aimed at deliberately and continually creating new markets.

6
Innovation Through Boundary Management: The Creation of a New Business Model

Hi-tech markets in such fields as system LSI technology led by Japanese semiconductor manufacturers and digital household appliances led by Canon, Matsushita, Sharp and other companies have been rapidly emerging in recent years due to the strength of demand for digital products in Japan. Matsushita has been achieving new heights in profits and market share particularly with hi-tech products in which semiconductor, software, opto-electronics, broadband communications and other technologies have been integrated. Matsushita has captured global market share by adopting such revolutionary production reforms as cell production and speedy new product development through core technology black-boxing and flexible, modularized designs. (Matsushita holds the No. 1 position in global market share for DVD recorders.)

In fiscal 2001, Matsushita Electric, a traditional Japanese manufacturer of general electrical appliances, recorded the largest loss in its history. Then, following drastic structural reforms, the company's business results experienced a rapid V-shaped recovery. By transforming its product development strategy from the old technology-led type to a customer-led type and implementing far-reaching organizational reforms, Matsushita emerged as a global leader in the field of digital household appliances. Matsushita's new product development capability was founded on the formation of a number of SCs, which represent the organizational boundaries within and outside Matsushita Group companies, and on the organizational integration of these SCs. In this chapter, the author uses a detailed case study to describe the mechanism of boundary management that enabled Matsushita Electric to simultaneously establish a new market position and achieve competitively advantageous capability in the hi-tech field of digital appliances by balancing vertically integrated SCs and horizontally integrated SCs.

Destruction, creation, and the great leap forward

On 9 January 2004, Matsushita Electric announced their 'Great Leap 21 Plan,' a mid-term management plan for the coming three years starting with fiscal 2004. This plan set targets of ¥8.2 trillion in consolidated sales and a consolidated return on investment (ROI) of better than 5 per cent for fiscal 2006. Since his appointment as president of Matsushita Electric in June 2000, Kunio Nakamura has been implementing reforms under the theme of 'Destroy and Create.' Though Matsushita Electric recorded the largest profit loss in its history in fiscal 2001, it has enjoyed a sudden V-shaped recovery in business results after it instituted drastic structural reforms.

Dismantling the business department system, one of the pillars of the reform, allowed the company to select and concentrate on management resources and business domains. The Marketing Division, for instance, amalgamated development and production into a strategic product planning and business unit to create an organic organizational operation structure that freshly questioned the existence of the value of making things from the users' points of view. This reform led the way to the so-called 'V products' which were digital appliances such as DVD recorders, digital TVs, and digital cameras.

President Nakamura's strong faith in the revival of Japan's manufacturing industry was reflected in the structural reforms at Matsushita:

> The manufacturing industry was declining in recent years and we had to do something about it. From now on, it is important to concentrate on what potential there is in technology and to transform ourselves into a manufacturer of distinction. During the '90s, Matsushita Electric was a dispersed, autonomous type of company and the R&D layer was thin. During the period of mass production, it was fine for us to be imitating other companies, but now with the growth of digital technology, we need to develop distinctive products quickly. The most important point in a strategy is to do what other companies are not doing. To achieve that, we need to concentrate on black-box type technology development and I believe Japan will then again become a manufacturing nation. (President Nakamura)

The 'V product' cited in Matsushita's 'Great Leap 21' has three features: Black box technology, environmental considerations (energy-saving, recycling), and universal design. In fiscal 2004, Matsushita has been selling

71 'V products' with the aim of capturing No. 1 market share and of generating sales income of ¥1.5 trillion. Supporting the marketing, development, and production of 'V products' has been a positive activity of middle management and young employees with vision, something that had not been well developed under the old business department system. One of the features of the structural reform is that the pyramid organization of the old business department system was changed from a structure with up to 13 layers to one with 4 layers, creating a flat, web-type organization. New posts such as Business Unit Manager and Team Leader were also established, providing an environment in which ambitious young employees ('chiefs' or 'managers' who are also union members) can play major roles. This 'Nakamura Reform' gave birth to SCs in which middle managers and young employees could participate responsibly in business projects.

Rapid growth and the business model of DVD recorders

In the first quarter of 2003, Matsushita Electric expanded their operating income to ¥43,500 million, a 2.2-fold increase over the same period a year before. Sales of DVD recorders, plasma TVs and other digital household appliances have been strong. Matsushita's global market share for DVD recorders is currently No. 1, at 45.2 per cent, and for plasma and LC TVs, it is ranked No. 3.

In his management policy announcement for fiscal 2002, President Nakamura stated his aim of using 'V products' to either capture or maintain top market share and to realize a V-shaped recovery in profits. The DVD recorder, positioned as a representative V product, records and plays back digital video images, replacing the video tape recorder (VCR). Matsushita predicts that DVD will surpass VHS in 2005. With the expansion of the market for DVD recorders, Matsushita is also aiming to make DVD-RAM a *de-facto* worldwide standard.

Matsushita Electric's primary strength is the value chain it has built using the vertically integrated business model that combines production stages from basic research, component development and product development to production, sales and solutions (Porter, 1980, 1985). The following are the structural elements of this vertically integrated model: the development of next-generation technologies aimed at becoming future digital appliance technologies, the black-boxing of core technologies, the development of products supporting multiple models, cell production as a reform in manufacturing, a sales system for gaining dominance in the domestic market and a system for developing business models aimed at new solutions.

Matsushita's second strength is the building of a horizontally integrated business model. This includes the establishment of a sales system using global management to effect simultaneous vertical launches on a global level aimed at capturing global market share, the horizontal development of a technology platform through such means as transferring Matsushita's knowledge of core technologies or providing OEM supplies of parts and sets (products), and the development of new business through Group management aimed at launching network or environmental business or through strategic links with other companies (Figure 6.1). By balancing these vertical and horizontal business models, the Matsushita Electric of today was able to simultaneously capture resources and skills that are superior to those of other companies and to establish a competitively advantageous market position and core technologies in the field of digital household appliances.

Matsushita Electric's organizational dynamics

Behind these vertically and horizontally integrated business models is Matsushita's unique integration of organizational boundaries. In other words, the optimum SC design is SC vertical integration and SC horizontal integration (Figure 6.2). The vertically integrated SCs consist of an R&D SC, a Product Development and Production SC, a Product Planning SC, a Sales SC and SCs with customers. These SCs are strongly interdependent. The vertically integrated SC network is bound by strong ties that enable actors (organization leaders or managers) to share and create knowledge, both tacit and explicit.

The horizontally integrated SCs, on the other hand, consist of a Global Management SC, a Group Management SC, a Technical Platform SC and SCs with Firms of Different Industries as strategic links. However, in addition to the strong ties of the vertically integrated SCs (Kodama, 2005a), these also include a network of SCs with loose, weak ties (Granovetter, 1973). Once a new opportunity comes, weak ties enable actors to effectively embed structural holes with weak ties so that actors in SCs on both sides can access new knowledge of a different nature and build completely new business relationships that have never existed before (Burt, 1992). For example, Matsushita Electric today has brought under its umbrella Matsushita Electric Works, a company with which it has had a loose capital relationship in the past, and is working very hard to harness Group management synergy toward the launching of a future residential space business.

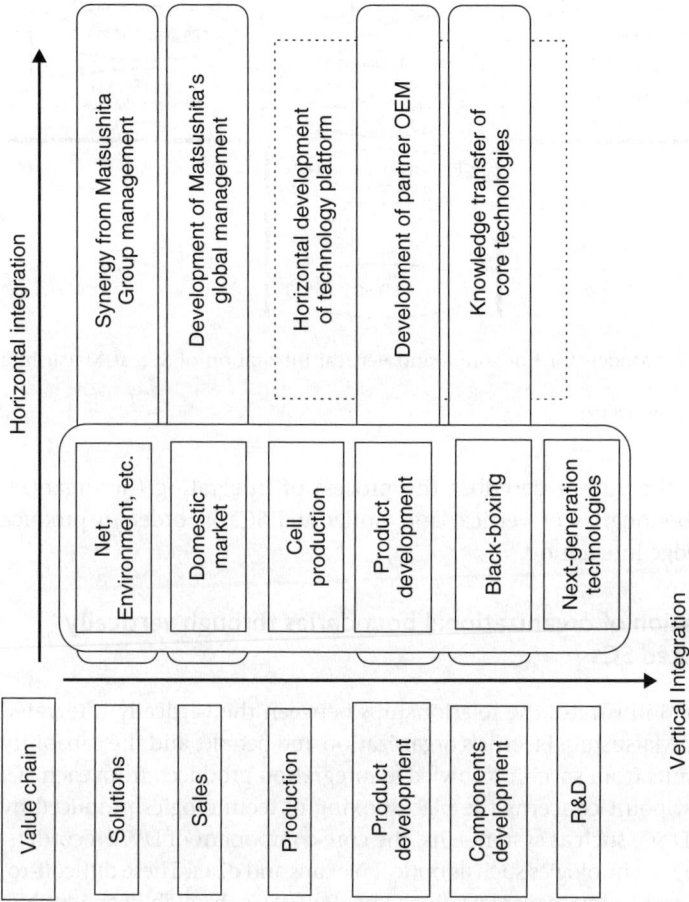

Figure 6.1 Matsushita Electric's digital home appliance business model
Source: Kodama (2007).

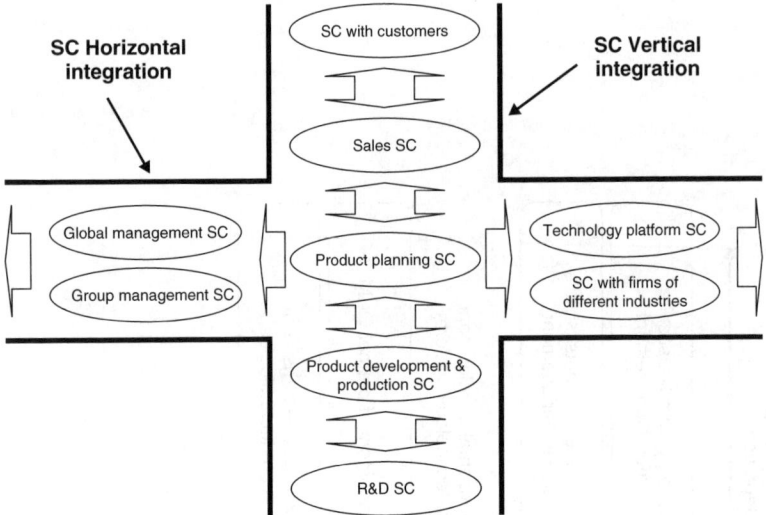

Figure 6.2 Models for horizontal and vertical integration of SCs at Matsushita Electric
Source: Kodama (2007).

Next, the author describes the process of integrating the organizational boundaries of vertical and horizontal SCs in order to produce knowledge integration.

Integration of organizational boundaries through vertically integrated SCs

Figure 6.3 illustrates the relationships between the vertically integrated SCs and Matsushita Electric's organization and people, and the capability that results from specific knowledge integration produced from each SC. The first point concerns the black-boxing of technologies produced by the R&D SC, such as system LSIs, the core component of DVD recorders, and other technologies such as optical pickups and discs. These difficult-to-imitate technologies were produced by dense SCs through deep involvement and deep embeddedness between the product development teams of AVC Networks' Development Center and Matsushita Semiconductor Company's development group.

In developing system LSIs, one of the black-boxed technologies of DVD recorders, both divisions of AVC Networks and Matsushita Semiconductor always shared technology roadmaps and developed in-depth discussions at

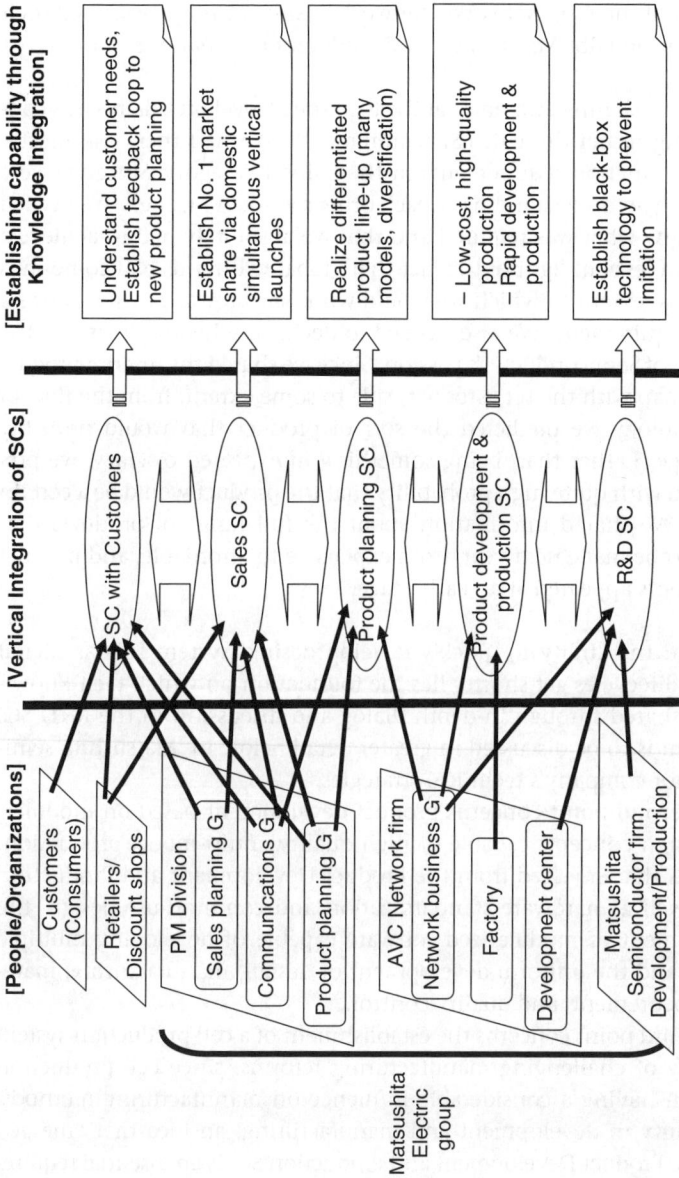

Figure 6.3 Knowledge integration through vertical integration of SCs
Source: Kodama (2007).

various management levels, including business manager level, department manager level and head of development team level. Mr Matsumoto, Manager of the AVC Networks' Network Business Group, described their collaboration with Matsushita Semiconductor Company as follows:

> We were sharing awareness at the team-head level on a daily basis concerning rather difficult LSI requirements. We had them ask mostly about function requirements in the chipset category. Since we were gaining an understanding of each other's work or business, we needed to know what was required and that we absolutely had to achieve a certain level in light of the fact that global LSI trends had come thus far. The extent to which we would work hard toward this goal was a key requirement. We also needed to decide a schedule. This was the depth of Semiconductor's passion. Since we shared the interim product roadmap with the set (product) side to some extent, from the flow of technology we predicted the sort of product that would probably emerge. Rather than being something unexpected or crazy, we predicted with quite high probability that the product would be a certain way. We shared information about the full range of products that would be made next year, from expensive to affordable, and product concepts appeared at an early stage.

Behind the ability to quickly develop desired system LSIs as digital product lifecycles get shorter lies the foundation on which tacit knowledge is shared through in-depth dialog and discussion in the R&D SC. This item is to be discussed in greater detail below in 'Matsushita semiconductor company's technical strategies.'

The second point concerns product development based on modularized design concepts capable of high-quality, multi-model production, concepts that emerged from the Product Development and Production SC, as well as hardware standardization and common-use design, the development of modularized software capable of developing multiple models and the uniform development of design, manufacturing, materials procurement, and quality control.

The third point concerns the establishment of a cell production system as a way of challenging manufacturing reforms, since cell production has been having a considerable influence on manufacturing methods. Uniformity in development and manufacturing, an idea that emerged from the Product Development and Production SC, is an essential requirement for accelerating the speed of bringing new products to market and improving quality. Though it takes a bit less than a year starting from the initial concept stage to bring one DVD recorder model to market, it is important to improve and overcome problems with cell production at the current plant at an early stage. A unique feature of Matsushita's method is to create close links between plant engineers and technicians from the initial concept stage and finally to provide them with details of the design and manufacturing process. Before the die is made, the manufacturing side receives feedback from the development division about a variety of ideas and issues, such as how the product, including prototypes, can be made more easily or how the manufacturing process can be improved. Feedback from engineers comes because this is cell production.

In addition, the move toward internal manufacturing of production equipment, a new production management system, is currently enabling the ratio of personnel, original cost repayment and other fixed expenses in manufacturing costs to break 5 per cent. Another of Matsushita's advanced technologies is the black-boxing of technology. This SC lies in the close dialog and ability to act with AVC Networks' Development Group and the plant. Concerning this point, Mr Matsumoto, Manager of Business Unit and a key person at AVC Networks, states the following:

> The following three points are basic to R&D procedures. The first point concerns standardization and modularization, the second point concerns the integration of key devices and the accumulation of know-how through close links between the Set (product) Division and Matsushita Semiconductor, and the third point concerns black-boxing and other technologies in an easy-to-manufacture process brought about through close links between design and manufacturing. Even when new DVD recorder features are added or old ones are changed, schedules are moved forward, or other events suddenly occur, there is a system in place to absorb these surprises and respond accordingly. Since advanced functions and low prices have passed these three conditions, we achieve our objectives as a result. There is never any compromise.

It can be said that the current technology innovations in DVD recorders are due to this strength in Matsushita's development and manufacturing. The changes in the PC boards of DVD recorder models E-10 through E-50 are all hidden (Figure 6.4). In miniaturizing the PC boards from E-10 to E-20, the encoding functions that compress analog video and audio signals into digital signals were amalgamated from 7.5 IC chips to one chip. The decoding functions were also amalgamated this way, from 6 chips to one chip. In the E-10, 9 wires were used to connect the PC boards to the motherboard that was placed at the bottom of the product's interior. In the E-30, this design was improved, allowing the PC board to be inserted with pins directly to the motherboard. And to shut out noise from the PC board, the LSI packing technology was reviewed (changed from the typical quad flat package with a peripheral terminal array to a compact, high-performance, multi-pin chip-size package), reducing not only the package area but also the number of steps in the assembly process. In this respect, a major feature of Matsushita's DVD recorders is this success in reflecting advances in the company's own system LSI development and high-density packaging technology, advances that have enabled Matsushita to balance the contradiction of greater functionality in the product and lower prices.

AVC Networks' developers are not simply acting passively in response to demands from the Panasonic Marketing (PM) Division. Those men (and women) are aware that at the same time as they are developers and engineers they are themselves customers and consumers. The new DVD recorder models incorporate functions proposed by the technical side.

MPEG4 functions were inserted in DIGA SD cards from the E100 Series. These functions were inspired by a proposal from the field side of technology (a young technician). If we ask what they are, the development side is always studying what kind of functions are to be introduced in the next year or two. Somehow the idea that this is what has to be done in order to sell the next DVD recorders has been created on the technical side of the field and the concept if formed while the PM Division is being sounded out on the suggestion that this could be done next year. In other words, various demands are being answered because the possibility has been studied beforehand to some extent on the technical side. It is a result of brainstorming, not just a development from a customer. In cooperation with Mobile Communication Company, which is developing mobile phones, the development was immediate by adjusting FOMA's MPEG4 file format. Actions between and within domains have been simplified by lowering the barriers. (Project M Leader, Kawamura)

Promotion and publicity by the PM Division is essential. A novel function is a function that the customer does not yet know. A new method of use due to the new function (involving a development expense) is to be offered in a manner that the customer can understand. Various trial and error methods such as catalogs and magazine articles are employed. Selling involves transferring new functions and new methods of use to the customer by the transmission of information

E20 Digital PB 230×88 mm

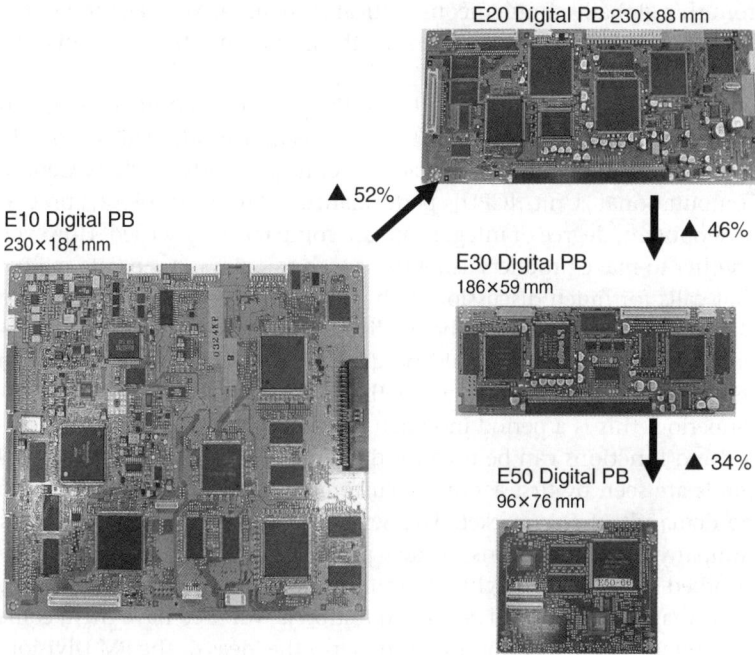

E10 Digital PB
230×184 mm

▲ 52%

▲ 46%

E30 Digital PB
186×59 mm

E50 Digital PB   ▲ 34%
96×76 mm

Figure 6.4   Changes in the size of DVD recorder PC boards
Source: Matsushita Electric.

from the manufacturing side to the selling side in this way. At first, the manufacturing side assimilates the demands of the selling side and puts them into practice. Next, when the manufacturing side has been able to introduce this function with this technology, the fact that this can be done is put to the customer in a meaningful way and selling proceeds. At the time of divisional organization, there were organizational boundaries and it was very difficult to make comments such as this. It is much easier to handle now. Everyone understands that the aim is for collaboration and acts spontaneously. (Business Units Manager, Matsumoto)

Moreover, key devices such as system LSIs were designed to handle all the different voltages and broadcasting systems in each country and DIGA, which was launched in March 2003, achieved globally simultaneous vertical launching. The realization of the marketing power and technological strength to achieve the continuous conception of new products is necessary in order to achieve the market supremacy that was derived from this globally simultaneous vertical launching. Mr Matsumoto, the Business Units Manager, is suggesting the importance the power of organizational linkages:

'The PM Division at the front line is the present customer demand. In that regard, there are also ideas from the technical side. This is done in consultation with the PM Division. Technical trends (such as Central Computational Unit [CPU] performance, core technology, process development, degree of integration) are comparatively settled. However, whether to make products using these technologies is a separate matter. That calls for much discussion with the PM Division. The Set Division will propose a base that can be predicted by technology. Which combination of technologies should be used for producing a product is an important matter for discussion with the PM Division. Unlike the analog period, this is a period in which an assembly of essential technologies and functions can be used for digital products. However, technical trends are seen by first assuming customers' needs in accordance with the demands of the market. The Set Division and the Semiconductor Company make provisions for new products. A small departure can be absorbed by deeper thought and immediate revision. However, because of the many options available, the question is where to have them come together. It is probably important to merge the ideas of the PM Division, the Set Division, and the Semiconductor Company.'

The third feature is the existence of the Product Planning SC that plans the product concepts underlying the DVD recorder line-up in response to customer needs. The Panasonic Marketing (PM) Division that has been split from the various sales departments is the organization that aspires for a new product strategy aimed at creating post-VHS businesses. As a product supervision division, the PM Division is responsible for the planning, marketing and sales of a product, as well as buying back all the products. This point represents a significant reform from the days of the old business department system at Matsushita Electric. In those days of mass production and the business department system when it was easy to sell just about any product they made, this confidence game between sales and technology was fine, but in this world of digital technology where product lifecycles are short, this sort of approach is no longer valid. At the PM Division, personnel responsible for products are committed to the entire process of a new product, from planning to sales.

The core of sales and marketing is 'people.' Ever since the PM Division was inaugurated, Mr Ushimaru, the Director of the PM Division, has boosted the sense of unity within the PM Division through thoroughgoing discussions with company members by arranging for the joint ownership of values towards innovation and the creation of new markets. Then, with the flattened web type organization, all 600 employees of the PM Division were placed closer to the customers in aiming at the rapid and flexible vertical launching of V products.

The organizational structure of the PM Division is described next. Primarily in charge of the marketing of A/V products is the Product Planning Group. There is also one team, the Home A/V Team, which has been divided for each product category. Mr Ishihara is responsible for DVD recorder marketing and product planning. Alongside the Product Planning Group is the Communication Group, in charge of public relations (PR), advertising, sales promotions, Web sites and other areas. Mr Osaka is responsible for the PR Team in charge of DVD recorder PR and advertising. There is also the Sales Planning Group, which governs sales companies and outlets and manages sales for all products. During the age of the business department system, before the PM Division was established, the business departments pursued their operations independently and an overall synergy at Matsushita could not occur. After the PM Division came into being, the flattening and web of the organizational structure stimulated much faster sharing of information and decision-making.

Product planning in the days of the business department system began with all concepts in the range of single products. With video for instance, video only was considered as a single item for sales and development as well as production. Public relations and publicity were also bundled into that department. A point of major change, however, is that information sharing has become close, and in organic links with public relations and publicity under the wide-ranging idea of digital networking with the Panasonic brand as the product axis, the extensive view seems to have become the optimum overall image as a product. Moreover, with the flattening of the organizational levels, there is less distance between the Director and the operational forces, and the communication of ideas is better and faster. At that time we also changed suddenly to the PM Division and gathered business people from all operational departments, but the ways we had each been working up to this time were all different. Out of that we searched in many ways to find the best approach to act as the PM Division and finally settled on a common method. Then management became easier with the flattening of the organization as the people responsible for each product became more clearly defined. We were able to gain a mutual understanding of the intentions of the relevant sections with whom we dealt regularly and could plan for products that would stand up in the view of the market. (Mr Ishihara, Home A/V Team)

There were many disconnected separate levels at the time of the business department, but with the PM Division they came together in a flattened organization. Information had been very difficult to transmit up to then, but now the matching of understandings and the making of decisions are quickly settled. With the PM Division, the people responsible for the product have the authority and, with regard to public relations for DVD recorders, Ishihara and I pool our understandings and report to our superior. Key people have been appointed with regard to the products, and important matters can be settled by talking between a few people. (Mr Osaka, Communications Group Public Relations Team)

To pursue ideal product planning without compromises between AVC Networks and the PM Division, the Product Planning SC formed an SC to engage in constantly intense discussions. The Product Planning SC establishes a strong linkage between technology and the market through which it carefully listens to feedback from the market and incorporates the ideas into product development. In this way, it is possible to quickly respond to changes in customer needs and engage in rapid technological innovations. Two key persons at the PM Division provided the following statements:

Since we are close to the market, we receive a constant stream of various information from customers. In our efforts to plan new DVD recorders, we monitor changes in the market and engage in various interactions with the AVC Networks development team. The PM Division provides advice on what needs to be done to make a product that will sell. Though it is important to study trends at other companies as well as to listen to feedback from customers and the market, it is also important to incorporate our own ideas in the products. Since the PM Division is responsible for taking delivery of the product and selling it, it cannot expect AVC Networks to buy back products that were difficult to sell. The PM Division's expanded right to speak has only added to the weight of its responsibilities. There are times when a product's specifications or design will change even just before it goes to market. We never compromise the content of a product plan. Technical issues that remain difficult at the end are solved with conditions attached. (Mr Ishihara, Home A/V Team)

Until now, sales people simply sold whatever the business department made and anything it couldn't sell was returned to the business
division. In the relationship between sales and technology, even if
the technology had been made, sales would say they wouldn't be able
to sell it and the tug of war between sales and technology ended up
with both sides blaming each other. After the PM Division and the
buy-back system was set up, though, if a product didn't sell, the PM
Division has to take responsibility for it and this has made it possible
for the PM Division to tell AVC Networks that they wouldn't buy a
product if they didn't make it in the way they wanted it. AVC Networks
then says they understand the requests and would do their best to
make the product, so the discussions now go in a more positive, constructive direction. In the past, sales mainly followed a product-out
concept in which they simply sold whatever was made. I can feel the
huge change that has occurred in the quality and speed of interactions between the PM Division and AVC Networks after the organizational structure was revamped. AVC Networks is asking about some
very stringent requests concerning both technology and price. The
two sides are also providing feedback to each other concerning distribution as early as the product planning stage, so the work now progresses very smoothly. As a result, relationships of trust can now be
built between the various organizations. (Mr Osaka, Communication
Group PR Team)

The fourth feature is the Sales SC that implements vertical launches of
DVD recorders on the domestic market. Until now, the PM Division had
been implementing a completely different sales strategy for DVD
recorders. The new sales strategy was named 'vertical launching.' It
refers to selling large quantities of new product at the time of release and
capturing high market share within about a month. When sales of that
model begin to lag, large quantities of the next new product are sold.
This means that market share continues to grow as this process is
repeated. Speed is of the essence in this sales strategy (Figure 6.5).

The PM Division released Matsushita's first DVD recorder, the E-10, in
June 2000 at a price of ¥250,000 and as a result of thorough marketing
surveys and customer trends, the second model, the E-20, was released
in July 2001 for ¥135,000. After that, the E-30 was released in March
2002 for ¥93,000, dropping below the ¥100,000 barrier, and the E-50 followed in March 2003 at a street price of around ¥60,000 (recommended
retail prices were no longer used by this time). In just three years, 'vertical
launching' enabled Matsushita to stimulate the DVD recorder market in

Market Share

Secure
large
share

Release   1 month

Time

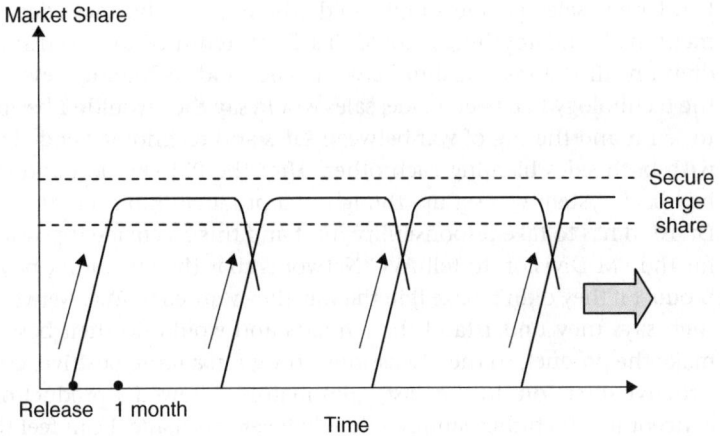

Figure 6.5   DVD recorder 'vertical launch' strategy
Source: Kodama (2006).

Japan in a significant way and to capture the No. 1 position in market share (Figure 6.6).

Behind the success of this 'vertical launching' was the organic collaboration with the Sales SC that linked its advertising and sales activities with the Product Development and Production SC and the Product Planning SC. A major feature of this organic collaboration was that it came as a result of dense, multi-layered SCs that were formed among a variety of organizations. For example, an organic, multi-layered, cross-functional SC of various sections (the Product Planning Group, Communication Group, Sales Planning Group, and others), spanning marketing, product planning, sales and advertising was formed within the PM Division and various strategies and tactics were narrowed down toward the 'vertical launching.' SCs were also actively formed with Group companies Matsushita LEC, Matsushita CE and other sales and distribution companies, which shared with the PM Division detailed customer and consumer information from volume discounters and specialty shops.

The SC with Customers, the final SC, obtained the views, requests and potential needs of consumers through direct marketing activities at events and exhibitions and over the Internet, and a system for providing appropriate feedback to the Sales SC and Product Planning SC was established.

Single vertical launch

50.8%
49.0%
46.2%
44.0%
40.5%
38.0%
36.8%
27.4%
10.1%

E50

Vertical Launch

(Share)

Release 3/2 3/9 3/16 3/23 3/30 4/6 4/13 4/20 4/27 5/4 5/11 5/18

50.0%
40.0%
30.0%
20.0%
10.0%
0.0%

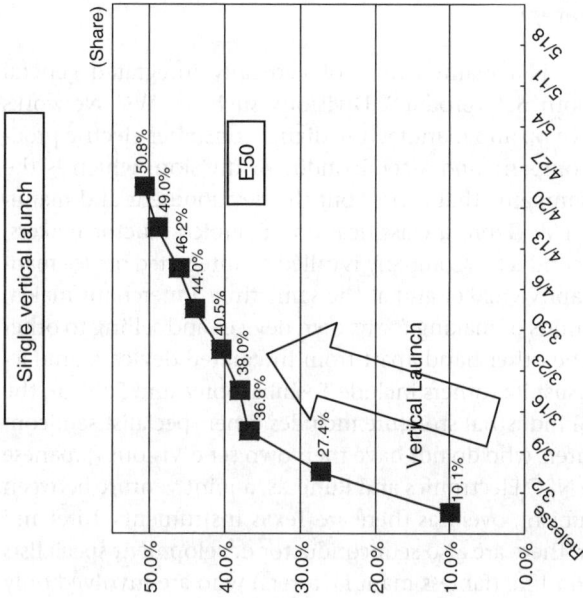

Single Type: Model with standard functions

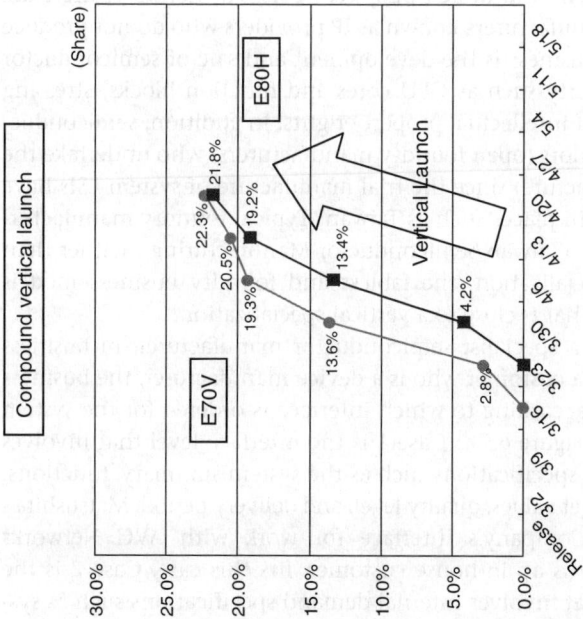

Compound vertical launch

21.8%
22.3%
20.5%
19.2%
19.3%
13.4%
13.6%
4.2%
2.8%

E80H

E70V

Vertical Launch

(Share)

Release 3/2 3/9 3/16 3/23 3/30 4/6 4/13 4/20 4/27 5/4 5/11 5/18

30.0%
25.0%
20.0%
15.0%
10.0%
5.0%
0.0%

Compound Type: Standard DVD recorder model with various optional functions

Figure 6.6 DVD recorder 'vertical launch' results
Source: Matsushita Electric.

Technical strategy of Matsushita Semiconductor Company – black boxing strategy

Matsushita Electric is a manufacturer of vertically integrated general devices having both Set (product) Divisions such as AVC Networks Company that develop and manufacture digital consumer electric products within the company and a semiconductor division, which is the Semiconductor Company, that carries out the development and manufacture of system LSI. (From a classification of semiconductor makers, Matsushita's Semiconductor Company is called an integrated device manufacturer. It is a captive maker and at the same time a merchant maker, having both functions of making for its own devices and selling to other companies.) On the other hand apart from integrated device manufacturers such as Matsushita (others include Toshiba, Sony, and Fujitsu), the present system LSI industrial structure includes other specialist semiconductor manufacturers who do not have their own set divisions (Japanese examples include NEC Electronics and Runesas, a joint venture between Hitachi and Mitsubishi; overseas there are Texas Instruments, Intel and others). Moreover, there are also semiconductor development specialists with no production line (fabless manufacturers) who are involved only in the development and design of system LSIs. Furthermore, there are development manufacturers known as IP providers who do not produce LSIs but whose business is the development and sale of semiconductor intellectual property such as CPU cores and function blocks, stressing the importance of intellectual property rights. In addition, semiconductor specialist vendors (open foundry manufacturers) who undertake the work (LSI manufacture) since the trial manufacture of system LSIs have begun to appear in places such as Taiwan. Typical foundry manufacturers include TSMC (Taiwan Semiconductor Manufacturing). Rather than a horizontal specialization, the fabless and foundry business models have a structure that is close to a vertical specialization.

In the case of a specialist semiconductor manufacturer, in business discussions with a customer who is a device manufacturer, the business details will vary according to which interface is ordered for the system LSI design flow (Figure 6.7).[1] Case 1 is the interface level that involves external demand specifications such as the system summary, functions, performance, target values, quality level, and delivery period. Matsushita's Semiconductor Company's interface for work with AVC Networks Company, which is an in-house customer, fits this case. Case 2 is the interface level that involves internal demand specifications such as system LSI block diagram architecture design sheets. Case 3 is the interface

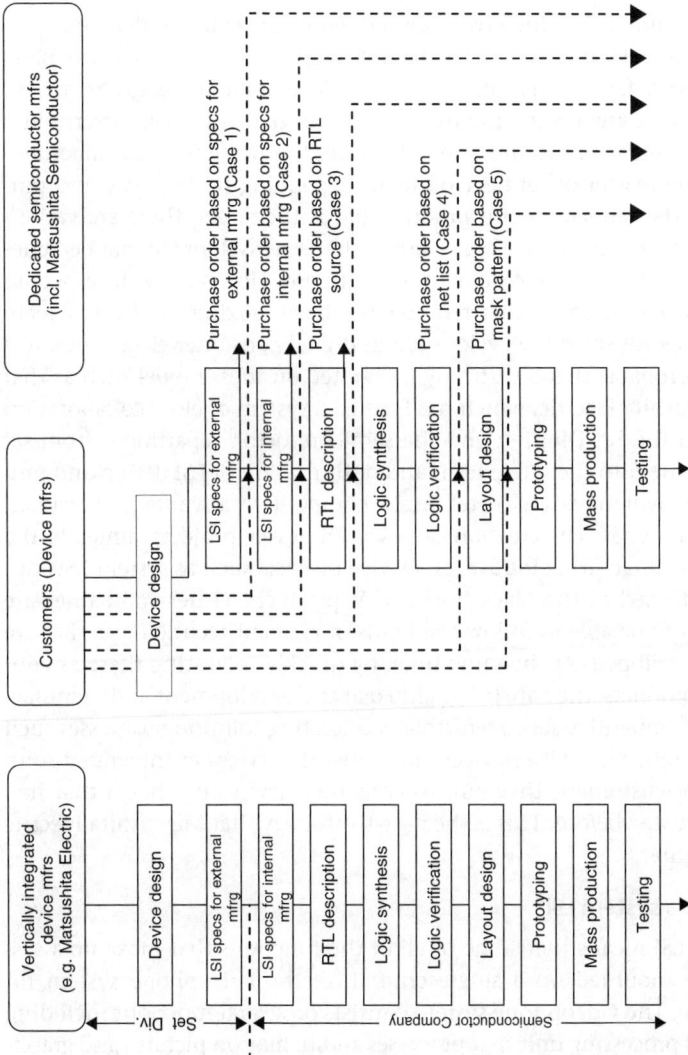

Figure 6.7 Manufacturing process and business structure of system LSIs
Source: Prepared by author based on interviews with semiconductor-related people.

level that involves the register transfer language source code[2] and is in the charge of the semiconductor specialist manufacturer following logical synthesis. Case 4 is the interface level that involves logical circuit diagrams (net lists) and is in the charge of the specialist semiconductor manufacturer following layout design. From the external demand specifications level of Case 1 to the layout design of Case 4, there are many cases for a fabless manufacturer of a development design model to undertake. Case 5 is the interface level that involves mask patterns and is in the charge of a foundry manufacturer following trial manufacture.[3]

On the matter of set development, depending on the type and purpose of the semiconductor product that is the target, there are various options as to which interface to use to share the system LSI that becomes the core with the semiconductor department. However, with respect to product development that requires the black boxing of element technologies with short life cycles such as digital consumer electronics, it is highly probable that a vertically integrated business model such as that of Matsushita Electric, which has formed a system of close collaboration between the Set Division and the semiconductor department from set development to the integration and optimization of LSI design and production, will have an increasingly competitive advantage. President Nakamura cites 'The creation of powerful device projects' aimed at the super manufacturing industries. Device projects such as system LSIs can be positioned as the black boxes of V products. Other companies are unlikely to be able to follow the kinds of element technologies that are being developed. At the same time, by quickly mounting these as consumer products, they are being aimed at the development and manufacture of competitive sets. By further accelerating solution businesses such as sets embedded with devices and network services as integrated solutions for customers, they aim to construct new value chains that had never existed before. This is the growth strategy that Matsushita Electric is targeting.

What is a system LSI?

System LSI means that some or all of the functions that make up a system are mounted on a single chip. Take the videophone system for example. The videophone system consists of several functions including a digital processing unit that processes audio, motion pictures and graphics, a CPU section that controls the entire videophone system, and a memory section for the storage of data. Up to now, LSIs have involved only digital logic (the so-called hardware section). Because of the limitations on the degree of integration in an LSI, system structures achieve

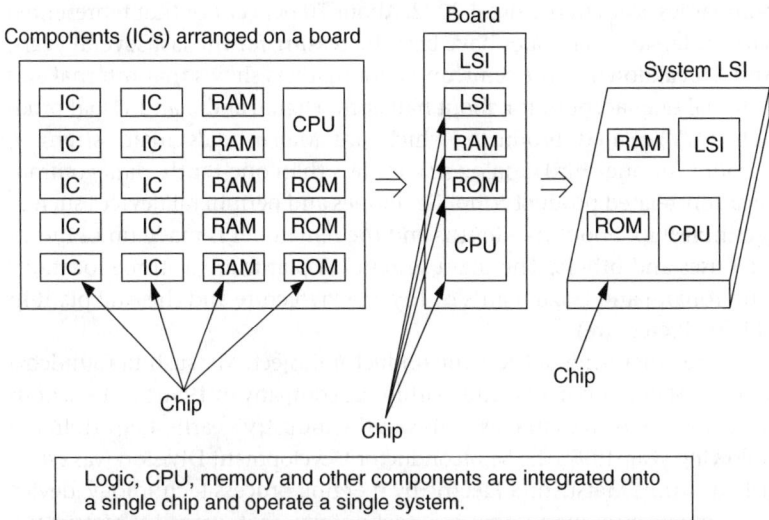

Figure 6.8   What is a System LSI

one function by combining several LSIs. Nevertheless, when the degree of integration increased not only was it possible to integrate in one chip all of the digital signal processing function that make up digital logic but functions other than the control section and memory could also be mounted in the chip (Figure 6.8). This is system LSI, also known as system-on-a-chip (SoC).

A Semiconductor company that supports system LSIs

For the last several years as director of a semiconductor company, I have devoted all my energies to the launching of a system LSI project in particular. As a result, system LSIs were suddenly connecting across products in various fields. Even if semiconductor development and device development are cut, they are not cut off. Perhaps many in-company engineers are beginning to feel that. When the semiconductor is powerful the device is powerful and if you look at history, it is plain that the converse is also true. (Makoto Koike, Representative Managing Director, Matsushita Electric Industrial)[4]

Semiconductor Companies support the development and manufacture of system LSIs, which lies at the heart of Matsushita's consumer electronics products. System LSIs accounted for about 50 per cent of semiconductor companies' sales in the fiscal 2002. About 70 per cent of that represented sales in Japan. Asian sales have been increasing for the last several years, and a breakdown of the semiconductor markets shows that internal and external sales account for about half each. Digital audio and visual products (A/V)-related products, which are Matsushita's main strength, account for one-third, analog A/V for less than one-tenth, data communication-related products (mobile phones and peripheral devices such as facsimiles) for about two-tenths and the remainder is made up of industrial uses and others. The main system LSI plants are at three locations (the Tonami and Uozu plants in Toyama Prefecture and the Arai plant in Niigata Prefecture).

As a restructuring of the semiconductor project, Matsushita founded a system LSI development center within the company in 1996 for the serious development of system LSIs. This was the industry's earliest effort. In the following year, 1997, the Semiconductor Development Division was established within Matsushita Electric by merging process technology, device technology and manufacturing technology that were in Matsushita Electric Industrial. Then the Semiconductor Operations Division was established independently from the Matsushita Electric Industry Operations Division. This strengthened the semiconductor project and eliminated duplication within the Matsushita Group. From about 1996 there was a great slump in demand for DRAMs and Matsushita formally withdrew in 1998. The operations division and the development division were absorbed in 2001 to establish the Semiconductor Company, an internal company, with an integrated system embracing development, manufacture and marketing. The Semiconductor Company is positioned as a leading example of the Nakamura 'Destruction and Creation' reformation. In 2002, the industry's first and largest scale mass production of $0.13\,\mu\mathrm{m}$ was started. In this way, the rapid structural reformation of Matsushita's Semiconductor Company and the strategic conversion to system LSIs put the operational retreat from DRAMs into the background. The Semiconductor Company not only has the most open Set Division in the Matsushita Group, it has grown into an organizational system that is also collaborating with outside customers and proactively pioneering in the field of digital consumer electronics.

In the system LSI business, 'technical development style marketing' becomes important to forecasting the potential market and deciding which key businesses can be developed based on the knowledge that is the core of one's own company. To raise system LSI development productivity (discussed later) as much as possible, a business management system with the capability for coherent vertically integration from

Future evolution of semiconductors depends on new market creation and ability to take the lead.

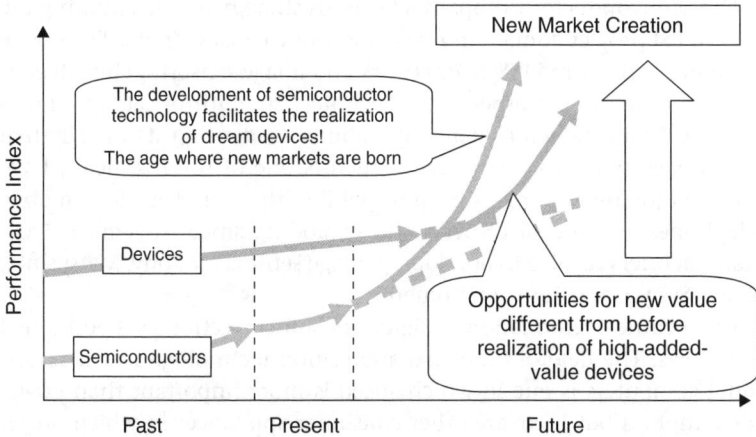

Figure 6.9 New market creation
Source: Matsushita Electric.

upstream to downstream, from design to software development to devices to processes to production, becomes necessary and indispensable.

By comparison with the growth of sets up to now, the development of semiconductors has followed with very great difficulty but the miniaturization of semiconductors has gathered pace suddenly in the last several years and it has appeared possible that they will outstrip the future demand for sets. Consequently, when set performance and semiconductor performance have crossed in the future, for the Set Division and the semiconductor division to come together and create new markets is a major issue for Matsushita Electric (Figure 6.9).

System LSI business domain and strategy

At Matsushita, taking the average growth rate for all sets to be 6.8 per cent per year, within which the growth rate for digital consumer appliances is seen to average 12 per cent per year or twice the growth rate for all sets. System LSIs have a growth rate of about 18 per cent, and this is where Matsushita's strategy is focused. The field of digital consumer appliances in which system LSIs are the nucleus includes a variety such as DVD, digital TV, digital cameras, mobile phones as well as car navigation systems and in addition, due to broadband, the world expects these sets to be joined seamlessly by networking.

The Semiconductor Company's business strategy is concentrating the system LSI project domain in five fields (optical discs, digital TV, mobile communications and ITS, SD/network and image sensoring) by integrating market growth prospects, the technical strength of sets (products) and the Semiconductor Company's ability to develop its own system LSIs. Image sensors in particular, which is one of the five fields, have been enjoying strong demand while the market for mobile telephones and digital cameras was exploding since November 2003. Manufacturers capable of developing image sensors are Sony, Matsushita, Sharp, Sanyo, and Texas Instruments.

The technical reformation of digital consumer electronics is positioned as follows. The field of industrial application technologies such as personal computers is one in which speed is more important than power consumption but there are other consumer appliances in which power suppression and increased quality are more important than speed. However, for digital consumer electronics the various issues that must be integrated include fast processing of high-grade complicated signals, ease-of-use and low cost. The resolution of these issues involves system LSI. The highest technology and most closely limited costs are sought for Matsushita's system LSI. Moreover, the major competition for system LSI is on the time axis. In the case of DVD-ROM at present, the product life-cycle is being curtailed to about three months. In the period of analog video VHS, one technical platform could be in use for two years and a few improvements could ensure the life of the product life for about one year. But with digital consumer electronics, major paradigm changes are breaking in with specification changes in as little as three months.

The Semiconductor Company differentiated between the five fields that emerged following a process of selection and concentration based on wisdom and time, and focused on the following three points. In order to execute de facto formation and multifaceted recovery (including the recovery of invested development costs), it is important to sell OEM boards and semiconductors not only for own-company brand sets but also for those of other companies. Also, there is the sales promotion of intellectual property (IP). Even Matsushita has not been all that proactive about IP in the past, but sales of SD cards, for instance, are overwhelming, and the security and coding in these are Matsushita's IP.

Differentiation of the first point concerns system technical strength (system architecture, system design and software technology), process technical strength (detailed processing technology, multi-layer wiring technology and packaging technology) and LSI design technical strength (memory mixed loading technology, analog mixed loading technology and low power technology), which provide customers with a total solution based on a system LSI single chip solution that depends on this three-level integration of technological strength. Differentiation of the second point concerns the establishment of a development mechanism with a development precedence semiconductor roadmap not only for the Set Division within the company but also to be shared with external customers and made available to future key customers aiming at the same goal. This is a system LSI business model connected with black boxing, which is the final goal. In particular, the AVC Networks Company, which is the biggest in-company customer, implements large scale conferences at least twice each year to interchange awareness from top management to each business unit manager and development chief and to arrange for the development road map to be shared periodically with the Set Division and the Semiconductor Company, which are the final product development side:

> The Semiconductor Company's road map is frequently discussed and shared by the Set Division, the laboratory and each management level. On behalf of the Semiconductor Company, we are watching product trends ten years hence and semiconductors that will be important in the future will be precisely developed. The Set Division is making a similar road map. (Nishijima, Semiconductor Company System LSI Development Manager)

Differentiation of the third point concerns conversion to the importance of development productivity. There is a tendency for increasing design production costs and development expenses associated with the expansion of the scale of system LSIs due to the real advent of the age of digital networking consumer electronics. Therefore, in order to improve development productivity and provide customers with timely solutions, it is important to bring actual design productivity closer to Moore's Law. Moore, CEO of Intel Corporation in the US, predicted that in three years, gate scale and capability will be four times greater, and this trend is still continuing at present in the semiconductor industry. Going one-chip like system LSI has great benefits such as higher functionality and reduced size, but on the other hand, miniaturization is accompanied by increasing difficulty of design (known as the so-called design crisis). Improving design productivity means somehow plugging the gap with LSI scale. The Semiconductor Company's target is to increase design productivity by

136

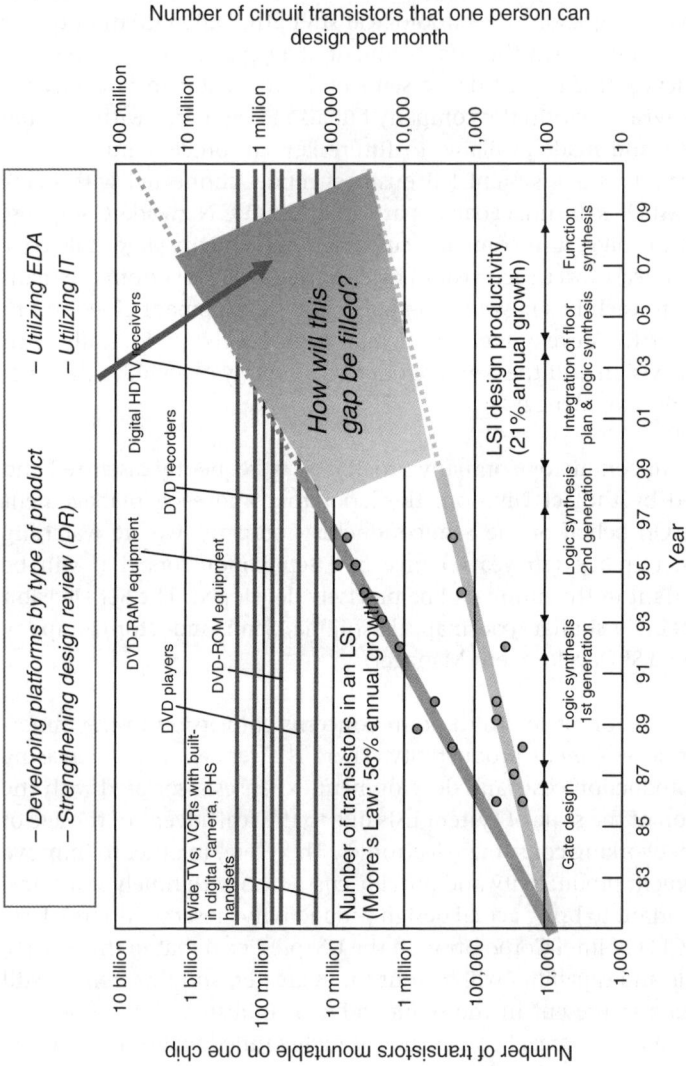

Number of circuit transistors that one person can design per month

100 million
10 million
1 million
100,000
10,000
1,000
100
10

– Developing platforms by type of product — – Utilizing EDA
– Strengthening design review (DR) — – Utilizing IT

Digital HDTV receivers
DVD recorders
DVD-RAM equipment
DVD-ROM equipment
DVD players
Wide TVs, VCRs with built-in digital camera, PHS handsets

How will this gap be filled?

LSI design productivity (21% annual growth)

Number of transistors in an LSI (Moore's Law: 58% annual growth)

Gate design
Logic synthesis 1st generation
Logic synthesis 2nd generation
Integration of floor plan & logic synthesis
Function synthesis

Year

83 85 87 89 91 93 95 97 99 01 03 05 07 09

Number of transistors mountable on one chip

10 billion
1 billion
100 million
10 million
1 million
100,000
10,000
1,000

Figure 6.10 Moore's law and growth in design and productivity
Source: prepared by author based on SEMATEC.

building a platform for each product area through the effective use of design assets (IP), fast verification of large scale logical circuit designs as well as intensified design reviews through electronic design automation and improving development speed through the sharing of information on development processes through the Intranet. By these means, somehow the company's competitive strength on the time axis will be increased, and it will quickly take the lead over other companies and proceed to sell superior products (Figure 6.10).

Mr Nishijima, head of the Semiconductor Company's system LSI development department, comments as follows on the background that enables Matsushita to release so many types of DVD recorders on the market so quickly:

> Firstly, marketing has ended and we should now be able to sell these sorts of products. Once that is done, they can be made into sets. Good. Let's make them. Next, it's a matter of making LSIs, but actually, if you ask why Matsushita can finish quickly and get into the game, it's because it can only start when you have all the parts in the palm of your hand. The development of DVD recorders has a long history. Around 1992 Matsushita decided that optical discs would be the main business company-wide. At that time, the idea of making DVD recorders such as we have now had not yet been reached, but from that time, Matsushita's laboratory and Semiconductor Division have been devoted to making the essential element technology. Later, around 2000, the Marketing Division and the Set Division came in and specific product development began. An important factor for speed is that up to that time we had been building up an accumulation of element technology. Then a platform for DVD recorders was created on the basis of this element technology and through the pursuit of new element technology, such as expanding existing platforms or designing new special circuits, a speedy response to specifications demanded by the Set Division has been made. Accordingly, the technology for 70 to 80 per cent of system LSIs is already in hand with existing IP. The important point is whether the future can be seen somehow and element technology developed and accumulated.

Activities for creating knowledge required for system LSI development

Taking Japan's semiconductor industry from the viewpoint of competitive strength, for DRAMs there is a manufacturing value-added system that was revived by improvement, which is Japan's strong point. For system LSIs, however, this is the core component of various digital consumer electronics, and an intellectual value-added system gains in importance. With the acquisition of intellectual property rights, how to somehow launch the product on the market quickly becomes a problem. In addition, design is important with system LSIs, and factors such as design yield rates and design production costs are different from digital random access memory (DRAMs). For that reason, improving the accuracy of design and reducing design production costs with IT or electronic design automation (EDA) tools can be one way to strengthen competitive advantage. On the other hand, although specialist semiconductor designers are initiating young designers with their technological proficiency in the design reviews that are conducted at each design step, it is important to have an ongoing system (between system LSI function blocks and between modules as well as verification of the entire system, requirement specifications and confirmation of performance) in which all members are united as one. System LSI development engineers are required to have expertise in matters such as the height of the degree of completion of the hardware description language that exactly reflects function specifications, methods of implementing ideas for new design techniques and circuits (such as reducing the scale of circuits with algorithms improved by trial and error instead of entrusting logic synthesis to IT, raising performances to the utmost limit) as well as analog circuit technology:

> For system LSI development, the further upstream a process is, the greater is the know-how required. In other words, if we consider the horizontal axis showing production cost and the vertical axis showing LSI capacity, in a highly abstract situation, LSI capacity will be settled between 80 and 90 per cent. If the basic architecture and algorithms do not have a high-quality RTL, system LSIs with good performance cannot be achieved. Moreover, EDA tools all have unique characteristics. Whether or not the result is efficient depends on how they are used, and engineers must build up various types of expertise and share it with everyone. In the standard design flow, which tool to use and how to use it is to be determined from a manual or other instructions. Design methodology is clearly determined and know-how on the use of tools is to be built up by individuals. The design flow is to be amended when a new tool appears. Then the individual's know-how (tacit knowledge) is to be formalized. In a design review, a multifaceted check of the design process is to be made piece by piece (architecture

level, RTL level, logic level, layout level, and so on) with respect to product specifications by all of the various engineers (specialists). System LSI development is a wide ranging area from software engineering to quantum mechanics, and the product is useless if even one of the 5,000 transistors is faulty. Such a fault cannot possibly be grasped by a human. Accuracy must therefore be increased as formal knowledge using IT such as computer simulation. Since the failure of one design involves several hundreds of millions of yen, the design process must be of high quality. System LSIs are not simple like memories. Development is a game that involves many complicated essential inspection processes by the design and emulator (simulation by hardware) in accordance with the degree of abstraction. Consequently, who will do it and when it is to be done must be determined precisely beforehand. It's like a space program that shoots a rocket with computers in full operation. (Mr Nishijima, head of the Semiconductor Company's System LSI Development Department)

Another point that should be noted concerning the basis for the background to the creation of Matsushita's competitive digital consumer electronics products is the sharing of deep tacit knowledge and the great creative energy between the Set Division and the Semiconductor Company. When the decision was made to withdraw from DRAMs, then President Koike considered that in addition to the Semiconductor Division's hitherto accumulated strengths in LSI design and processing technology, its technological strength would need to be boosted towards strengthening the system LSI project in order to make timely responses to the demands of outside customers (such as device manufacturers). Then some excellent engineers with skills in system technology were transferred from the Set Division to the Semiconductor Division to improve their technical strength in Semiconductor Company algorithm design, software development and architecture design, and at the same time to promote positive collaboration between the different organizations by breaking down the barriers with the Set Division:

At Matsushita, some engineers have been shifted from the Set Division to the Semiconductor Company. This means the engineers will have a very high level of tacit knowledge and understanding concerning sets. Since they were originally familiar with semiconductors as the main constituents of consumer applications, the engineers' level of recognition and awareness of consumer appliances is very high. Although they are making a road map, before that, they all had the impression, as tacit knowledge, that the Set and semiconductors divisions would change in that way. Based on that tacit knowledge, they are probably aware that element technology such as this must be developed on the Semiconductor side in the future. This is the result of collaboration and synergy between the Semiconductor and Set divisions, which is only possible in Matsushita Electric. They both feel that they are in a win-win situation. (Mr Okada, Semiconductor Conductor Company Business Group Manager)

The importance of training project leaders (silicon masters)

The existence of a project leader, called the silicon master, who is responsible for the design review, is of particular importance for system LSI development. Under the project leader, there is a number of specialists who are responsible for subtasks. If the project grows in size, the project organization will be stratified by the appointment of a sub-leader. However, a pipeline system will be implemented whereby a specialist for each process will fluidly participate in their process on a number of projects:

> This kind of project management style is being implemented from the past accumulation of Semiconductor Company experiences and is different from the semiconductor business models of other companies. In the case of Matsushita's Semiconductor Company, they made a road map and improved development efficiency while forming tie-ups in advance of the Set Division. However, even though the specifications were vague, full efforts were made to commence development. A specialist semiconductor company that has no set division but receives purchase orders based on the customer's final specifications has a form for development organization and a form for administration that are clearly different. It is also fundamentally different from DRAMs. (Mr Okuda, Group Manager of the Semiconductor Company Planning Group)

The project leader is the one who holds the key to system LSI development. The number of system LSI projects a business has is determined by how many great leaders it has. This may also be considered to hold true for the competitiveness of its sets. With the development of nano-level semiconductor manufacturing technology, LSIs have already exceeded 50 million transistors in 2000, and on the basis of $0.1\ \mu m$ technology, it is expected to reach 200 million components in 2005. This means that it will become practically possible to accumulate all technically essential functions on one silicon chip in nearly all digital consumer electronics products. In other words, microprocessor, memory, analog circuits and logic circuits will all be incorporated. At the same time, they will work faster and consume less power. Furthermore, improvements to microprocessor efficiency will also include improvements to the operating range of add-on software. Accordingly, among such technical trends as these, with respect to various issues such as the complexities of development costs, higher efficiency design and faster function verification stemming from the expansion of LSI design scale, the existence of high-quality project leaders who can foresee the entire development process is indispensable. Project leaders are required to have a wide range of experiences and skills including an understanding of system algorithms and silicon technology trends and experience with both software and hardware, having a wide range of experiences from upstream design to downstream design, a thorough knowledge of EDA tools as well as being versed in analog circuit design. The role of the project leader is not simply the progressive administration of the project. This is also a person who has various technologies and experiences, and can precisely carry out the technical management of the project.

Integration of organizational boundaries as horizontally integrated SCs

Matsushita's horizontally integrated SCs are roughly classified into four types. Figure 6.11 shows the capability that results from concrete knowledge integration emerging from the relationships between the horizontally integrated SCs and Matsushita Electric's organization and people and also the various SCs.

The first type, the Global Management SC, develops strategic sales and PR strategies centered on AVC Networks' overseas sales locations and Matsushita's sales companies in order to promote the simultaneous launch of DVD recorders worldwide. The second type, the Technical Platform SC, develops global sales through OEM supplies of system LSIs and other semiconductor products, PC boards and sets (products) that form the core of digital household appliances. This strategy not only secures profits from the company's own completed products but also from the company's components that are used in the products of other companies. The third type, the Group Management SC, stimulates maximum synergy from knowledge possessed by the Matsushita Group and produces paradigm reforms for new businesses aimed at developing products and services or business models in new fields such as future broadband and mobile businesses, IT household appliance businesses and environment businesses.

The recent creation of subsidiaries at Matsushita Electric Works has created the possibility that new businesses could be generated by merging the household appliance and semiconductor technologies of Matsushita Electric and the residential space and other technologies of Matsushita Electric Works. Both companies have set up the '21st Century Collaboration Committee' which is currently looking into future collaboration businesses in a number of themes such as strategy, organization and technology. As a result of this effort, Matsushita Electric Industrial and Matsushita Electric Works released the 'Collabo V Product,' merging a wide range of black-boxed technologies held by both companies. The first stage of the 'Collabo V Product' release occurred in December 2004 and consists of bathrooms, toilet rooms, kitchens and living rooms, creating comfortable residential spaces for customers.

Panasonic Mobile Communication (formerly Matsushita Communication Industrial) was created as a business merging mobile phones and electric household appliances. For example, collaboration between Panasonic Mobile Communication and the Development Division of AVC Networks has enabled a moving picture format stored on SD memory cards to be used between a DVD recorder and a 3G mobile phone.

The fourth type of SC, the SC with Firms in Different Industries, fosters the expansion of business models linking, for instance, car electronics (car audio, car navigation, semiconductors, batteries, CCD for car bodies, multimedia products, etc.) and telematics and other technologies in the automobile industry. Panasonic Automotive Systems, representing the unification of car electronics businesses in the Matsushita Group, was established in January 2003 and has already achieved annual sales of ¥460,000 million in fiscal 2003:

> From now on, completely new products and technologies related to cars will no doubt be developed and the need for systems linking various areas is likely to appear. We will need to incorporate the Matsushita Group's internal resources to make new things such as semiconductor LSIs and sensors, batteries and digital A/V technologies. In this respect, Panasonic Automotive Systems is an extremely fortunate company. We will be tapping Matsushita's strengths in the car electronics industry as well. (Mr Takami Sano, President of Panasonic Automotive Systems)

In addition, as a recent case in strategic linking, Matsushita is aiming to expand the production of LC TVs through joint production efforts with Hitachi and Toshiba as a way to counter the expansion programs of Sharp and Korean and Taiwanese manufacturers.

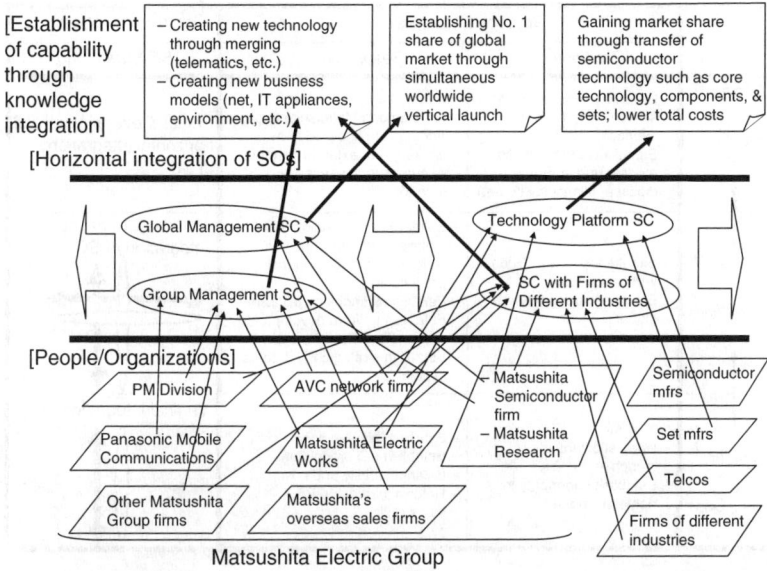

| [Establishment of capability through knowledge integration] | – Creating new technology through merging (telematics, etc.)
– Creating new business models (net, IT appliances, environment, etc.) | Establishing No. 1 share of global market through simultaneous worldwide vertical launch | Gaining market share through transfer of semiconductor technology such as core technology, components, & sets; lower total costs |

[Horizontal integration of SCs]

Global Management SC

Technology Platform SC

Group Management SC

SC with Firms of Different Industries

[People/Organizations]

PM Division

AVC network firm

– Matsushita Semiconductor firm
– Matsushita Research

Semiconductor mfrs

Panasonic Mobile Communications

Matsushita Electric Works

Set mfrs

Other Matsushita Group firms

Matsushita's overseas sales firms

Telcos

Firms of different industries

Matsushita Electric Group

Figure 6.11   Knowledge integration through horizontally integrated SCs
Source: Kodama (2007).

Matsushita Electric's strategy dynamics

In this section we will discuss the building of strategic dynamics in Matsushita's digital appliance business of DVD recorders from the viewpoint of a chronology of SC formation (Figure 6.12).

Matsushita released the world's first DVD-RAM recorder in June 2000 and by about the end of 2002 had achieved a line-up of models featuring new functions and low prices at the same time. In order to promote vertical launches on the domestic market from the viewpoint of organizational dynamics, Matsushita had to first promote the vertical integration of SCs. Matsushita also continuously worked at shortening development lead times and meeting customer needs. Referring to this period as Stage 1, Matsushita achieved the No. 1 position in market share and sales on the domestic DVD recorder market. From the viewpoint of strategic dynamics, during Stage 1, Matsushita was able to establish a competitive advantage in the domestic market and a solid market position (Porter, 1980, 1985).

From the resource-based view (Prahalad and Hamel, 1990; Barney, 1991), along with its success in black-boxing core components such as system LSIs required in the development of DVD recorders, Matsushita also

	Strategy Dynamics		Organization Dynamics
	Positioning	Resource	SC Structuring
Stage 3 (2004 – Future)	– Establish new solutions strategy (products -> services) – Establish new business models (e.g. merging digital appliances with net)	– Synergize resources and skills among Matsushita Group – Accumulate knowledge by working with external partners – Accumulate advanced core technologies	Partial & overall vertical & horizontal integration of SC
Stage 2 (2002–2003)	– Simultaneous worldwide vertical launch – Establish superiority in global markets	– Solidify modularization (hard-/software) design concepts – Reform manufacturing (cell production) – Establish technology platform – Establish uniform development system: Dev-Prod-Res-Qlty – Establish strategic PR & sales system	Vertical & horizontal integration of SC
Stage 1 (2000–2001)	– Domestic vertical launch – Establish superiority in domestic market	– Establish black-boxing – Establish cell production – Balance quality and cost – Reform marketing, PR, sales skills	Vertical integration of SC

Figure 6.12   Matsushita Electric's strategy and organization dynamics
Source: Kodama (2007).

firmly established the completely new manufacturing method of cell production at its plants. As a result, in the areas of product development and manufacturing, Matsushita was able to obtain and accumulate the skills and know-how of sales activities and PR in a new, unprecedented business style that has succeeded in obtaining and vertically launching superior resources and capability compared to other companies.

During Stage 2, from 2002 to 2003, Matsushita rebuilt the integration of organizational boundaries in the form of SC horizontal integration in addition to the existing SC vertical integration with the aim of achieving simultaneous vertical launches worldwide. The focal point in Stage 2 was placed on a strategy for developing DVD recorders that met the needs of various countries and improving product line-ups. To achieve this, the R&D SC and the Product Development and Manufacturing SC, both vertically integrated SCs, engaged in further improving technologies compared to Stage 1 with the aim of obtaining and accumulating resources and capability of higher quality. For example, Matsushita optimized the supply chain of development, cell production, and materials procurement with the aim of thoroughly modularizing hardware and software, reducing costs, and improving quality for products tailored to various countries.

In addition, Matsushita succeeded in further advancing black-boxing technology by balancing higher functionality and greater miniaturization in systems LSIs, the core component. Matsushita also achieved collaboration with local subsidiaries worldwide and overseas sales companies in the form of horizontally integrated SCs that also enabled the company to obtain and accumulate sales skills and other know-how through the establishment of a worldwide PR and sales system. Matsushita achieved the No. 1 position in the global market as well.

Stage 3 is the step that aims for future business expansion. To achieve this, it is important not only to optimize the individual parts of vertically integrated SCs and horizontally integrated SCs as organizational dynamics but also to design the integration of organizational boundaries so that they can bring out the synergy of overall optimization that combines both groups of SCs. It is important to create and accumulate new knowledge by promoting cooperative work within Matsushita and the Matsushita Group and with external partners. In this way, it is possible to establish a business model as new positioning. Representative examples of this are DVD recorders linked with Panasonic Mobile Communication and products linked with 3G mobile handsets (e.g. NTT DoCoMo's FOMA) and broadband. Products made in collaboration with Matsushita Electric Works and new multimedia-related products made in collaboration with automobile manufacturers such as Toyota, Nissan and Honda are also representative examples.

New insight derived from the case

Establishing competitive advantage through the integration of organizational boundaries

After World War II, Matsushita Electric was able to capture market share by riding the wave of rapid economic growth during this time and relying on mass production and high-volume sales through the business department system that divided products into categories. It may appear at first glance that the business department system is able to optimize the overall business process of development, manufacturing, and sales by having top management delegate authority. Looking from the total viewpoint of corporate activities, however, company-wide optimization was insufficient as seen in the higher costs due to duplicate development occurring in the various business divisions (inter-division barriers); gaps in awareness among employees in different divisions, such as the development division, the manufacturing division and the sales division in the same business department (function barriers) and, though partial optimization was achieved in each division, the lack of speed and sharing of information due to the formation of hierarchies in various layers of management (hierarchy barriers).

As a result, during the late 1990s, Matsushita Electric's business department system was having difficulty keeping up with changes in the external environment caused by the growing diversity of customer needs and the development of digital technologies. This difficulty occurred because the information and knowledge held by individual employees was not well distributed despite the high quality of the company's human resources, and the integration of knowledge and synergy rooted in shared corporate value did not effectively create new knowledge.

As one condition of an organizational form demanded by corporations like Matsushita Electric that are constantly requiring new strategies for rapidly changing environments in such areas as market structure or technology innovations, it is necessary to build a multi-layered structure in which SCs that represent the boundaries between individual organizations in each business process comprising the value chain are vertically arranged. At Matsushita, however, these SCs do not necessarily exist independently but are organically linked (Figure 6.13).

The first point is that SCs linked with the R&D SC and the Product Development and Production SC are able to generate products of many

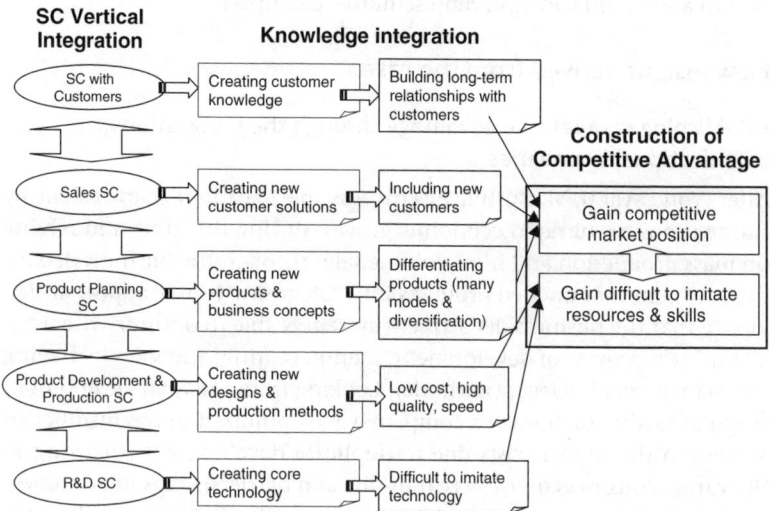

Figure 6.13   Establishing competitive advantage through SC vertical integration
Source: Kodama (2007).

models in small quantities with difficult-to-imitate technological advantages based on new design concepts (simultaneously pursuing speed, quality, cost, etc.) that consider core technologies and manufacturing processes. In addition, the strong linkage between these SCs is capable of achieving not only partial optimization in individual SCs but also overall optimization of company-wide technical strategies. As a result, this enables shorter lead times and higher quality in product development and makes it possible to achieve product innovation. It is also possible to release many models in small quantities.

The second point is that links with the Product Development and Production SC, the Product Planning SC, the Sales SC and the SCs with Customers not only strengthens sales and marketing capabilities but also makes it possible to obtain new customers as well as maintain existing customers over the long term by quickly understanding potential customer needs, creating concepts for diversified new products and balancing the speed and ability to diversify new products that make this technologically possible.

As noted above, it is possible to achieve product development capability that is linked to the market, to the difficult-to-imitate technological capability that supports product development and to the manufacturing capability that fosters cost leadership and, at the same time, to build a unique value chain in which global sales capability is different from competitors and to gain a unique, highly competitive market position as well as difficult-to-imitate resources and capability.

These SCs are mainly comprised of actors who produce corporate visions in response to changes in the environment and new meaning and pragmatic boundaries for strategic goals. An important point for the actors is for each of them to thoroughly understand and share the different contexts at the various SCs to which they are committed and then to dynamically yet flexibly change the contexts of individual SCs. They also make instantaneous decisions about whether to have their own company respond to the changing environment or to form a completely new environment on their own and form new SCs and links. The SC dynamics of SC formation and linking are necessary for the acquisition of new knowledge and this simultaneously achieves and updates new market position along with resources and capability for Matsushita Electric.

There are two objectives for Matsushita Electric in building horizontally integrated SCs (Figure 6.14). One objective is the aspect of best practice that horizontally, across the globe, fosters knowledge creation achieved by vertically integrated SCs through cooperative work with various partners. This applies to global simultaneous vertical launches

Construction of Competitive Advantage

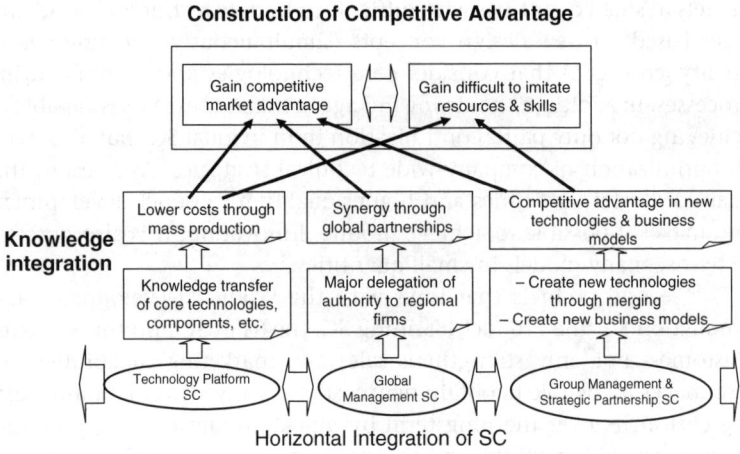

Figure 6.14   Establishing competitive advantage through SC horizontal integration
Source: Kodama (2007).

and the development of technical platforms. The second objective involves strategic links with Group companies, competitors, different industries and others, with the aim of creating new knowledge (e.g. searching for new business models). Though one case of the second objective may be the creation of knowledge at the level of sharing each other's know-how and other tacit knowledge through the formation of SCs with strong ties, it is conceivable that new knowledge could also be created by maintaining the formation of SCs that have weak links with firms of different industries or other entities.

Concerning the point in the Global Management SC, regional companies to which full authority has been delegated from the head company share a Group-wide vision and mission while at the same time, their partial optimization in the implementation of operations according to regional conditions, is balanced with full, Group-wide optimization. The Technical Platform SC, the second point, aims for cost leadership in reducing overall product costs by accelerating the horizontal development of the company's own technologies and products through proprietary core technologies, OEM sales and by other means. The third point is the Group Management and Strategic Links SC. The greatest aim of this SC is to innovate technology and create new business models by merging different technologies through collaboration with partners. This SC makes it possible to generate competitive advantage in new technologies and business models through the innovations of synergy and time.

Though the timing for the building of these horizontally integrated SCs is determined by a corporation's environment and future vision, Matsushita Electric forms and links these horizontally integrated SCs at the same time as it builds vertically integrated SCs. The SC dynamics of building vertically integrated SCs and horizontally integrated SCs make it possible for Matsushita Electric to build a dynamic view of strategy for acquiring new market position and new resources and capability.

Hierarchies and SCs

A major problem for company employees under the hierarchical organization in the era of business departments was their difficulty in seeing the faces of the users. The one point of organizational reform of the Nakamura reform this time is the dismantling of conventional business departments and the introduction of a light, fast flat-and-web type organization. The pyramid structure with up to 13 levels was flattened to 4 levels. While the introduction of IT naturally made management more efficient, the main aim was to speed up the sharing of information and knowledge from person to person.

New posts such as business unit (BU) managers, category owners, group managers and team leaders are in the middle management layer. BU managers have the rank of senior executive manager and are responsible for projects that bring together categories such as areas of merchandise. They have the authority for centralized management of capital investment and recovery common to a category by making decisions and strategically spreading resources between categories. Also, each merchandise category has a category owner with the rank of group manager who is finally responsible for investment, recovery, sales, income and expenditure and market share. From the point of view of driving the project, he is the leader who concentrates the power of group members in their ordinary work. Group manager is a senior executive post with responsibility for the functioning of a group, displaying maximum efficiency and having the duty of regulating the strategic distribution between business units and categories. A team leader has the rank of section chief and is responsible for driving the work force of his category.

In the four layers of the flat-and-web type organization, the middle layers have been compressed into two layers, above and below which are a final decision-making layer at the top and lower layer of general company employees added below (Figure 6.15). In the PM Division, for instance, the four layers are: the director of the PM Division, group managers, team leaders, and general employees. In the AVC Networks Company the layers are: the company president, business unit managers, category

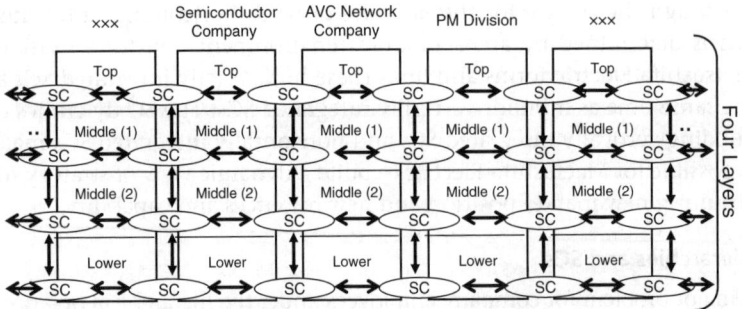

Figure 6.15 Flat- and web-type organizations and SC formation (conceptual diagram)

owners and general employees. This is extremely simple. The middle management layers have been given greater authority than they had before, which has greatly increased the motivation of all company employees. A noteworthy point is that the business awareness of those concerned has also been increased.

The 'web' of flat-and-web means that the transmission and sharing of information within and between organizations is to be implemented by an open environment like the Web of the Internet. It suggests that various multi-layered SCs are organically networked within each organization and between organizations. These networked SCs give new meaning to interactive information and knowledge between organizations, including client and partner companies in particular, and will become a source of knowledge creation as a new dynamic context.

One of the conditions of organizational form demanded of businesses that take environmental changes such as market structure and innovation to be violent and constantly requiring new strategies is that the features of SCs will be integrated as a flat hierarchical organization and network like Matsushita. Networked SCs ensure creativity and compatibility when corporate vision and strategic objectives are to be expressed in specific duties. Networked SCs also have a hierarchical structure but this too is one of the techniques for the sharing and creation of context with the key persons belonging to various layers within and beyond the organization in order to effectively reach fast creativity. On the other hand, the flat hierarchical organization guarantees speed and efficiency when duties are performed positively. In order to adapt to the uncertainty of the environment, the key is either to differentiate the uses of bureaucracy and network or by simultaneously implementing and integrating them, cause the structure of the organization to change flexibly and spontaneously. In the case of Matsushita, having the network and bureaucracy coexisting within the same enterprise and integrating them produces the maximum synergy of the features of each.

Realization of the Road map of knowledge

Riding the wave of high postwar economic growth, Matsushita Electric acquired market share with mass production and mass marketing under a business department system that was divided by products. One glance gives the impression that the succession of business processes from development to production to sales, with delegation of authority from top management, may be generally most appropriate. However taking the viewpoint of total business activities as seen in previous Matsushita Electric, there were cost increases due to redundant developments between each business department (interdepartmental barriers), as well as differences of awareness between individual employees in the development department, production department and sales department within the same operational division (functional barriers) (partially optimized by each department but) in addition because of deficiencies in speed and the sharing of information due to the stratification of each management layer (hierarchical barriers) optimization as a total enterprise had not been achieved. As a result, the business department system of Matsushita Electric of the late 1990s found difficulty in following changes to the external environment brought about by the diversification of customer needs and the introduction of digital. Even though very talented people were kept within the company, this has been caused by the giving out of the information and knowledge of individuals, and by new knowledge creation not being produced effectively from the accumulation of knowledge and synergy rooted in common company values.

With regard to the three previous barriers, the Nakamura reformation over the last several years, is making and achieving major management reforms under the corporate vision 'Destroy, Create and Leap Forward.' However, President Nakamura's management ideas are immutable. In his management reforms he declared: Smash everything other than 'the idea of management.' The idea of management of the founder, Mr Konosuke Matsushita, is that its basic objective and reason for existence determines the general plan, knowledge command, administrative procedure and the way company employees should be. In addition, the way of thinking with respect to the company as an expression in strong plain language based on this 'idea of management' is also determined by the basic management guidelines of Matsushita Electric. The 'idea of management,' which is Matsushita's basic value, is being transmitted and is permeating to each company employee through dialog with top management and through research and other activities in various management layers.

The undercurrent, 'Create and Leap Forward,' is filled with the keywords: 'improve social life and contribute to the development of world culture,' 'our mission as producers,' 'honest management' and 'people are important,' which are basic ways of thinking about this 'idea of management.' The ideas embodied in the expression 'improve social life and contribute to the development of world culture' question the existence of a company facing a target of 'creation of new markets,' which was turned towards the ubiquitous society of the future. On the other hand, the concept of 'our mission as a producer' also questions a return to the original source of a manufacturer which is to revive the act of making things from the standpoint of customers. An important viewpoint is for various layers of management represented by top management to take a fresh look at corporate ontology concerning the question of how the company wants to be in the future. Through this process, companies will be able to determine new strategic goals that will embody their vision as a company. At Matsushita, this sort of questioning for the future results in concrete strategic goals involving 'vertical launches' in the former case and 'super manufacturing and black-boxing' in the latter case. In the DVD recorder business case, the PM Division, the AVC Networks Company and the Semiconductor Company each questioned itself as to the basic value of its existence as a business and formed a strong will and resolve towards specific strategic objectives that must be created in future. This induced the organizations to reflect on their past, and at the same time the past and future became one, leading them to think at this point in time, 'What should we do?,' and move to specific action. On the other hand, for the implementation of strategic objectives, the 'people are important' idea of management is fundamental, and as a result they will also return to 'honest management.'

Matsushita's DVD recorder strategy is filled with visions such as 'creation of a DVD culture,' 'videotape revolution' and 'from square to round.' On 9 March 2004, Matsushita released a line of five new models of DIGA DVD recorders. These new products are lavishly provided with Matsushita's exclusive black box technology and high-density mounting technology, as well as 'direct launching' that is the previous selling strategy up to now and 'super direct launching' that must be further accelerated as a future target. In order to win in the competitive environment of the digital consumer electronics market, the company must continue to produce a succession of new knowledge, and the 'road map of knowledge,' which crystallizes the justification of knowledge, must be put into tangible form. Where will the energy for the organization for the continuous creation of this new knowledge come from? In the end, aren't masses of 'people' who hold their own vision, faith and feelings the source of knowledge creation?

'People' have a variety of world outlooks and values, but at the root of an individual's way of life there is a pattern of thoughts and actions that is a fixed paradigm based on past personal experiences. Due to interactions that have passed though dialectic syntheses of their own subjective viewpoints (viewpoints that try to perceive potential demand by assimilating with the customer) and objective viewpoints (analyses of competing products and customer data), the marketers of the PM Division are unceasingly producing new perceptions. 'We must plan products that provide customers with new value' and 'How shall we grasp customers' potential needs and connect them with merchandise planning?' However, this does not mean that the marketers are completely devoid of technical viewpoints. Always grasping technical trends both inside and outside the company, the idea that 'It is full of uncertainty, but if such a technology were to be realized, customers could probably be provided with functions and services such as these' concerns a potential form of use that customer themselves have neither noticed nor made an effort to verify. At the same time, the marketers' new perceptions are deliberately forming various stratified networked SCs within the PM Division, including customers and external partners. Through productive conflict and creative friction with regard to the networked SCs, from the marketers' viewpoint, they will proceed with introspection on the drawing up of a 'road map of the market' and the creation of a product concept.

On the other hand, due to interactions that have passed though dialectic syntheses of their own subjective viewpoints (beliefs and feelings that they themselves would like to develop this) and objective viewpoints (concentration and selection based on analysis and evaluation of technical trends), the engineers of the AVC Networks Company and the Semiconductor Company are unceasingly producing new perceptions: 'We must develop technology that satisfies customers' and 'We must develop core technology that other competing companies cannot imitate.' This does not mean that the engineers are also completely devoid of feelings for the marketing viewpoint. Offers are made to customers because of original and certainly feasible seeds oriented way of thinking by the engineers. The facility for exchanging image data by such means as SD cards for digital cameras, FOMA and DIGA are typical examples of this. At the same time, with the engineers' new perceptions, densely multi-layered SCs are being formed deliberately between the AVC Networks Company and the Semiconductor Company and through discussion and practice with SCs they are engaged in creating core technology concepts and introspection at the same time as a 'Road map of technology' is being prepared and shared from the engineers' viewpoint.

Then, new energy is being produced in the PM Division and AVC Networks Company SCs because of creative and productive conflicts of the paradigm as marketers and the paradigm as engineers and context of a higher order will be formed. Marketers and engineers each understand a diversity of values and outlooks on the world and though dialectic interaction between different organizations they will produce mutual agreement and establish rules. Then, through abduction the 'Road map of the market' and 'Road map of technology' will be integrated and knowledge, which is a new product as a transcendental hypothesis, will be created and realized (Figure 6.16).

The absorptive competence of knowledge difference

This author would like to take up the absorptive competence of 'knowledge difference' with respect to the ideas of the engineers for realizing the

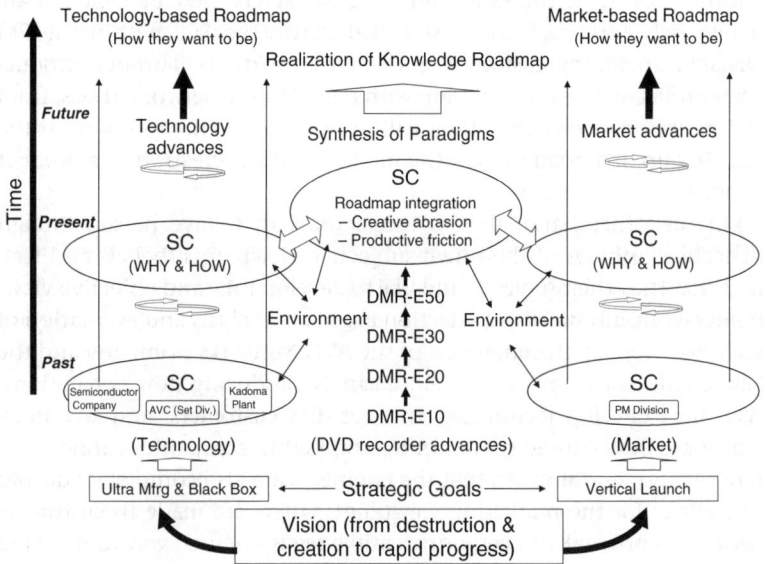

Figure 6.16   Realizing the knowledge roadmap (case of Matsushita Electric)

'Road map of knowledge' through the rapid development of new products using ongoing knowledge creation activities. Generally, more than half the items that are to become new products or services are not items that appear suddenly but are based on intellectual assets that have been built up over a long time within the organization and have been nurtured and developed incrementally. If the 'road map of knowledge' is redefined from a technical viewpoint, it is a history of technology that has been tangibly realized as goods or services. DVD recorders, digital TV, digital cameras, mobile telephones and others, which are typical digital consumer electronics appliances, are largely supported by the accumulated results of past core technology development, and if we look back over history, these merchandise groups are items that have achieved incremental technical progress from analog technology to digital technology. Taking the progress of the 'road map of knowledge' shown in Figure 6.16 to mean the extent of technological innovation, it does not necessarily mean only the upgrading of technology. Rather, it is building up new knowledge gradually on a foundation of existing intellectual assets.

As discussed in Chapter 2, 'knowledge difference' can be divided logically into 'a newly developed element,' 'an improvement of an existing intellectual asset' or 'a diversion of use of an existing intellectual asset.' An engineer must have the ability to divide, analyze and/or reconstruct the elements of a product that is targeted for development into 'new elements (including improvements to existing knowledge)' or 'existing elements (knowledge)' on the basis of existing tacit knowledge (experience and know-how of an engineer and a group of engineers) and existing explicit knowledge. In other words, 'knowledge difference' is one of the capabilities that engineers have acquired through thorough discussion in order to materialize new concepts, for perceiving the three rough categories: (a) diversion of existing technology, (b) improvement of existing technology, and (c) new element development. The important point for an engineer is the need to be able to quickly and accurately ascertain the degree of new element development (how difficult, how big), as these will determine how much the development will cost and how long it will take.

In this case, SCs have been formed between various organizations. In these individual SCs, the engineers of various organizations participate together in sharing and understanding the context beyond the environment of the organization and new development elements will be discovered on the basis of the common knowledge between engineers (in this case, this includes technical terms related to DVD technology and used between engineers such as architecture, audio and video technology, semiconductor technology and software technology as well as the past experience and know-how possessed by individuals; with this formal knowledge and tacit knowledge, the content that can be mutually perceived and understood). Dynamic contexts at SCs, such as 'What sort of architecture would be good for realizing the new product concept? And what sort of component technology or software development would be required to achieve this?' are shared among engineers to give birth to new contexts.

At Matsushita, various black-box technologies such as system LSI development technology, optical pickup technology and high-density mounting technology are knowledge assets that have been accumulated from the past. An important point is to somehow make them the foundation and discover new knowledge difference so they will be absorbed through fast accurate abduction. At Matsushita Electric, with past knowledge assets as the foundation, the absorptive confidence of knowledge difference that can accurately materialize core technologies that reflect various customers' needs in new products and functions is high. This is why it is possible to quickly develop and realize an ongoing lineup of products.

Conclusion

As a concluding remark, hi-tech corporations of the 21st century that need to build new business models by merging different technologies or different services must synthesize a variety of boundaries, both within and outside the corporation, from multiple viewpoints and continuously create new knowledge toward the corporation's goals. Through this case of Matsushita Electric's digital household appliances, this paper presented the concept of strategic communications as one practical method of organizational boundary management aimed at innovation. Innovation, a core capability, emerges from pragmatic boundaries where professionals are in various specialized fields inside and outside the corporation. Strategic communities that have integrated, or networked, many pragmatic boundaries inside and outside the corporation promote knowledge integration or knowledge transformation and, as they produce the capability of competitive advantage for the corporation, they are also able to establish a competitively advantageous position in the market at the same time.

7
Knowledge Creation Through the Networks of Strategic Communities

This chapter provides a new point of view regarding the knowledge management and leadership theory of NPD, a high-tech field requiring the merging and integration of different technologies. As in-depth case studies, the author examines the dynamism of the knowledge creation process in NPD at Fujitsu Ltd., a traditional Japanese telecommunications manufacturer, as it merges and integrates the different elements of broadband network technology, computer and software technology, and multimedia processing technology. In a short period of time, a strategic team at Fujitsu, consisting mainly of undisclosed cross-functional middle managers transcending Fujitsu's business divisions, formed SCs inside and outside the company, including customers, and then formed a network that transcended the SCs' boundaries. In this chapter, the author identifies four factors that are important in integrating the different bodies of knowledge that various SCs have. This chapter also points out that the dialectical leadership of community leaders that form the leadership-based SC produces synthesizing capabilities as networked SCs, and that these capabilities integrate the knowledge that is the core technology of each SC, build a new business model, and create new knowledge in the form of successful NPD.

Summary of an in-depth case

In Japan, a number of Japanese manufacturers engaged in NPD with the aim of offering new video distribution services for use with FOMA, NTT DoCoMo's new third-generation (3G) mobile phone service that was launched in October 2001, the world's first 3G service to become commercially available. At that time, the NPD team at Fujitsu's Network Division was engaged in the development of a new video streaming platform and live video camera that could stream the same video content simultaneously to FOMA mobile phones, personal digital assistants (PDAs), and notebook computers (equipped with wireless cards) (Figure 7.1).

This NPD, however, required the merging and integration of three basically different technologies: broadband network technology, computer and software technology, and multimedia processing technology. Such NPD was not at all possible with systems within Fujitsu's business division. The NPD team at the Network Division therefore needed to create knowledge in the form of new, compound knowledge by merging and integrating elements of technology in the possession of NPD teams in their own and other divisions, namely the broadband network technology of their own Network Division, computer and software technology of the Software Division, and multimedia processing technology of the Fujitsu Laboratories.[1] To this end, a cross-functional team (Figure 7.2, SC-a) that transcended the boundaries of the business divisions was quickly formed within Fujitsu. The Sales Division with marketing and sales capabilities joined to participate in SC-a, and while engaging in close collaboration with the other divisions aimed at developing the target product. They also started marketing activities aimed at all types of customers including communications carriers such as NTT DoCoMo, ASP/ISP and corporate customers. (Figure 7.4, Phase 1). The NPD teams of the Network Division and Software Division in particular formed an SC with the video business planning and development at NTT DoCoMo, a customer, from an early phase of NPD (SC-b). These teams communicated and collaborated closely in order to study the technical aspects of interface conditions required for building a 3G communications network and achieving inter-operability for multimedia communications with 3G mobile phones. They also actively collected data on customers' needs for use in the NPD. Links between the SCs and SC-a and SC-b were established as well (Figure 7.4, Phase 2).

In the process of pursuing technical investigations in greater detail and solving a number of technical issues, Fujitsu formed collaborative relationships with best partners around the world. Specifically, in developing a wireless video gateway system in Figure 7.1, the NPD team of Fujitsu's Network Division formed a strategic alliance with NMS Communications of the United States to promote joint development (SC-c).[2] Also, to partially supplement the function of Fujitsu's own product under development with the video streaming server in Figure 7.1, a technical tie-up was established with Packet Video of the United States with the aim of integrating their product with Fujitsu's product under development (SC-d). SC networks linking SC-a through SC-d were formed in this phase (Figure 7.4, Phase 3), and various technical discussions were conducted within the networked SCs.

Next, the possibility of developing a live camera with MPEG-4 moving picture technology stimulated discussion on the possibilities of a business model where providers could charge a fee to provide live video content (such as images of sightseeing spots, day care centers, business process monitoring and progress of events) over a wired broadband network to the 3G mobile phones, PDAs and computers of 'anywhere, anytime' end users. Six manufacturers developing live moving picture cameras (Japanese manufacturers: Megatips, AlphaOmega, Hitachi Kokusai Electric Canon; Taiwanese manufacturers: Leadtek and @utoTOOLS) joined a new SC (SC-e) (Figure 7.2, SC-e) networked with Fujitsu and an expanded network of SCs centered on Fujitsu came into being. Next, a variety of technical issues (new technologies to be developed such as multimedia video processing and communications protocols) related to end-to-end (camera-to-3G mobile phone/PDA/PC) transmission of live video images were thoroughly discussed (Figure 7.4, Phase 4). By April 2002, the NPD in Figure 7.1 was completed through the phases described above. The system could now be supplied to NTT DoCoMo, the customer, tie-ups could be formed with the sales SI vendors, and sales to ISPs/ASPs and large corporate customers became possible. The NPD in Figure 7.1 became the world's first example in which knowledge was created by merging and integrating knowledge from around the world (Japan, United States and Taiwan).

Following the completion of NPD, DoCoMo launched a one-to-many video streaming trial service called 'V-Live' beginning April 2002.[3] The trial service was provided via the 3G mobile network and both live and archived video content was streamed to 3G mobile phones and PDAs. One of the representative business models involved live broadcasts aimed at corporate member customers and the distribution of archived videos such as new product information. The other business model involved real-time monitoring of stores or young children at child care centers, a new application that received high qualitative support from customers. For consumers as mobile handset users, video content included music, sports highlights, news, animation, tourist information and more. Closed content was available exclusively to the customers of content providers or members of corporate users. Examples of this content include English conversation lessons, internal information for employees, security services (observation from a remote location) and investor relations tools. Content providers or corporate users of closed-content systems were charged a fee for system construction.

Following the DoCoMo V-Live service, the project team in Fujitsu Software Division actively discussed the video streaming systems with KDDI Development Department, and the new SC (SC-f) between the

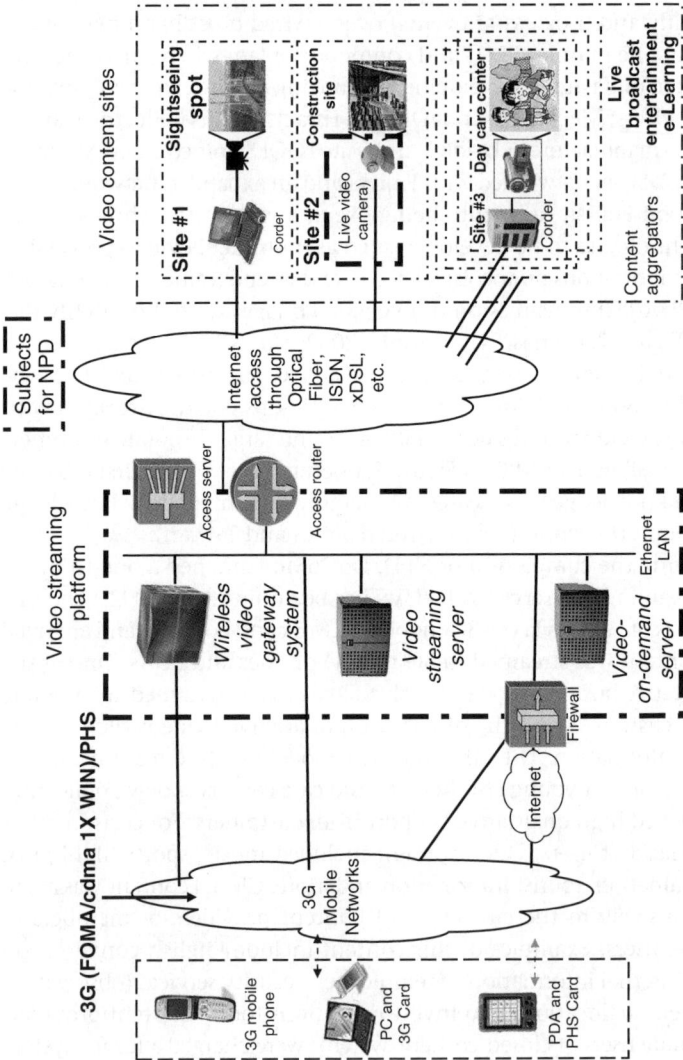

Figure 7.1 NPD targets for NTT DoCoMo and KDDI
Source: Kodama (2005a).

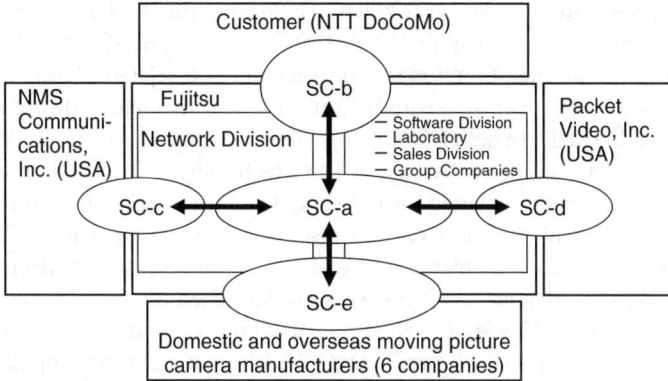

SC-a: Fujitsu Group's SC comprising Network Division, Software Division,
    Laboratory, Sales Division, and Group companies
SC-b: SC with NTT DoCoMo, a customer
SC-c: SC with NMS Communications, Inc., of the USA
SC-d: SC with PacketVideo, Inc., of the USA
SC-e: SC with 6 domestic and overseas moving picture camera manufacturers

Figure 7.2   Networked SCs including NTT DoCoMo at Fujitsu
Source: Kodama (2005a).

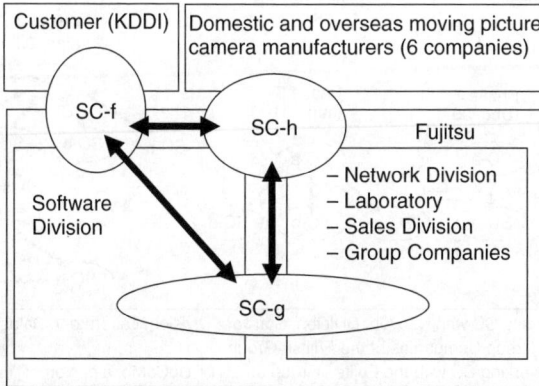

SC-f: SC with KDDI, a customer

SC-g: Fujitsu group's SC comprising Network Division, Software Division,

    Laboratory, Sales Division, and Group companies

SC-h: SC with 6 domestic and overseas moving picture camera manufacturers

Figure 7.3   Networked SCs including KDDI at Fujitsu
Source: Kodama (2005a).

Fujitsu Software Division and KDDI was formed for the basic survey of product development (Figure 7.3). At this point, a new SC (SC-g) in Fujitsu as an informal cross-functional team including all related divisions was also immediately formed to study and propose a new video distribution platform for KDDI in detail. So the joint development for 3G mobile video streaming service started, based on CDMA technology with KDDI development team and immediately the networked SC linking SC-f, SC-g and SC-h was formed, and various technical discussions including manufacturers developing live moving picture cameras (SC-h) were conducted within the networked SCs (Figure 7.4, Phase 5). KDDI launched the nationwide service of CDMA 1X WIN, a new 3G service that enables high speed data communications of up to 2.4 Mbps.[4] CDMA 1X WIN will allow the popular 3G web access services and EZ video-mail, a faster delivery. In addition, the service will host a new series of rich services dedicated to CDMA 1X WIN, including video distribution channel, an innovative service that automatically distributes various genres of program, and Live Camera, a service that delivers desired video content in real time.[5] To support to the content volume that will grow with the availability of high speed data communications, KDDI will introduce the world's and the industry's first fixed packet communications service rate plan that will enable users of services, including email, unlimited usage for a fixed monthly charge of 4,200 yen.

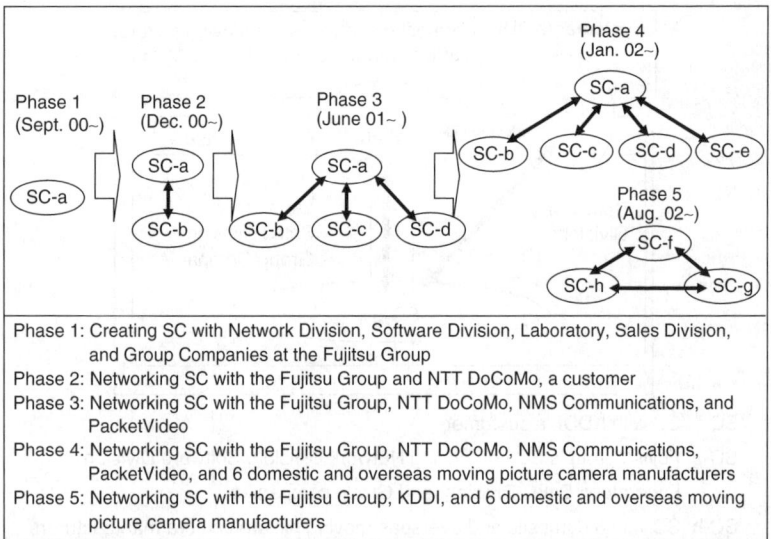

Phase 1: Creating SC with Network Division, Software Division, Laboratory, Sales Division, and Group Companies at the Fujitsu Group
Phase 2: Networking SC with the Fujitsu Group and NTT DoCoMo, a customer
Phase 3: Networking SC with the Fujitsu Group, NTT DoCoMo, NMS Communications, and PacketVideo
Phase 4: Networking SC with the Fujitsu Group, NTT DoCoMo, NMS Communications, PacketVideo, and 6 domestic and overseas moving picture camera manufacturers
Phase 5: Networking SC with the Fujitsu Group, KDDI, and 6 domestic and overseas moving picture camera manufacturers

Figure 7.4   Networked SCs at Fujitsu
Source: Kodama (2005a).

Dynamics of networked SCs

The NPD in this case required hardware and software elemental technology as well as technologies in a wide range of fields including broadband network technology, mobile network technology, computer and software technology, multimedia processing technology, and network operation technology. It was absolutely impossible for this NPD to be completed with the knowledge of only one company. Companies had to follow two steps to complete this NPD. The first step involved knowledge sharing. Along with gaining a clear understanding of partners' capabilities, it was necessary to judge whether a partner's core technology was suitable for satisfying the technical needs in the NPD, and it was important for engineers to gain a deep understanding that transcended the area of information sharing. Information and knowledge could be shared between both parties through close dialog and discussions. It is necessary for engineers to thoroughly understand the core technologies. The second step involves knowledge integration and knowledge creation which is based on knowledge integration. This step, based on the thorough mutual understanding of core technologies achieved in the first step, involves the integration of the core technologies of one's own company and the core technologies of the partners. This naturally includes knowledge transfer. However, the most important point, as seen in this case of NPD, is that the core technologies are integrated and further improved (adding technical value), or that the integrated core technologies lead to a process of knowledge creation in which new technology is developed. The two steps of knowledge sharing and knowledge integration are therefore both important in this case.

In this section, the author uses six concepts derived from the research method (See Appendix) to consider what sort of impact the SC networks and the integrative competences through dialectical leadership of the community leaders had on new knowledge creation, the output of Fujitsu. As a first angle, the author analyzes the characteristics of SC networks that became the trigger causing the merging and integration of knowledge diffused from the boundaries of individual SCs that were distributed from the four concepts of their involvement in collaboration, embeddedness in collaboration, resonance of values, and the speed at which the SCs were formed. As a second angle, the author discusses the integrative competences through dialectical leadership that the leadership-based SC comprising community leaders within networked SCs uses to dialectically synthesize the different knowledge of SCs that is distributed in the new knowledge creation process in NPD from the aspect of two concepts derived from the research.[6]

Characteristics of networked SCs

Information and knowledge within communities is both sticky and leaky. It is important, however, that the networked SCs make the leaky aspect of knowledge in communities work in a positive manner and that community leaders of all SCs promote the sharing and inspiration of knowledge beyond the SCs' boundaries. The act of transcending boundaries stimulates deep, meaningful learning, which in turn opens possibilities for the generation of new knowledge and creativity. Radically new insights and developments, such as the NPD in this case, often arise at the boundaries between SCs (Grant and Baden-Fuller, 1995; Grant, 1996b). In particular the dilemma faced by firms is the need to reconcile rapid access and integration of relevant new knowledge, with the long time frames needed for knowledge creation and integration. Networked SCs based on deep inter-firm collaboration can offer a possible solution. The need for businesses to transcend the boundaries of SCs has been increasing in recent years as markets in their industry become more uncertain and technology changes more rapidly. One practical experience and the knowledge of a single organization does not need to be embraced in order to solve the complex sort of problem of merging and integrating technology that is shown in this case. The community leaders of organizations need to actively build SCs inside and outside the company, including customers, and then to transcend the boundaries of the SCs and network them in a speedy manner.

One important element in the formation of networked SCs is collaboration. The presence of deep interaction among community members, the presence of a strategic partnership among the organizations that form networked SCs, and interactive information and knowledge sharing within networked SCs are not the only conditions required for deep collaboration as defined by DiMaggio and Powell, since high levels of involvement in the collaborative process, i.e. the development of a strong mutual awareness that SC members are involved in a common enterprise, are also essential. Figure 7.5 shows the results when the author evaluated the networked SCs of Fujitsu with weight given to the factor of high involvement.

The second important element in the formation of networked SCs – embeddedness – describes the degree to which collaboration between SCs is enmeshed in inter-organizational relationships. This element highlights the connection between the collaboration and the broader inter-organizational network. Instances of highly embedded collaboration between SCs were observed as an expanded network of SCs centered on Fujitsu came into being (Figure 7.5).

The third important element in the formation of networked SCs is the resonance process of resonating values in the community. This is the process whereby all community members, in their effort to fulfill the networked SCs' mission and goals, share and resonate values aimed at achieving the business model. This idea of the resonance of values is also the same as the hidden value, espoused by O'Reilley and Pfeffer, that enables the shared values within the formal organization or community to produce new knowledge or competences (O'Reilly and Pfeffer, 2001). The resonance of values in networked SCs with partners inside and outside the company and in networked SCs with partners (Kodama, 2002) leads to dialectical ideas and strength to act among community members, and turns into a capability for generating community competences, knowledge that forms the new core for the networked SCs. High levels of resonance value were observed in the networked SCs of Fujitsu, which had succeeded in NPD (Figure 7.5).

The fourth important element in the formation of networked SCs is speed. This element of speed in the formation of networks was not discussed in any depth in research on inter-organizational networks. This element must be considered, however, by businesses in industries undergoing rapid change or whose technologies are rapidly advancing. In this case, a major feature of Fujitsu's success is the fact that they formed their networked SCs very quickly (Figure 7.5). The decisive factor behind this rapid formation of networked SCs is improvisation, an especially important concept when developing innovative products and services in an environment where market needs are uncertain due to ongoing rapid changes and technology is also changing (Brown and Eisenhardt, 1998). Speed and flexibility are particularly essential when making organizational decisions in tie-ups with external strategic partners. From the viewpoint of strategic logic, companies need to jump into the confusion, keep moving, and seize opportunities quickly as they pursue opportunities in unpredictable, rapidly changing, ambiguous markets (very characteristic of the 3G mobile phone market in this case study) (Eisenhardt and Sull, 2001). Fujitsu needed to ride along with this flow (the speedy pattern of forming networked SCs).

Next follows a supplementary explanation of the four factors of the networked SCs obtained from this field study mentioned above. High involvement, the first element of networked SCs, refers to the condition in which specialized engineers in the networked SCs are thoroughly understanding and sharing each other's knowledge in the various core technologies that were created in each SC through concerted dialog and collaboration among members in networked SCs. The specific knowledge of core technologies that was created in each SC is as follows.

The core technology created in SC-a came as a result of the merging and integration of network technology and software operation technology within the Fujitsu Group. SC-b, comprising members from the Fujitsu Group

and NTT DoCoMo, constructed the new business model for mobile terminals (3G mobile handsets and PDAs) and developed the service architecture.
In SC-c, Fujitsu's Network Division and NMS Communications, Inc., of the
United States jointly developed the core technology for converting protocols, and in SC-d, the Software Division and other members from Fujitsu
along with Packet Video, Inc., of the United States jointly developed the
core technology for the large-capacity video distribution system. SC-e,
comprising the Fujitsu Group and five camera manufacturers, developed
the core technology for a live camera encoding system. The development
results (core technologies) that were created by these SCs became knowledge
that was deeply shared through close dialog and collaboration within
the networked SCs in each of the six cases. Much of the data from interviews
and other sources confirm that a condition of high involvement had been
attained. For example, a Fujitsu technology manager reported:

> We had to integrate a number of core technologies that we jointly
> developed with many partners and to further pursue new development,
> but in order to do so, we needed to achieve a deep and thorough
> understanding of these core technologies, otherwise we wouldn't be
> able to know how to apply them. Sharing knowledge at a deep level is
> of first and foremost importance.

High embeddedness, the second element, refers to the condition in
which knowledge created in each SC transcends the SCs' boundaries and is
deeply shared among them, and is then generated as new knowledge by
integrating the various bodies of knowledge from the networked SCs.
The main feature in the networked SCs of each case is that the element of
high embeddedness facilitates the integration of the core technologies of
each SC and creates concrete new knowledge as results of development.

High resonance of value, the third element, refers to the condition in
which networked SC members deeply share and sympathize with a vision
for development that the members of each networked SC aim to achieve
through close dialog and collaboration. This observation was obtained
by the author from discussions with many community members. A Fujitsu
community leader, for instance, commented: 'It is important for both parties to thoroughly understand each other's core technologies and to deeply
share and sympathize with ways to develop the target system, philosophies
about the system and the other uniform values of partner members.'

The feature of the fourth element, SC formation speed, is the speed with
which all partners organized themselves into networked SCs, which in these
cases took around 10 days. A comment by a manager at Packet Video of
the United States indicates that improvisation was a value when forming

networked SCs: 'In order to develop faster than anyone else in the world, one has to think while running.'

For the analysis mentioned above, community members including community leaders need to build a platform for resonating values and creating relationships of mutual trust (Vangen and Huxham, 2003) while also engaging in ongoing mutual exchanges, deep collaboration, high involvement, high embeddedness and high speed formation at the boundaries of multiple, different SCs. An evaluation of networked SCs can be found in the representative pattern of Fujitsu which has quickly networked its SCs and realized high involvement, high embeddedness and high resonance value within these SCs. These effects can establish the leadership-based strategic community between community leaders and produce integrative competences based on their dialectical leadership (Figure 7.5).

Integrative competences of leadership-based strategic communities

In SCs and networked SCs, however, as knowledge-based organizations, the skills as an organization to always stimulate knowledge sharing and knowledge creation, a vital issue in promoting knowledge management, are important. This burden is carried by the leadership of leaders as an organization. Leadership is about setting direction, motivating and inspiring staff members, and is mostly about people (Hooper and Potter, 2000). When knowledge management is a crucial issue, leaders must devote time and attention to knowledge sharing and knowledge creating activities such as NPD and other important issues (Popper and Lipshitz, 2000). Leaders must also manage many knowledge workers with specialized expertise and skills, and must become role models of the desired behavior for knowledge workers (Pam and Scarbrough, 1998; Burtha, 2001). Leadership in a knowledge-based organization is thus of great importance, and different leadership styles and roles such as instructors, coaches, servants, stewards, and mentors that encourage, motivate, and support knowledge workers to learn, have been recognized as appropriate for leading a knowledge-based organization (Maccoby, 1996; Marquardt, 2000).

Struggles and conflicts are a common occurrence among networked SCs. These elements are harmful factors in the effort to merge and integrate the knowledge possessed by the SCs. This integration is thus promoted by the leadership strategic community (LSC) which we describe below.

The role of the LSC is to merge and integrate the knowledge of all SCs on the network that were formed by community leaders (made up of personnel from various levels of participating firms: top management, middle management, etc.) and to generate integrative competences, the combined network power of all SCs (Figure 7.6). The LSC needs to balance

Characteristics of networked SCs	Integrative competences	New knowledge creation
– Involvement High – Embeddedness High – Resonance of value High – SC formation speed High	High – Presence of solid LSC – Developing dialectical leadership	High – NPD completed – Business model established

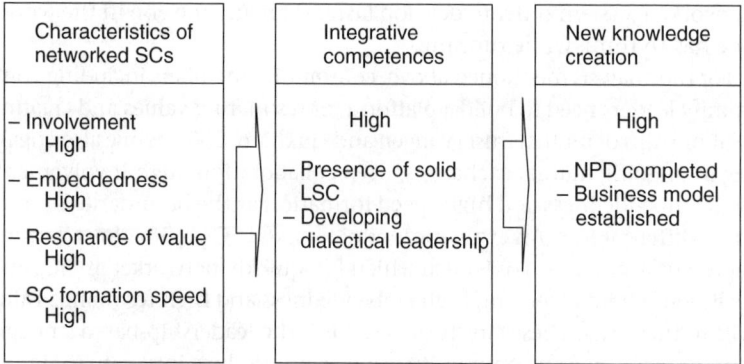

Figure 7.5 Evaluations of new knowledge of creation in the case

Figure 7.6 Integrative competences through dialectical leadership of community leaders
Source: Kodama (2005a).

the various paradoxical elements and issues within SCs on the network in order to realize these integrative competences. The LSC also needs to enable community leaders to consciously conduct dialectical management and engage in constructive dialog to solve the various differences and issues that result from learning among the community leaders. As a result, the LSC actively analyzes problems and resolves issues, forms an arena for the resonance of new values, and creates a higher level of knowledge. Dialectical management is based on the Hegelian approach, which is a practical method of resolving conflict within an organization mentioned in Chapter 2.

The balancing of paradoxical elements and issues involves the synthesis of mutually divergent views among organization members coming from different corporate cultures on the one hand, and the synthesis of a variety of divergent business issues (such as the procedures of different management, technologies, or business models). In the case of Fujitsu and Company A, for example, syntheses were required in four areas: 1. the values of many employees possessing a broad diversity of viewpoints and knowledge shaped by the different corporate cultures to which they belong, 2. the different elements of technology acquired by engineers from different organizations who aim to merge and integrate system technology elements diffused among the various SCs, 3. balancing proprietary development and development with other companies (or transferring knowledge of the technology belonging to other companies), and 4. balancing wired broadband business and wireless business models. The LSC plays a central role in synthesizing the paradoxical elements and issues in the specific areas of human resources, technology elements, technology management, and business. The new ideas and approaches of the community leaders who have adopted the methods of dialectical management in their efforts to synthesize paradoxical elements and issues make new knowledge creation and innovation possible.

The LSC promotes active dialog and discussion among community leaders in order to cultivate a thorough understanding of problems and issues. By communicating and collaborating with each other, community leaders become aware of the roles and values of each other's work. As a result, community leaders are able to transform the various conflicts that have arisen among them into constructive conflicts. This process requires community leaders to follow a pattern of thought and action in which they ask themselves what sorts of actions they themselves would take, what sorts of strategies or tactics they would adopt, and what they could contribute toward achieving the NPD and the innovation of a new business. And in achieving this innovation, the LSC promotes the sympathy and resonance of the community leaders' values, and the combined synergy and dialectical management of leadership among the community leaders have resulted in the high levels of synthesizing capability that has enabled Fujitsu and Company A to realize NPD and form new business models.

In another sense, it can be seen that Fujitsu and Company A have used the resonance of values among community leaders in their SCs and their leadership synergy to form the LSC and high levels of integrative competences, which in turn generated a solid network of SCs.

In the remarkably short period of about a year and a half, Fujitsu succeeded in the NPD of a large-scale system and created new knowledge at high levels that led to the establishment of business models with communications carriers and sales SI vendors (Figure 7.5).

Developing dialectical leadership: toward the realization of SC-based firms

Through these case studies, we would like to emphasize that innovative companies in the 21st century need to be SC-based firms. In other words, we believe that it is important for innovative companies to create ongoing innovation through business activities that involve the formation of SCs based on creative knowledge assets and the networking of these SCs. Knowledge, or management resources, aimed at strategic innovation is created from SCs, a wide range of knowledge both inside and outside the company, including customers and strategic partners, is merged and integrated via the network, and new knowledge that never existed before is created to become a new source of competitive advantage. To that end, it is important for community leaders who form the LSC to find a new value aimed at innovation with customers and leaders of strategic partners inside and outside the company as the company endeavors to achieve its desired vision and mission. The newly created value is then shared, sympathized, and resonated by all community members through constructive dialog and discussion within the LSC. The philosophy of an interactive learning-based strategic community, where members teach each other and learn from each other, is an important part of this process. This approach promotes further dialectical consideration and becomes the driving force for producing high levels of synthesizing capability.

The community leaders in the LSC use integrative competences through dialectical management to create innovative, creative NPD, business concepts, and reforms in business processes. The governance and control mechanisms within the SCs and networked SCs, including customers and external partners, are related in a big way to the behavior of the leadership of community leaders that form the LSC. The LSC is an informal SC made up of community leaders from the various SCs, and they are positioned above the layer of networked SCs (Figure 7.7). The LSC gives greater strength to the cross-functional or inter-corporate integration characteristics that the SCs and networked SCs have. The LSC's role is to boost NPD performance, and to fulfill this role, community leaders in the LSC need to have the element of dialectical leadership. They need to have not just the elements of the participative leadership style and a flexible approach discussed thus far in the literature on NPD (McDonough and Barczak, 1991; Dougherty, 1996), they will also need to balance creativity and efficiency or participative control and directive control (Shenhar and Dvir, 1996; Eisenhardt and Tabrizi, 1995). This sort of issue on behavior or dialectical management by individual leaders or among a number of leaders has not been discussed in the past in research on CTF or project management in NPD. More recently, however, Lewis *et al.* (2002) have been maintaining that a balance of a number of paradoxes is required for successful product development. They clarify the frequent but ambiguous calls for subtle control: Effective managers provide strong leadership to keep teams focused and on schedule, while empowering team members to foster motivation and creativity.

In our own field studies as well, we were able to glean some rich data from dialogs and discussions with community leaders concerning their dialectical considerations and actions. A community leader from Fujitsu, for instance, commented:

> This development and turning it into a service product requires element technologies in a variety of fields, and collaboration among internal members and external players is important. As the person responsible for my team, I had to devote development resources both strategically and deliberately in order to pursue development according to a target schedule. There were also many technically difficult areas, requiring both know-how and creativity from specialized engineers in the various fields both inside and outside the company. Since new ideas and creativity from capable engineers are important, as an organization, we had to exhibit flexible management. Development cannot just be forced.

A community leader from Fujitsu and another Japanese company commented:

> Since development encompasses a variety of technical fields and new business models, communication and ties with specialized engineers and persons in charge both inside and outside the company are necessary. Though leadership and management that can guide development team members in our own company and pull them along is also important of course, at the same time it is important to empower and motivate young members of our own team and to build cooperative

relationships and a daily support system with leaders and engineers among players in other divisions and external organizations.

A chief engineer in Fujitsu and another Japanese company commented:

Technical development in fields such as digitalization, broadband, and multimedia has recently become extremely difficult. Ten years or so ago, business models could exist in individual technical fields, but now it's impossible to generate new business models without merging various technologies. To generate these business models, we need to form ties with specialists in many fields both internally and externally, and to build the capacity to integrate technical and business model aspects. It's important to pursue various contradictions at the same time.

A community leader from a Taiwanese manufacturer commented: 'We need to overcome technical issues and build a business model simultaneously. Innovation will not emerge unless we tap the knowledge of both engineers and marketers and collaborate closely.'

The same sort of issues and views that people at the forefront of development struggle with on a daily basis as they work to cultivate new markets in a rapidly-changing environment of technical innovations and business models were received from eight other community leaders, chief engineers, and others. The demand for community leaders in SCs and networked SCs to exercise dialectical thinking and behavior is growing stronger than before. The sort of leadership required, gleaned from much of the data we obtained, can also be expressed as below (Figure 7.8).

As a first important element regarding the dialectical leadership which synthesizes the different leadership behaviors of leadership's dominant dualities, the community leaders in the LSC, who use synthesizing capability, do not only exhibit their 'strategic leadership' as directors based on integrated, centralized leadership which can produce long-term strategy, focus on the big picture and perform efficiently, but also exhibit their 'creative leadership' based on autonomous, decentralized leadership which can produce creative thinking and behaviors of community members. As a second important element, community leaders do not only exhibit their 'forceful leadership' as directors who can take charge and control community members, but also become listeners, recipients and collaborators based on collaborative leadership (Chrislip and Larson, 1994; Bryson and Crosby, 1992), empowering community members through enabling leadership and enhancing intrinsic motivation (Osterlof *et al.*, 2000) among community members in their knowledge creation activities. Their role

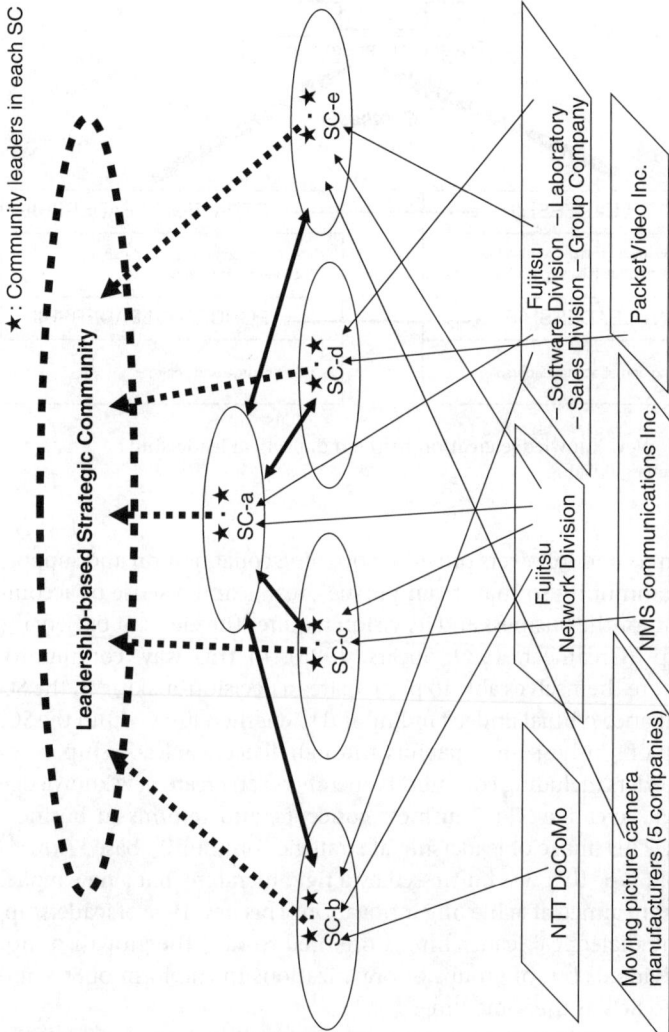

★ : Community leaders in each SC

Leadership-based Strategic Community

SC-e

SC-d

SC-a

SC-c

SC-b

Fujitsu
– Software Division – Laboratory
– Sales Division – Group Company

PacketVideo Inc.

Fujitsu
Network Division

NMS communications Inc.

NTT DoCoMo

Moving picture camera
manufacturers (5 companies)

Figure 7.7 Formations of strategic community networked SCs and LSC
Source: Kodama (2005a).

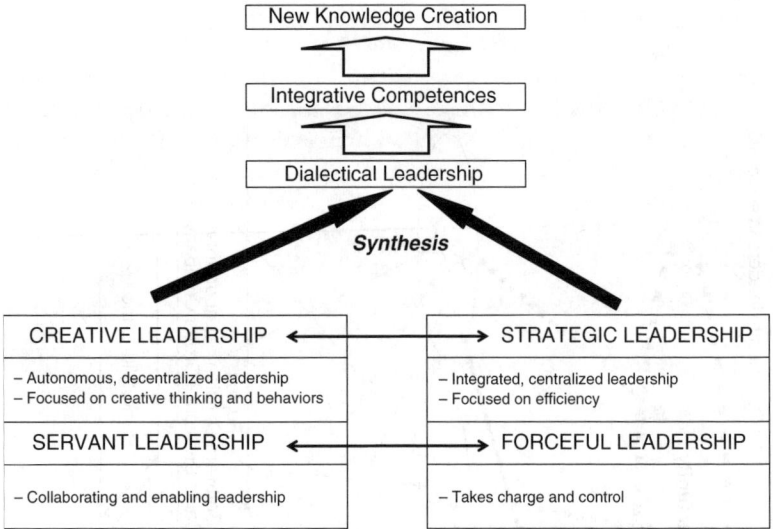

Figure 7.8   New knowledge creation through dialectical leadership
Source: Kodama (2005a).

as supporters and followers providing ongoing collaboration and support for the community so that it can pursue dreams and a sense of accomplishment for the business and its vision requires the element of 'servant leadership' (Greanleaf, 1979; Spears, 1995). In this way, community members are themselves able to participate in decision-making in the SC and to enhance mutual understanding and strengthen links within the SC. As a result of synthesizing capability through dialectical leadership, community leaders including community members can create new knowledge of strategic, creative NPD, business concepts, and reforms in business processes. This image of leadership at strategic community-based firms is not the old type that was buttressed by a rigid hierarchy but a new model of leadership aimed at achieving innovation. This new type of leadership, that is the dialectical leadership, is oriented toward the growth of not only individuals but of groups or organizations in the form of SCs and networked SCs at the same time.

From the viewpoint of leadership and organizational development, the key issue for companies of the 21st century aiming to achieve innovation is how to nurture and produce many community leaders who possess the dialectical leadership based on the concepts of being creative and strategic, and the ability to act. And the formation of SCs that can continuously generate innovation via the capabilities of individual community leaders, the number of community leaders from each level of management, and the abilities of these leaders to exercise their skills, along with the networking of these SCs, determine whether or not a company is able to build integrative competences through dialectical leadership.

8
Innovation by Strategic Community-Based Firms

Integration of different economies

Recently, markets in the hi-tech field such as system LSI are suddenly in the process of being started up by Japanese semiconductor manufacturers and firms such as Canon, Matsushita Electric and Sharp, who are large Japanese manufacturers in the digital consumer electronics field. The characteristic points about these companies lie in the accumulated know-how resulting from core technical strength, thorough-going cost reductions and quality improvements due to production reforms. In the United States, on the other hand, the dynamic growth of dot-com companies such as Intel, Microsoft and Dell and traditional American companies such as IBM and GE is eye-catching, though the characteristic points about these rapidly growing companies are that they are simultaneously pressing for and attaining inconsistencies in economies of scale, economies of scope, and economies of speed in their individual industries. Together with the development of ICT, when transaction costs and interaction costs are lowered, it becomes difficult to pursue three different economies at the same time, and the company is forced to specialize its business domain by 'concentration and selection' (Hagel and Singer, 1999). This is the proper argument for implementing strategy under established conditions. On the other hand, however, creative and productive frictions and interactions between and within companies acquire new competences that transcend the existing core competences and also hides the possibility that new innovation may be produced. Therefore, instead of asserting that interaction costs within and between companies are simply costs, it is important to think of them as a source of innovation. Is it not possible that this way of thinking will enable the three different economies to be pursued at the same time?

	Economy of Scale	Economy of Scope	Economy of Speed
Matsushita Electric / Sharp Canon	• Production revolution using cell production → Injection of cost leadership and high-quality products • Created ideal supply chain for parts procurement, etc. • Concentrated capital investment	• Expanded product line-up • Established global sales structure for simultaneous global launches	• Black-boxing of core technologies • Rapid development of multiple products through hard and soft modulation • Concentrated R&D investment
Toyota	• Toyota production system → Balancing cost and quality • Concentrated capital investment	• Expanded product line-up • Established global production and sales structure	• Established ideal global development and production structure → Injected IMV • Concentrated R&D investment
Microsoft Intel	• Concentrated capital investment (hard and soft) • Created ideal supply chain	• Established global sales structure • Established common (de facto) platform for IT devices, applications, content, networks, etc.	• Possesses difficult to imitate technologies • Concentrated R&D investment • Ongoing new product development
Dell	• Established cost leadership with unique supply chain • Concentrated capital investment	• Expanded customer demographics (consumer & corporate users) through direct sales and high-grade customer service	• Promoted standardized development aimed at modularization of IT devices • Concentrated R&D investment in high-end & network products

Figure 8.1 Simultaneous pursuit of different economies

For instance, as shown in Figure 8.1, due to investment concentrated on research and development at Microsoft and Intel, economies of speed are being realized by materializing the development of new products that will not be discontinued because of difficult-to-imitate technology. At the same time, through concentrated capital investment (in hardware and software) and global private company organization and strategic partnerships with other companies, economies of scale and scope are also being achieved. Moreover, Dell has materialized an economy of scale thanks to an exclusive supply chain and simultaneously reached an economy of scope by means of an expanded customer base due to high-grade customer service, while at the same time pursuing an economy of speed in new product development that includes high-end products and network products of many kinds.

On the other hand, Toyota Motor Corporation, which is an excellent company representing Japan, has an expanding economy of scale due to the a simultaneous pursuit of cost reduction and quality improvement by means of the refined Toyota production system while at the same time it is executing the pursuit of an economy of scope with a global production and supply system. In addition, the global development and production system for innovative multipurpose vehicles (IMV), which is aimed at the establishment of a global simultaneous development and production system, is at the same time reaching an economy of speed by further shortening the life cycle of new products. Furthermore, in the field of digital consumer electronics, while earning revenue and market share, Matsushita Electric, Sharp and Canon are in pursuit of economies of scale by means of the dramatic production reforms of cell production, and in pursuit of economies of scope with simultaneous global vertical launchings, as well as reaching economies of speed by rapid development of new products by means of black-boxing and flexible modularization of core technologies.

The foundations of the simultaneous pursuit of these different economies are the integrative competences that are possessed by SC-based firms. The author will apply the term 'knowledge architecture' to the framework that perceived the mechanisms to give rise to these integrative competences from the viewpoints of strategy and organization. 'Knowledge architecture' is the framework that provides the driving force for corporate activities that create and implement new concepts in a ceaseless spiral through interaction with the original strategic dynamics (to be called 'strategic architecture') and the original organizational dynamics (to be called 'organizational architecture') that SC-based firms possess (Figure 8.2). In this chapter, we aim to construct new strategic theories that have not previously been conceptualized as well as organizational arguments that are indispensable to these theories, and we wish to consider logic that can rhythmically reconstruct strategy and organization dynamically under any kind of environment.

Knowledge architecture

For a company to continue to achieve a dynamic invasion, it must unceasingly create new intellectual capital. SC-based firms have a different viewpoint from previous business and strategic theories, whose origin was how to make new business values in the knowledge period. A practical systematized framework is essential for an SC-based firm that must create a business concept of goods and services with absolute value where there were none previously. This systematized framework is 'knowledge architecture'. On acquiring integrative competences, the firm will build a knowledge concept platform by building strategic and organizational architecture, and proceed to create and practice new business. Having a built-in framework of 'knowledge architecture' inside and outside the company, the firm can acquire the resources and capabilities that bring dynamic value and competitive status and can create and put into practice new business concepts.

In addition to providing continuous value to customers, essential knowledge acquisition for an SC-based firm lies in dialectical thought and action. 'Knowledge architecture' is composed of the concept that the actors must create and put into practice with dialectical thought as the basis, plus the concept platform and the strategic and organizational architecture that are the driving force of this concept platform, as well as the dynamic networked SC formation that gives rise to these two architectures, plus four specific factors. How the firm designs from the viewpoint of strategy and organization under a dynamic environment then creates new knowledge and puts it into practice from the practical viewpoint is essential for an SC-based firm.

Essentially, architecture means 'systematized technology,' but with a broader interpretation as 'a systematized business system' we shall take it to be not only technology but a systematic method that embraces a wide range of goods and services as well as business models. The architecture that a firm possesses is the most suitably designed strategy and organization that is required for the goods and services and other matters that are the final form of knowledge to be created and put into practice by a knowledge integration process and then provided to customers.

Knowledge architects

The author will refer to leaders of organizations that construct 'knowledge architecture' as knowledge architects and wishes to make general comments relating to their mission. (Knowledge architects correspond to leaders in each management level, each department and project including the top layer.) Knowledge architects are leaders among knowledge workers. They drive the knowledge integration process through the formation and networking of SCs that have subjective values. The knowledge architects question the merits of the company's existence and have a sense of mission and commitment to absolute value visions. Then vision, dialog, friction and conflict, and practice through various hierarchical SCs display dialectical leadership that turns into resonance with environmental (market) knowledge. The knowledge architects tolerate various paradoxes inside and outside the organization, and SCs that transcend the boundaries of the organization are formed to expand the general mobilization of knowledge. The pursuit of the corporate vision and the corporate mission is the knowledge architects' essential objective, and the compatibility of maintaining the company's dynamic competitive dominance (securing strategic market positioning) and at the same time updating and storing internal resources that will become the core (securing strategic internal resources) are connected as a result of activities centered on the knowledge architects.

In discussions up to now in the academic world, deciding on strategy from the viewpoint of outlooks of both market positioning and resources, and implementing them at the same time, has given rise to arguments from businessmen that each is difficult due to differences in context. Thinking as a businessman from a business context, the author's idea on the reason for this is as follows. A background associated with the swelling of the organization, stratification and specialization of systems, specialization and subdivision of technical domains and the simultaneous need for amalgamation of technical domains, diversification, and complication of a business model that has cut across different industries due to acceleration of net business, makes demands on businessmen for diverse specialized technical knowledge that exceed the capacity of one individual businessman. Moreover, acquiring the expanded range of this specialized knowledge adds to the actual pressure and business uncertainties associated with the diversification of last year's customers' needs are increasingly limiting the scope of businessmen's thoughts and actions. The author wonders whether the result of this is connected with a reduction in the businessman's senses as a realist.

If we may mention a slightly negative opinion, generally head office staff make strategic decisions, but do they have enough daily interaction with the market (customers)? It is important for strategic decision-makers to have thorough perception and awareness of their own company's goods and services from the viewpoint of the customer through constant on-the-spot personal experience with customers. Head office strategic decision makers analyze the market to pick out the market positioning views that have competitive predominance, and although they draw blueprints in the form of medium to long-term plans and thoroughly discuss the merits and significance of the company's existence in terms of what, why and how, do they have on hand sufficient points of view to translate these into practical action? Furthermore, although the strategic decision-makers may collect and analyze market data in detail, are they not succumbing to the analysis paralysis syndrome and falling into the world of formal logic as onlookers or critics of a risky business? If not, completed strategic decisions become very much the static conclusions of onlookers and the spirit becomes an unconfined 'pie in the sky.'

On the other hand, company employees in service fronts nearest to the market (customers) and field employees in development and production divisions engaged in the storage and transmission of skill and know-how as tacit knowledge, have their thoughts blocked by the scope of their own work; are they not lacking thoughts and actions at the company-wide strategic level that everything is for the best? Although Japanese companies in the past had the strength of tacit knowledge due to the accumulation of design and operation know-how at the field level of development and production, in this world of explicit knowledge, does management out in the field have in hand a stock of logical thoughts and actions that would develop the kind of market positioning that has been providing ongoing competitive advantage? It is next to impossible for new innovation to emerge at a company if many employees simply disappear into the closed worlds of their own daily tasks or defensive positions and are mere onlookers to any world outside while the company is trying to establish competitive advantage and acquire resources and competences. An important point with respect to the future and present of one's own company: stretching the temporal ideas of 'how should it be, how do you want it to be, how will that be done?' around strategic and practical aspects, all company employees must behave towards the totally ideal management of their own company as if they were actually present.

Mr. Toshifumi Suzuki, President and CEO of Seven & I Holdings, is investigating 'management that considers the present from the future.' In other words, from a time when the future is predicted by analyzing the past and present, he has entered into a time that considers what kind of present we must have in order to produce a certain kind of future. The company is not able to challenge new matters unless this is done. When the present is considered from the future in the position of a customer, a completely different world appears for people who are really present. As knowledge architects in an SC-based firm, middle managers (including top management) are not in the position of onlookers. Instead, they are

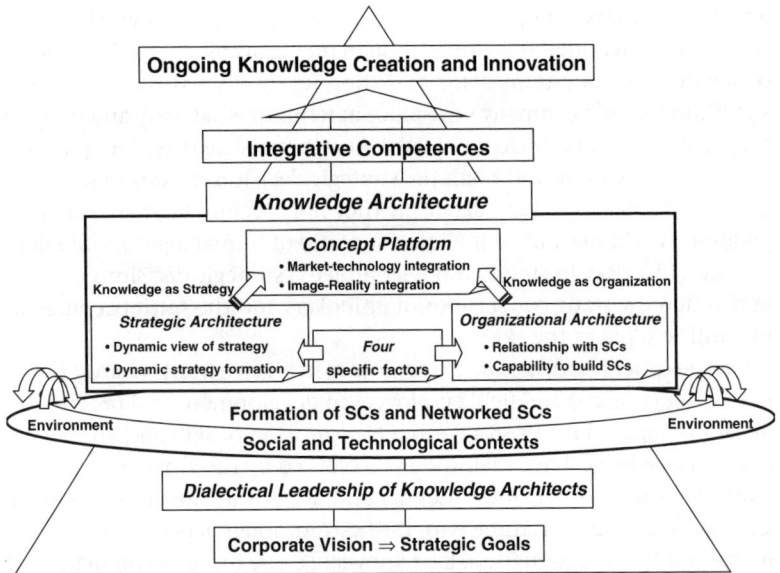

Figure 8.2   Strategic community-based firm

in the position of people who are really present, always aiming at totally optimum management with their thoughts and actions devoted to the pursuit of ideal values. With the viewpoints of integration of strategic decisions and practices (implementation) and the integration of management level with position (the front line of business), they proceed to construct 'strategic architecture' and 'organizational architecture.' Then, as a result of having acquired the integrative competences that are necessary for knowledge creation and innovation, they are able to make the two opposing items of market positioning with competitive predominance and the accumulation of very precious internal assets coexist.

Creation and practice of business concepts in a concept platform

Integration of market and technology

'People power' is the source of new knowledge for knowledge architecture and knowledge workers. There, the formation of hierarchical SCs becomes the platform needed for the creation of value by the creation, use, and sharing of knowledge. In that case, how do they form SCs and how do they proceed to create new business concepts? As Simon once pointed out, people have limited abilities for perception. That is the reason why organizational hierarchies and functional segregation were established in the world of management.

Certainly, corporate activities are formed from various business processes (including basic research, applied research, marketing, product development, production, sales, distribution and after-sales service) and the context of each business varies. No one company employee has all the basic capabilities and no-one who can do everything from development to the selling of new goods and services. It has been made clear from the case analyses in this book that the formation of multi-layered SCs is indispensable for the creation and practice of superior business concepts. Therefore, knowledge architects and knowledge workers of the departments that are at the core of new merchandise development, such as marketing, research and development and production, have plans to create and share a dynamic context that transcends the boundaries of the organization. In this way, they will be able to create and put into practice new knowledge (business concepts such as new goods and services).

Individual knowledge architects and knowledge workers of each department also have various views of values and of the world. At the foundation of an individual's way of life there is a form of thought and action as a fixed paradigm based on previous personal experience (such as working in a particular department engaged in marketing, research and development, and production). Through the dialectic integration of the interactions of their own subjective viewpoint (the viewpoint that assimilates with the customer and tries to understand potential demand) and their objective viewpoint (analysis of competing goods and customer data), knowledge architects in charge of marketing are ceaselessly producing new perceptions such as 'products that provide customers with new values must be planned' or 'how to grasp customers' potential needs and relate them to the planning of goods.' However, they do not necessarily have the technical viewpoints on hand. They are always grasping technical trends inside and outside the company. In the circumstances of 'it's full of uncertainty but if this technology is materialized, customers can probably be provided with equipment and services such as this,' the concept is a potential form of usage of which the customers themselves are not aware and they have even neglected making the effort to verify.

On the other hand, through the dialectic integration of the interactions of their own subjective viewpoints (faith and desire of developing this themselves) and objective viewpoints (concentration and selection based on analysis and evaluation of technical trends), the R&D and production knowledge architects are ceaselessly producing new perceptions of 'technology to satisfy customers must be developed' and 'core technology that competing companies cannot imitate.' The engineers also do not necessarily have market outlooks on hand. They can also be proposed to the customer from the engineers' original, certainly achievable, seeds-oriented concepts.

Then, knowledge architects and knowledge workers of every department subjectively form hierarchical SCs within the company. Each subject clashes from the viewpoint and context of market and technology, and the conflict of these paradigms creates new energy, and a higher-order context is formed. The knowledge architects and knowledge workers understand the diversity of each one's world outlooks and values, and mutual agreement and rules are created between different organizations through creative interactions and dialectical dialog. Then, however, the meaning of how new knowledge can be created by mutually understanding and sharing the thoughts and feelings of individual members and bringing self assertion and humility together is brought into question. In this way, individual people would be able to develop the next generation of higher ideas and thoughts. The 'roadmap of the market' and 'roadmap of technology' would then be integrated through abduction and business concepts created and put into practice as a transcendent hypothesis (Figure 8.3).

Synthesis of image and entity

The conversion domain of tacit knowledge and explicit knowledge represents the center of the creation of business concepts. Knowledge architects of the marketing field must perceive and experience social contexts that cannot clearly formulate knowledge such as market structural trends and the potential needs of customers. On the other hand, knowledge architects of the technical development field must create the kind of technical contexts (for example, reading as an engineer whether it is possible to cover the scope of the product image that is to be inferred from knowledge difference and knowledge integration) that will adapt (become familiar with) tacit social contexts (such as image and bodily sensation of the target product) through direct personal experience and close interaction on-site with the marketers. The question: 'Is it possible to materialize goods and services that give an impression such as this?' and creative and dialectical dialog between marketers and engineers are carried on through personal experience in abstracted space (the domain of the living world domain). Accordingly, in the abstracted time and space called image, the beliefs and thoughts of the knowledge architects come into conflict with each other.

However, it is also true that when closed in abstracted space, a definite concept and prototype cannot be materialized. Therefore, in abstracted

185

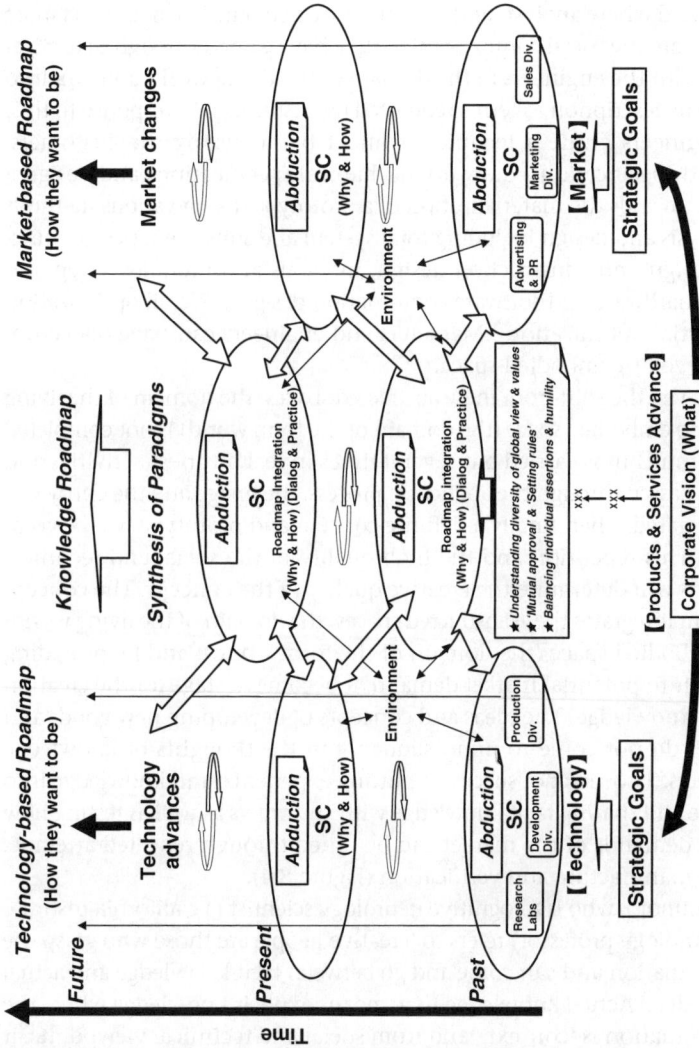

Figure 8.3 Synthesis of market and technology

space, images of the marketers and engineers must be incorporated into an actual form. This is embodied space (the domain of the world of form) the area where the image is converted by metaphor and analogy into formal knowledge (the customers' clearly verbalized potential needs and required terms) and where analysis and design are carried out. The marketers must incorporate the social context, which they have gained through dialectical dialog with the engineers in the domain of the living world domain, into a definite description as terms requested by customers. In response to this, the engineers create a technical context by analyzing the customers' demand specifications, draw up mechanical specifications and design a system towards the materialization of a prototype (using various methods of analysis and design including total system and subsystem design, function design and construction design, integrals and modules, open and closed, hardware and software coordination designs, overall optimization and partial optimization). Marketers and engineers can have dialectical dialog even in embodied space.

However, the shift from these abstracted spaces (the domain of the living world) to embodied space (the domain of the form world) is not completed at one time but is carried out several times in real business activities and having passed through the abduction process, the image and the entity will be integrated. Then finally a definite concept and prototype will be completed. This repetition and the high quality of the social and technical contexts will determine the creative quality of the concept. The concept platform integrates these abstracted spaces (the domain of the living world) and embodied space (the domain of the form world), and by providing insight into potential market demand, it becomes a stage for the creation of new knowledge. The ideas and concepts of developing new goods and services do not come to mind suddenly in the thoughts of knowledge architects. The secret of success is putting experience and knowledge into practice and sharing tacit knowledge with customers as well as testing how far the demands of the market can be tuned through repeated attempts at trial manufacture and verification (Figure 8.4).

Dr Shimojo, who is a cognitive neurology scientist (a California Institute of Technology professor) refers to 'creative people are those who grasp the entire situation and can come and go between tacit knowledge and actual knowledge.' Actual knowledge here means explicit knowledge where the entire situation is 'context,' and from social and technical viewpoints, it can also be called the global context. The driving force that dynamically induces the coming and going between tacit knowledge and explicit knowledge of the global context is probably the integrated competences held by the knowledge architects.

187

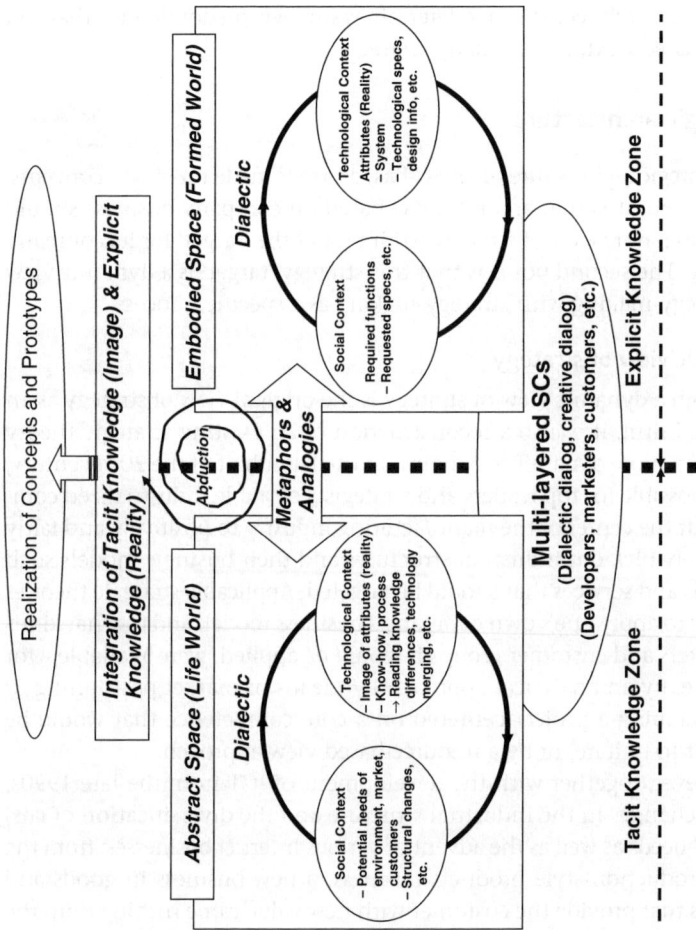

Figure 8.4 Concept platform

The business that is created by the subjective knowledge architects who have people power, and is put into practice by the concept platform, is one of the original strategic views (strategic theories) and organizational views (organizational theories) of SC-based firms. The building up of frameworks known as 'organizational architecture' that are related to the formation and networking of hierarchical SCs, and the building up of 'strategic architecture' that determines strategic predominance that will be discussed next, are mutually related.

Strategic architecture

The strategic architecture of an SC-based firm is made up of two concepts. The first point is that an enterprise based on company business should have a dynamic view of strategy to aim for as the 'target' for its company strategy. The second point is that this strategy 'target' is a dynamic view of strategy-making with strategy-making as a specific 'process.'

Dynamic view of strategy

Although a dynamic view of strategy is the original view of strategy as an SC-based firm, it is also a reconstruction of an existing strategic theory towards a more dynamic viewpoint. In the latter half of the 20th century, it was possible for top leaders and strategists of stable industrialized companies at the center of the manufacturing industry to positively and fairly accurately pick out industrial structures and their business models such as goods and services that should be targeted. Applicable strategic theories on how to apply one's own company's business model, and to what kinds of markets and customer groups it would be applied, were available – for instance, by an analytical approach by means of market positioning or by developing a project centered on a core competence that would be difficult to imitate, or by a resource-based view approach.

However, together with the development of ICT from the late 1990s, due to changes in the industrial structure and the diversification of customers' needs as well as the advent of various Internet businesses, from the mass-production-style products business, a new business in goods and services that provide the customer with new value came rushing onto the stage. The environment that surrounds those businesses changes dynamically (or turbulently), forcing the necessity for ongoing reviews of existing business models and the production of new values. The very strategy required under this kind of environment is for the company to continue activities that will create new knowledge on an ongoing basis. This is the strategic view of an SC-based firm.

Since strategic theory up to now was able to clearly define the markets and customers that should be targeted by a business in a comparatively stable environment, it has been possible to explain and predict the degree of strategic approaches derived from the analysis of industry structure and one's own company's core competences. However, if environmental changes are significant or unpredictable, a dialectical viewpoint will become necessary in which the company will always at high speed undertake an appropriate market-positioning view and an interactive and mobile review of the acquisition of necessary resources. On the other hand, the dialectical viewpoint of market (position) and organization (resource) is ignored by existing strategic theory, and the subjective side of humans who continue to remake their own environment by producing new perceptions was not considered at all by existing strategic theory. For example, the market-based view (Porter, 1980) and the resource-based view (Wernerfelt, 1984 and Barney, 1991, for example), which are two opposing items of traditional strategic theory, are both static models that do not consider dynamic environmental change. However, as discussed in the case analyses in section 4 of Chapter 2 and in Chapter 5, in SC-based firms, market position and resources are taken to be dimensions of 'knowledge' and the two opposing items of market position and internal resources are cancelled by the framework of a dynamic spiral knowledge integration process and they can now be integrated. In the SC-based theory of the firm, 'human dialectic thoughts and actions (subjective and objective mobility)' is a point that is incorporated into strategic theory.

By reconstructing strategic theory with a dialectic viewpoint, even with respect to any kind of environmental change, an SC-based firm will dynamically create and put into practice knowledge in a spiral, which is a new concept. It establishes and updates competitive predominance in the market, and at the same time is also able to acquire and update difficult-to-imitate resources (Figure 8.5).

In each case described in this book, the knowledge architects recognize their own mission and faith in the essential absolute values for their own company and dynamically execute interactions with the environment (such as customers) in real time. Then with respect to dynamic environmental changes, creative abrasion and productive friction with various hierarchical SCs not only improve existing resources and functions through dialectical dialog, but new knowledge is also acquired and business concepts created. Knowledge difference and common knowledge are essential for the creation of new business concepts (new products and new services). 'Knowledge difference' and 'common knowledge' are important elements

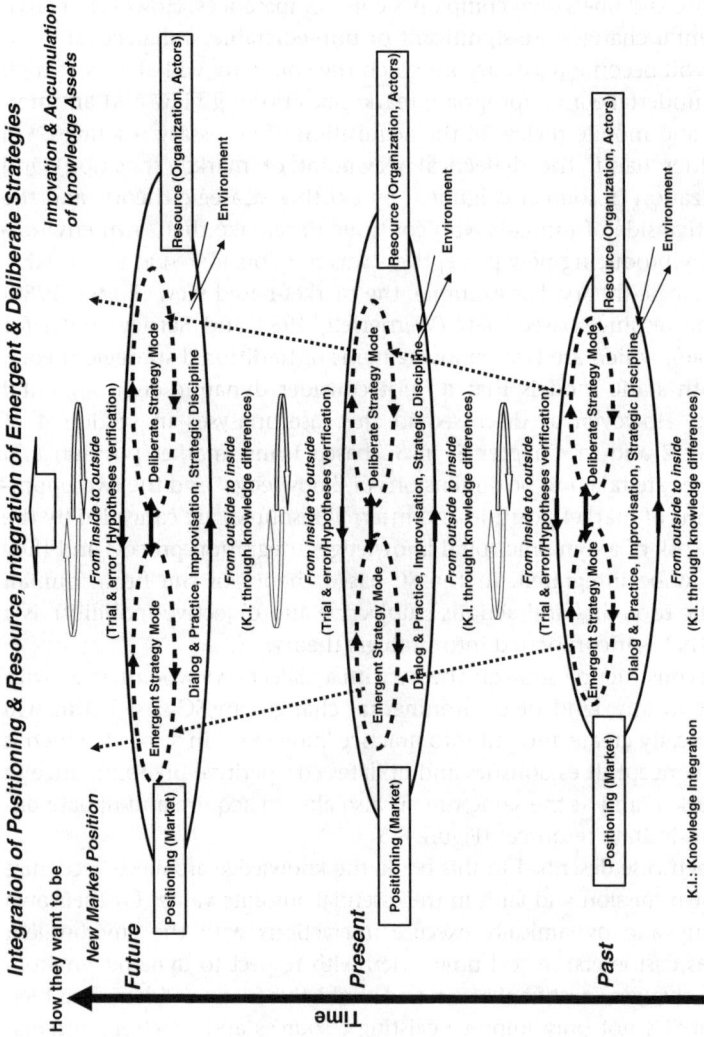

Figure 8.5 Strategic architecture

that stimulate the ideas and behavior of marketers and developers, who are the knowledge architects, from external points of view (realizing new market position dictated by new product concepts) to internal points of view (acquiring new capability in the organization). Therefore, creative dialog is to be promoted and improvised in order to cause dynamic changes in the context that must overcome the various contradictions that confront knowledge architects at the front line of business. The knowledge architects must implement decision-making by improvising a combined context of SCs and networked SCs inside and outside the organization in real time.

Improvisation means acting quickly to implement decision-making in real time with respect to an external environment that changes from one moment to the next. It is an action pattern whose 'entire strategic target is to proceed with orbital adjustments during repeated trial and error while sharing and running and thinking.' For members of the organization, it demands integrative competences of endurance and speed.

For example, knowledge architects will carry out improvised rearrangements of resources and competences through the speedy formation of SCs and the networking of these SCs, and the form of the organization of these SCs (organizational architecture: to be explained later) will be constantly reconstructed (Kodama, 2005a). Instead of simply coping with variations in the environment and conditions, improvisation is an act to cause subjective changes of the environment and conditions. If the environment and conditions vary, while the inconsistencies are being picked up, new inconsistencies will be discovered. Then the organization will acquire new resources and capabilities.

On the other hand, facing the embodiment of new products and services and the establishment of a business model, it is important that, through trial and error by experimentation and provisional inspection processes, the actors turn their thoughts and actions from the internal point of view (of acquiring new capability in the organization) to the external point of view (realizing new market position by bringing new products and services to market). By pursuing thorough efficiency by means of the supply chain management with integrated design and production methods as well as business processes that use IT, they go on to reach a market position that has competitive advantage. Then the knowledge architects will raise the degree of completion of the goods and services that are their development target. Then, at the same time as the knowledge architects are acquiring and accumulating new knowledge and know-how through merchandising, they proceed to touch off new knowledge by working subjectively in the environment (market) and by perceiving and reflecting on differences with the market. In addition, the knowledge architects integrate opposing values while always renewing their experience of past successes. Members of SCs acquire competences through interaction with introspective practices and the environment, but the important duties they are fulfilling here are the SCs and networked SCs. The knowledge that has been acquired by stimulating, acquiring, and sharing the various concepts in SCs is deeply embedded in individuals through the SCs and networked SCs. In this way, the formation and networking of SCs are for the company the acquisition of assets and competences that have competitive advantage and are at the same time linked to an appropriate market position. The driving forces for the formation and networking of SCs are the 'people power' of individuals and at the same time the integrative competences that express the spiral knowledge integrative processes (Figure 8.5).

Spiral knowledge integrative processes that have passed through the formation of SCs and networked SCs as described above are continuously producing new knowledge with respect to dynamic environmental changes and have the capability of constructing new 'strategic architecture' as a dynamic strategic view that proceeds to produce strategic advantage as a company.

Dynamic strategic views are at the foundations of SC-based firms, but in addition, how a company should continuously produce innovation requires a specific strategy-making process. What becomes important there are the power of improvisation and strategic discipline, which the organization possesses. These elements become the front line that produces effective and dynamic strategy for the company, which will be discussed next.

Dynamic view of strategy-making process

Dynamic strategy-making processes of the corporation can be largely divided into deliberate strategy and emergent strategy. Emergent strategy differs from deliberate strategy, where decision-making is at the top level of the company, and is defined as emanating from proposals from the field or from middle management. However, there are not many instances in the fields of real business where the meaning is purely emergent, and most of the matters taken to be emergent proposals from the bottom up are strategies that conformed to the company's summary mission or orientation. Speaking from that viewpoint, few emergent strategies are strategies conceived from ideas that suddenly emanate as thoughts of the proponent. They are created in the course of daily routine as a result of improvisation such as incremental reformation, improvement, and trial and error, or by accumulated daily training known as communicated practice.[1]

When we think from the viewpoint of a strategy-making process, a dynamic strategic view in an SC-based firm is a materialization of integrated strategy-making aimed at the coexistence of a paradox in that it is emergent and at the same time deliberate. Here, we would like to consider the matter of how deliberate strategy and emergent strategy would be integrated. Emergent strategy is based on the sharing of individuals' introspection and tacit knowledge. It is formed by concept creation through abduction. Knowledge architects share various dynamic contexts in hierarchical SCs and networked SCs and create new knowledge by improvisation. Furthermore, embodied concepts, crystallized by goods and services as explicit knowledge, proceed to implement deliberate strategy by company-wide decision-making. As to the true nature of the emergent and deliberate integration strategy-making process, members in hierarchical SCs and networked SCs, by means of dialectical dialog, creative abrasion and productive friction, reiterated a self-corrected hypothesis that emergently unfolded and formed creativity and imagination until finally the hypothesis came to be reliably, intentionally and systematically materialized. In an SC-based firm, this repetitive shifting from an emergent strategy process to a deliberate strategy process proceeds in spirals (Figure 8.5).

It is important for an SC-based firm that these two different strategy-making processes are made to coexist within the company simultaneously. Actually, the concept of various multiple goods and services groups is being created and put into practice by SC-based firms, and companies are always evolving main-strength products. In other words, not only improving the function and quality of the products but also new versions and new-function additions associated with innovation and market trends. Knowledge architects and knowledge workers in the various departments (such as marketing, development, production, sales, and support) involved with individual products are simultaneously developing exploitation activities for existing business in the past, present and future, and exploitation activities for new business development. From the viewpoint of dynamic strategy-making, this is also a repetition of emergent strategy and deliberate strategy.

Furthermore, this strategy-making change process is different in space and time for each individual goods and services item. For instance, in a manner of speaking, at a certain time there is product A in the case of the deliberate strategy mode and a separate product B in the emergent strategy mode. The top layer of management of an SC-based firm is always aiming at growth now (today) with deliberate strategy and at the same time searching for a mechanism of innovation for the future (tomorrow) with emergent strategy. For example, in a case analysis in this book, Matsushita Electric is an SC-based firm that develops and markets various groups of products such as DVDs, digital cameras and flat-screen televisions with a nucleus of semiconductor technology in the form of a system LSI at the core. The expansion of existing products (a deliberate strategy action) and the development of new products (an emergent strategy action) are being made compatible. Moreover, from the form – and also from the viewpoint – of the organization, the company has two different strategy-making processes which are linked and are being managed at the same time: emergent strategy with the laboratory, the product planning department, and the development department at the center; and deliberate strategy by the production department and the sales and public relations departments. In the same way, NTT DoCoMo and NTT are also expanding existing services (a deliberate strategy action) and developing new services (an emergent strategy action) and making them compatible.

Generally, however, the top management of the company breaks into deliberate strategy mode from emergent strategy mode and suffers a loss of memory once the business model is a success and falls for the illusion that 'we put a successful strategy into practice deliberately.' The result is that it becomes difficult to discover new business (such as the development of new goods and services) by reusing emergent strategy (Christensen and Raynor, 2003). This does not happen, however, with an SC-based firm. Even if deliberate strategy has been successful, the knowledge architects always return to the origin to carry out introspection. Then, when arranging for interaction with the market (such as customers) for a second time, they will be monitoring potential or disruptive technology at the same time. Then the knowledge architects, aiming at the absolute value of the goods and services and answering their own questions, will implement emergent strategy towards the creation of new concepts. Despite comments from many journalists and media criticism that NTT DoCoMo had blundered by switching over to the 3G mobile phone (FOMA) after a period of successful experience with i-mode, by strengthening the emergent strategy for a second time, DoCoMo has started up and is developing a new market for its 3G mobile phone service (FOMA).

Where is the front line for making emergent strategy mode and deliberate strategy mode compatible, as discussed above? In the end, it is the hierarchical SCs and networked SCs, which are the basis of spiral knowledge integration processes within organizations and between organizations that accumulate subjective items that have people power. It is the leadership-based strategic communities (LSCs) that are the groups of leaders (knowledge architects) in each management layer of the companies discussed in Chapter 2, section 5, who play a particularly important role. The knowledge architects of an SC-based firm will pursue company business and their own targets, carrying out self innovation due to their own internal motivation (the belief and thought of one's own innovation through daily work). This further creates SCs and networked SCs as a company as well as an organization. The SCs and networked SCs stimulate improvisation and entrepreneurship for creating abduction and concepts that are important in emergent strategies, and they then proceed to deeply embed strategic discipline[2] in the organizational routine or corporate culture as an orchestra for linking the vision in a practical way toward the securing of competitiveness and profitability in the deliberate strategy. The formation of SCs and networked SCs produce the company's integrative competences and also maintain a robust constitution and strategy for the company with respect to dynamic environmental changes.

'Strategic Architecture,' including dynamic strategic view and dynamic strategic formation, which has been discussed above, and 'Organization Architecture,' design guidelines for SCs, which follows next, are close complements and function as both wheels of a strategic community-based firm.

Organizational architecture

Forming and networking SCs

This author believes that organizational boundaries are intellectual platforms where actors share dynamic contexts (relationships between time, place, and people) and generate new knowledge. SCs as pragmatic boundaries represent time and space where context is shared by individuals through mutual use, and by changing this context, time and space are also created and changed. The SC is a practical time and space for engaging in dialog and sharing tacit knowledge. In this section, the author describes from a practical viewpoint how SCs are formed and linked.

Organizations and individuals are in dialectical relationships, and practitioners change organizations through the human powers of individuals while practical consciousness that is the here and now of space and the tacit knowledge in dynamic context become cyclically involved with the organization (Giddens, 1984; Giddens and Pierson, 1998). While people are subject to limitations by the very organizations they created, they have the power to transform the organization with their own behavior. The SC is a platform that acts as a bridge between individuals and organizations (companies). People in their micro existence bear influence on macro structures such as organizations, companies, industries and society overall through the formation (or disappearance) of SCs and networked SCs. The SC is thus positioned not only as an important linkage between the micro and the macro in societal networks, it is an important analysis unit from the viewpoint of how individuals in the relationships between individuals, organizations, SCs, companies, and industries can manage SCs, form and accumulate social capital (Coleman, 1988; Burt, 1997; Nahapiet and Ghoshal, 1998; Cohen and Prusak, 2000), and influence the performance of companies, or conversely, how individuals are affected by these influences (Figure 8.6).

On the other hand, social capital in the form of knowledge assets is generated mainly around SCs from the flow of knowledge management, and SCs are important also from the viewpoint of process clarification that transcends SC boundaries and is synthesized. SCs are also considered important to practitioners in the aspect of how new knowledge is generated in a practical way through the formation and linking of SCs.

The new viewpoint gained from the DoCoMo case study in Chapter 3 is that diverse, multilayered SCs of different contexts and the network structure linking them always exist within DoCoMo. These SCs were formed and linked (networked) by the actors who actively approached the environment (customers) and others inside and outside the organization. Though the actors may have consciously formed and networked SCs, what sorts of patterns are possible? The author would like to consider this question from two viewpoints: 1. the relationships among the SCs, and 2. the nature of the SCs' structures. (Figure 8.7)

Organizational architecture for the purpose of knowledge integration

Relationships between SCs

As this author mentioned in Chapter 1, with the advances of IT in recent years, there is a growing need to merge different technologies, to develop products and services that span different industries, and to build business models. In the past, innovations in technology have developed through the deep pursuit of specialized knowledge. Now, there are numerous cases in which the technology of one field has to be merged with the technology of another field in order to develop new products based on new ideas that had never existed before.

An important issue is how to integrate different knowledge from various locations. (From the viewpoint of technology, this issue concerns technology integration, i.e. how knowledge in different technical fields is

197

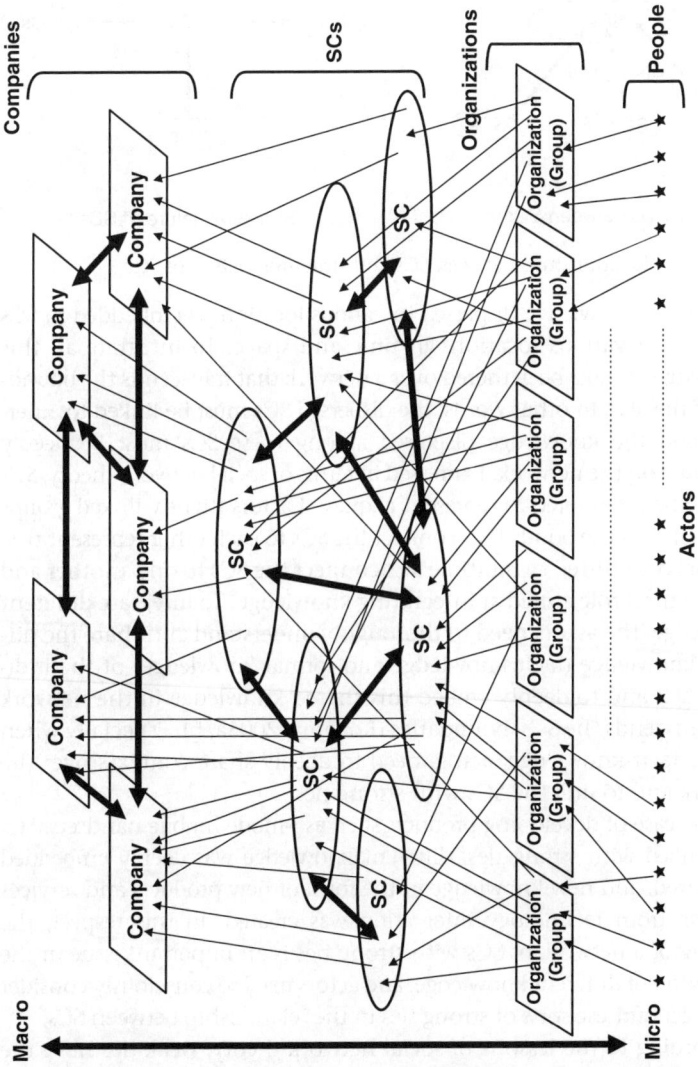

Figure 8.6 People, organizations, and companies centered on strategic communities (image)

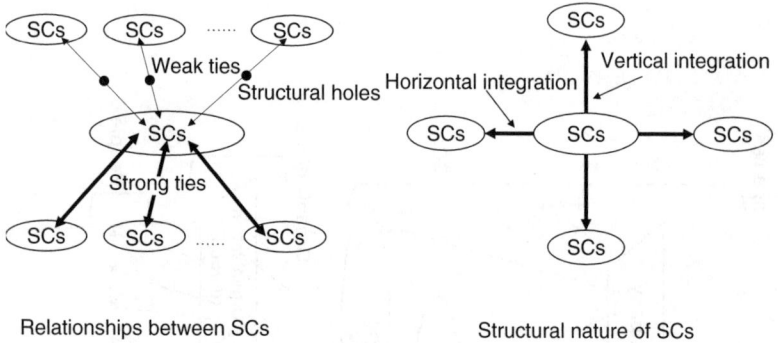

Relationships between SCs   Structural nature of SCs

Figure 8.7   Relationships between SCs and structural nature of SCs

integrated.) Knowledge dispersed in various locations is embedded in SCs dispersed in various locations in time and space. To integrate all this knowledge, it must be gathered over a network that transcends the boundaries of the SCs. In other words, the dispersed SCs must be linked to a network, and the knowledge dispersed among these SCs must be deeply embedded on the network. Expressed in terms of social network theory, SCs can also be interpreted to represent cliques of actors (tightly-linked groups of actors), and the bonds that connect the SCs to each other represent ties.

Actors committed to multiple SCs connect the SCs to one another and play a central role aimed at integrating knowledge. To integrate different knowledge, the actors need to thoroughly understand and share the different knowledge (tacit knowledge and formal knowledge) of the individual SCs and to deeply embed this shared knowledge in the network that transcends the SCs' boundaries (Kodama, 2005a, b). Especially when sharing tacit knowledge, actors need to deeply share contexts over the network and to link the SCs with strong ties.

In the case of developing products such as i-mode mobile handsets, SCs were linked with strong ties, different knowledge was deeply embedded and shared, and new knowledge in the form of new products and services resulting from technology integration was created. In this respect, the building of a network of SCs with strong ties is an important issue in the integration of different knowledge, and actors need to consciously consider the aspect of these sorts of strong ties in the relationship between SCs.

According to the lessons of social network theory, weak ties have the ability to transport a person to new knowledge of a different nature (Granovetter, 1973). In addition, Burt (1992) points out that weak ties with structural holes make it highly possible for actors to access new information and seize new business opportunities. This author is particularly concerned with identifying the sorts of cases in which building a net-work of SCs with weak ties could become an effective approach.

The development of i-mode being studied in Chapter 3 is one such case. The i-mode business model was produced through the integration of various knowledge in such endeavors as the development of a mobile handset, a technology platform, and content. Among these endeavors, the development of a mobile handset and a technology platform occurred as the result of various SCs being formed both within and out-side the organization and then being linked with strong ties (Figure 3.2).

Concerning the development of various content (such as text, games, music, or video), on the other hand, DoCoMo did not build any close network relationships with specific content providers (though DoCoMo engaged in deep knowledge sharing with content providers through a formal i-mode Web site). Instead, DoCoMo built a network of SCs with content providers on an informal Web site that had weak ties, accessed new content information, and used this information to take advantage of new content business opportunities (networked SCs of the content strategy in Figure 3.2).

The building of networked SCs in the platform strategy worked in a similar manner. Behind the realization of i-mode FeliCa, for instance, the world's first mobile e-commerce service for mobile phones, rather than developing this new business by maintaining a close network relation-ship from the beginning just with the Sony Group, FeliCa's promoter, DoCoMo was searching for future electronic money services for the mobile phone and started by maintaining relationships of weak ties not only with the Sony Group but various other related companies as well. By effectively embedding this structural hole, both DoCoMo and Sony actors were able to access new information and knowledge and success-fully create new knowledge that led to the new service. The result was a transformation to networked SCs with strong ties.

As seen above, in building an organizational architecture for realizing knowledge integration that eventuates in the development of a new business, an important issue is to not only build an SC network with strong ties but to also build one with weak ties. (This organizational architecture refers not to a company's formal organizational structure but to a design policy that defines the sort of organizational boundaries that should be formed and how these boundaries will be integrated.) At the same time, actors also need to consciously consider how to constantly balance (or utilize for specific purposes) these SC relationships with strong and weak ties. While the weak ties are being maintained, a network of SCs with weak ties is also formed to bridge structural holes on a timely basis and to absorb and integrate different knowledge. The i-mode business model can be said to have been made possible by the organizational architecture of ingenious SCs.

Along with the relationships of SCs and the structural nature of SCs that will be discussed below, the small world network of Watts and Strogatz (1998) and Watts (2003) that has recently been attracting attention sheds some practical insight into how an organizational architecture of SCs can be quickly and efficiently designed in order to achieve the creation of knowledge that becomes a new business.

Structural nature of SCs

To quickly create high-quality knowledge and promote the spread of knowledge, actors need to consider the structural nature of SCs as well as the SCs' relationships. The structural nature of SCs can be divided into two types: vertical integration and horizontal integration (Figure 8.7).

The vertical integration of SCs refers to their hierarchy. In this structure, the actors of various sections in the company form multiple cross-functional SCs which are also hierarchically networked at different management levels at the same time. This sort of structure is observed, for example, in cases of large-scale new product development. Professionals work together in a variety of specialized fields to perform such tasks as designing the overall architecture for the particular product being developed, designing various subsystems, developing software and hardware, and manufacturing the product. SCs are formed at all management levels, and these SCs are hierarchically structured.

As Henderson and Clark (1990) have pointed out, while the internal structure of the development organization reflects the technology structure that builds it, when basic technology is transferred (for example, when a business model or product and service architecture is changed), the response of the company can be protected by an existing organizational structure. The development of DoCoMo's i-mode in Chapter 3 also suffered from major limitations in its existing organizational structure as it aimed to meet large challenges and achieve its goals. However, by forming networks of flexible, organic pragmatic boundaries within the company, it was possible to respond to the challenges of new development.

It is possible for this sort of vertical integration of SCs, especially in a new product development process that requires the merging and integration of diverse technologies in high-tech fields, such as computer technologies, communications technologies, software technologies, multimedia processing technologies, LSI technologies, or human interface technologies, to become an effective organizational architecture. The individual autonomous SCs that are made up of professional groups in the vertical integration of SCs ensure creativity and flexibility the mission of developing a new product is expressed in concrete tasks. The hierarchy of SCs, on the other hand, ensures efficiency and decision-making speed when tasks are executed. In the i-mode development structure within DoCoMo, multilayered SCs that incorporated vertical integration were formed and contributed to the development of the new i-mode service.

Another interpretation of SC vertical integration that is different from a hierarchy within a company is also possible. This one involves a vertical relationship as a keiretsu network, or network of closely affiliated companies. In Japan, DoCoMo, a communications carrier, and existing mobile handset manufacturers are linked with strong ties in a keiretsu network. This same sort of network relationship between companies also exists between Japanese automobile manufacturers such as Toyota and parts manufacturers (Dyer and Hatch, 2004, for example). When developing a mobile phone, DoCoMo decides the detailed functions for the phone, the technical architecture to make the functions possible, the detailed specifications and the mobile handset manufacturer who then manufactures the phone based on these details and delivers the completed product to DoCoMo. DoCoMo and the mobile handset manufacturers that are linked in strong networked SCs share deep information and knowledge. Also, the business model of vertical integration in Chapter 6 can be interpreted as SC vertical integration in the same way as Matsushita Electric that is also materialized within the company.

Horizontally integrated SCs refers to SCs that work together with customers and external partners in relationships on an equal plane. There is little of the sort of hierarchy that is seen in vertically integrated SCs. In these cases, SCs expand knowledge that they have in common with partners, and they work together in relationships of equality to jointly develop new products and services. For example, through the organizational architecture of horizontally integrated SCs, DoCoMo expands to communications carriers in other countries the knowledge of i-mode and FOMA, the third-generation mobile phone format, that it has created and accumulated within the company (SCs formed with overseas carriers in Figure 3.6). Another aim of horizontally integrated SCs can be seen in the form of collaboration with other fixed communications carriers or Internet service providers (ISPs), including members of the NTT Group, as DoCoMo seeks to increase its revenues generated through synergistic effects from its future broadband and mobile businesses (SCs formed with external partners in Figure 3.6).

In developing mobile phones or technology platforms, DoCoMo also taps its leadership position to maintain the vertical integration of SCs and pursue activities aimed at accumulating knowledge and developing new services that require creativity and efficiency. By balancing the vertical and horizontal integration of SCs in this way, DoCoMo aims to leverage its integrative competences in the form of scale, range, and speed in the mobile Internet and mobile multimedia markets.

Now we have come to some concrete issues faced by practitioners on a daily basis, such as how they should build an organizational architecture that gives birth to new knowledge, how they can make it possible to access new knowledge, how they can generate new business ideas, or to what level relationships with partners should be nurtured. It is important, however, for actors to consciously and actively form and consolidate potential SCs (organizational boundaries) including customers and partners that are sources of context for knowledge hidden in the background between existing formal organizations, companies, industry structures, and even different industries, without being held captive by existing thought paradigms, and to focus on their own ideas and behavior with respect to viewpoints on an organizational architecture made up of relationships between SCs and their structures.

For the future, there is a need to promote more qualitative studies in various business or technology development contexts in order to test more generalizations of this theoretical framework. It is also important to observe the dynamism of SC and network formation that has been obtained from much data and to clearly understand the mechanism by which diverse knowledge dispersed both inside and outside the organization is integrated.

Another important issue for both future research and practical application involves the handling of 'time factors' in strategy and organizational theory.[3] How can organizations or strategies be rhythmically rebuilt in response to technology innovations, changes in market structures, or other dynamic changes in the environment? Or how can corporations on their own create new environments? Since business models that were once successful are bound to collapse, corporations must always continue to generate new value and create new products and services. To do this, they need more detailed theorization and practical methods for dynamically integrating strategies and organizations.

Four specific factors in the dynamic view of strategy for forming networked SCs: context-specific, people-specific, timing-specific, and network-specific

In order to continually generate new market position and new organizational capability through knowledge integration and knowledge transformation, the corporation needs to rebuild the network of SCs on a time-based axis to suit their vision and strategic goals. The following four points are important in this regard from the theoretical and practical view.

The first point concerns context specificity. Actors must constantly form and link SCs by identifying new meaning from dynamic contexts. SCs are also organizational platforms for creating and practicing new concepts through constructive and creative dialog into questions that ask why something is, how something should be, or how something can be accomplished, as members aim to achieve their vision or mission. Another factor determining the nature of strategic concepts is the nature of specific contexts. Overcoming contradictions occurring in the diversity of contexts gives birth to a further context, and an SC is formed and linked at the same time. The nature of this specific context determines the nature of the knowledge that arises as a result.

In Chapter 3, i-mode represents the creation of a new market, the vision for the future. To realize this vision, actors, as professionals possessing a variety of skills and backgrounds, question meanings either on their own or with each other, and then dynamically generate and share specific contexts.

The second point concerns people specificity. At the source of context specificity noted above are specific people who form and link SCs. This cannot simply be any person but rather a number of specific people with human skills to tirelessly pursue self reforms. Expressed in the context of engineers, they are specific people who share common knowledge (a common understanding gained through common language, knowledge, prototypes, or other boundary objects; Star, 1989, for example). These people use their own beliefs and ideas to independently produce contexts of specificity and to execute the formation and linking of SCs. Specific people are also leaders and members of management positions in organizations, leaders and members of partner companies, or progressive customers.

In Chapter 3, the aspect of 'people specificity' comprises Enoki, Matsunaga, Natsuno and other GBD members who are focused on building a new business model, the main members of content providers who are staking their success on i-mode, and DoCoMo engineers who are working on the technical aspects of i-mode.

The third point concerns the dynamics of generating and linking SCs in time and space, one of which is timing specificity, the time characteristic of SCs. The meaning of this point is who will form and link an SC with what sort of context in the specified time. The element of timing is important in strategy decision-making. This is because the questions of when and how the company forms and executes its strategy leads to widely varying results. The timing of SC formation and linking on the time axis extends considerable impact on the development decisions and market introduction of new products and services.

In Chapter 3, the i-mode strategy, which involves continually predicting new markets (with their attendant risks) and setting new goals, is determined by top management at DoCoMo. Based on a vision focused on 'From volume to value' and 'From voice to data,' Oboshi assigned to Enoki the responsibility of carrying out this project, and with specific timing, concrete service development was started.

In the case concerning Chapter 6, Matsushita Electric's digital appliances strategy is to constantly forecast new markets (along with their risks) and establish new goals. At Matsushita Electric, the roadmaps (including a technical roadmap for system LSI, optical, and circuit design technologies; and a new product roadmap aimed at the broadband and ubiquitous markets) relating to digital appliances are shared with all concerned organization members and all members are aware of the answers to when, who, and what must be done.

The fourth point, concerned with space characteristics, is the element of network specificity. This point represents the form of the human network as a structural element in the formation and linking of SCs, and is a specific network that creates valuable knowledge. This specific network is important for when actors rebuild on the time axis in accordance with strategic goals. It is thus more accurate to call it a changing specific network.

In Chapter 3, divisions within DoCoMo, content providers, manufacturers, carriers and others represent a specific network, and this network constantly changes as i-mode services evolve.

From the viewpoint of building a network of SCs, the above four specific factors are not independent of each other but are mutually dependent. The partial optimum of the four individual elements and their overall optimum build an ideal network of SCs and serve to create concepts for superior products and services and continually achieve the practical application of business processes.

DoCoMo was able to simultaneously obtain a competitively advantageous market position and organizational capability through a dynamic view of strategy by which SCs were networked according to the four specific factors. The most important process from the practical point of view is the one in which 'Specific people' dynamically build 'specific networks' by forming and linking SCs at a 'specific time,' which then dynamically generates 'specific contexts' through the sharing and integration of new knowledge.

Integrative competences of SC-based firms

The SC-based firm is the company image demanded of an innovation company in the knowledge era. What sort of thing was this as the way an organization should be? The important point in an SC-based firm is the concept of organizational design that envelopes within a dynamic structure a nature that reciprocates creativity and efficiency and the generation of meaning and the processing of information. In an SC-based firm, the integration of SCs having several heterogeneous and different properties is arranged. A feature here is that the functions of creative SCs that possess new knowledge resources of a different nature and of traditional SCs that possess knowledge resources accumulated over many years are merged and integrated in a good balance (Figure 8.8).

Emergent SCs are, under an unreliable dynamic environment, innovation-oriented. With creative power at the base, they are ceaselessly creating new knowledge of a sort that will enable the continuous creation of the concept of new business models (new products, new services, or new business frameworks). There, an emergent organization is improvised by the formation of several hierarchical SCs with strategic business partners including customers outside the company and proceeds to implement the emergent and entrepreneurial strategy of taking in knowledge from inside and outside the company under a high-risk environment. Individual projects within an emergent organization take autonomously dispersed organizational action, like a networking organization or an intermediate organization (semi-structure) that is somewhere between tightly-controlled and loosely-controlled, with the concept of new products and new services and prototypes being produced one-by-one through abduction and many incubations being implemented.

On the other hand, for timely and efficient investment, propagation and expansion of the markets that specifically do the merchandizing of these new products and services, commercial processes such as production, marketing, distribution and after-sales support become important. These business processes are the infrastructure that supports the traditional organization. The traditional organization, which is the hierarchical structure that attended to the system of command directives, based on strategic discipline founded on knowledge capital accumulated over many years, will proceed to implement deliberate strategy reliably as an orchestra. Hierarchical SCs at the center of deliberate strategy will incrementally improve and modify the efficiency of business processes, and the Community of Practice will also promote best practice in the workplace. The results of the innovative new products and services concept that the emergent SCs created will then be quickly, efficiently, and reliably propagated, expanded, and invested in the market.

In classifying these two types of SCs, they have the paradoxical elements of pursuing creativity and autonomy on the one hand, efficiency and control on the other, but inconsistencies will be picked up by means of creative and dialectic dialog, creative abrasion, and productive friction. In an SC-based firm, hierarchical and vertically integrated SCs are formed at each layer of management (the top management layer of emergent and traditional organizations, the middle management layer and their mixed management teams, cross functional teams, task forces, and so on) and the SCs are formed by each leader (knowledge architects including the CEO, directors, divisional managers, managers of each department and project leaders) in a process known as LSC formation. Then integrated competences are formed as SC-based firms by the uniting and integrating of knowledge by creative organizations and traditional organizations.

Within Toyota, for example, vertically integrated SCs are formed hierarchically as close functional task teams at each management level (group, division, department, section, director level). Group and division level task teams handle the resolution of chronic problems and technical issues, and task management teams of department and division manager class handle activities for creating solutions that can generalize without a stopping at particular cases. The total task management team at the director level handles activities to transfer effort and cooperation between sections to advanced high-grade technological creations for new global production systems. Moreover, a joint total task management team is formed that includes domestic and overseas suppliers (group and non-group), and SCs are formed for activities to ensure the high reliability of the products.

The linking of SCs in this way is not confined to technical departments. From the viewpoint of constantly providing better vehicles for customers, 13 departments from sales and marketing to development and design to production site work are linked in the total. In addition, the control divisions that manage these departments (including technical control, production control, procurement control, marketing control, information technology, quality control departments) and the business and indirect departments (including general planning, TQM drive, public relations and publicity, safety, health and the environment, client liaison, finance and accounting, overseas projects, personnel and general affairs departments) are individually connected and multi-layered. By activating the resources and capabilities within the company and linking with organic organizations, they are coping with both partial and total optimization

(Amasaka, 2004).[4] Thus, hierarchical vertically integrated SCs are in existence at various levels of management in Toyota, and the features of bureaucracy and networks are being integrated through vertically integrated SCs.

At Canon also, there is a 'morning meeting' made up of the top management where the LSC consisting of these leaders makes decisions on important matters and which are promptly implemented by various operations divisions and group companies. The source of Canon's integrative competences, which are thoroughly concerned with technical development within the company, is making things by means of a trinity of design, production technology and manufacturing. The product planning group, the product development group, the production technology group and the manufacturing group have come together to form vertically integrated networked SCs, and in addition, by grading these SCs at each management level, Canon is pursuing total optimized management. This recalls features in common with Matsushita Electric (Chapter 6), which promotes the strategy of making things in digital customer electronics by forming SCs.

SCs ensure productivity and compatibility when corporate vision is to be expressed in definite professional duties. On the other hand, the grading of SCs ensures prompt decision-making, efficiency, and speed when professional duties are performed. How to use both bureaucracy and networking differently in accordance with the circumstances in order to cope with environmental uncertainties, is in the place where the maximum synergy of the features of both is created through the vertical integration of the SCs. Therefore, the key is whether the structure of the SC organization is compatible and can be made to change by improvisation.

With hierarchical SCs, thorough understanding of problems and issues is advanced by means of dialectical dialog and discussion between knowledge architects. Through mutual communication and collaboration, each knowledge architect recognizes the role and value of the other's work. As a result, knowledge architects are able to convert the various conflicts that have arisen between knowledge architects to constructive conflicts. By this concept, facing the mission that should be their aim, the thoughts and actions that are demanded on each of the knowledge architects are: 'If it were I, what action would I take, with which strategy and tactics, and what could I contribute towards the innovation of the company?' Both self-assertion and humility are essential for creative dialog.

On the other hand, the CEO, who is at the top and is also the final decision-maker, at the same time as demonstrating top-down leadership in accordance with the situation in order to strengthen the linkage of

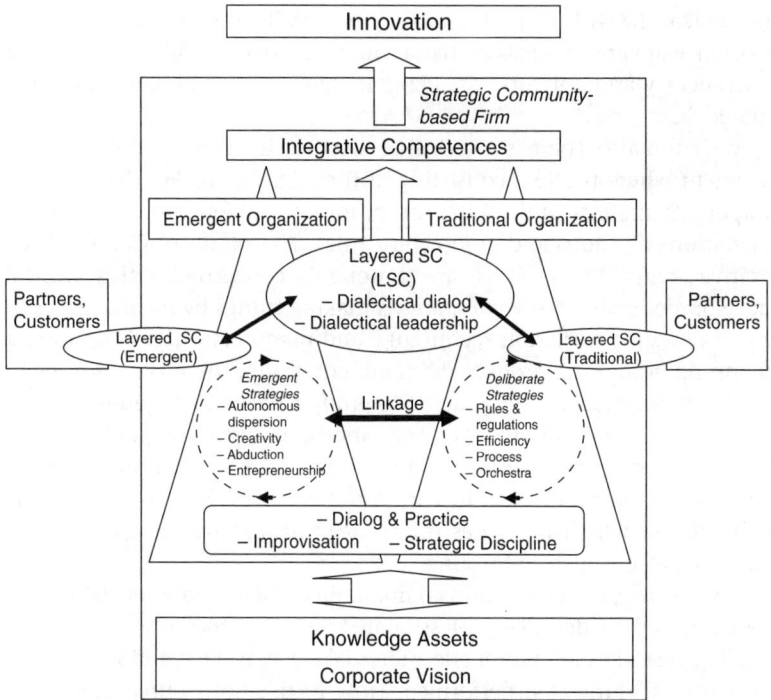

Figure 8.8   Strategic community-based firm

close collaboration between the company top and the knowledge architects, it is important to maximize the dialectical leadership coherence that
each knowledge architect possesses by make a proactive opportunity for
creative dialog and discussion with the SC. Then, in an SC-based firm,
towards attaining business called innovation, the resonance of values
(Kodama, 2001) of each knowledge architect including the company's top
management will be encouraged, forming a solid new business chain with
the integrated synergy effect of the leadership that each knowledge architect possesses and furthermore, it will be possible to produce new customer
value creation.

9
Toward a Strategic Community-Based Firm

New, practical viewpoints through case studies

This section discusses a new, practical viewpoint that was exhibited during the process of radical change within DoCoMo, as discussed in Chapter 3 and NTT in Chapter 4. Future research themes include whether or not the practical aspect of discontinuous transformation of these cases can be applied to other large corporations. It goes without saying that the actual discontinuous transformation method used by a specific large corporation depends on the environment, business type or form, and the existing organizational culture, as well as the value systems exhibited by top management, the leadership style, and so on. Based on the new perspectives obtained from the case studies, the following points are noteworthy in terms of the impact of innovation at other large companies as well.

Comparisons with leading research

Following the liberalization of NTT in 1985 and after the Mobile Communications Division was spun off from NTT to become DoCoMo in 1992, NTT and DoCoMo continued incremental change and achieved radical discontinuous transformation, with the intention to achieve re-orientation and in the process to become leading companies in the fields of digital net services and mobile Internet. In terms of the historic time axis, this is equivalent to the punctuated equilibrium model.

On the other hand, if we look only at discontinuous transformation, the following two similar points can be explained based on the ideological model of change process elucidated by Van de Ven and Poole (1995). The first point is a dialectic model where the MBD and the GBD input a new value system and at the same time abandoned the existing value system with a view to the future re-orientation of NTT and DoCoMo.

They also converted inter-organizational conflict with the traditional organization in such a way that knowledge management was practiced throughout the entire organization. The second point is the teleology model. By expanding Now-ISDN and i-mode promoting change at the same time, the MBD, the GBD and the corresponding traditional organizations were able to reach a consensus on the strategy, tactics, and competences required to achieve the expected target necessary to establish an advantageous competitive position. The fusion of these two models can be thought of as similar to the model describing discontinuous transformation in this case.

There is a long tradition in management and organization theory of using bipolar modes of thinking and action. The bipolar concepts are variously explained and used as paradoxes and dualities. Pettgrew (2000) reported nine key dualities that innovative firms use to simultaneously build hierarchies and networks, seek greater performance accountability upward and greater horizontal integration sideways, empower and hold the ring, maintain the discipline to identify knowledge and the good citizenship to share knowledge, and attempt to centralize strategy and decentralize operations, and so on. Their survey also showed that some firms were innovating simultaneously in many of the elements of the three areas of structures, processes, and boundaries, and that many of the innovative firms were exposing themselves to a range of dualities.

Through these case studies, a number of points can be observed as knowledge shared with important studies by Andrew. The first point is that the organizational structures of the MBD and the GBD feature a simultaneity in which a hierarchy and networks coexist. When NTT and DoCoMo are viewed overall, this point concerns the coexistence of a hierarchical line organizational body, which is the traditional organization, and the MBD and the GBD, whose organizational bodies have strong network elements in the form of strategic alliances with external partners and customers. The second point is that the important multimedia strategies are centralized in the organizational bodies of the MBD and the GBD, and that the many specific operations are decentralized in the line organizational body of the traditional organization. The third point is that company-wide knowledge management is promoted among the MBD, the GBD, and the traditional organization, thereby encouraging horizontal and vertical communications. The fourth point is that the top management team of NTT and DoCoMo empower the MBD, the GBD, and the traditional organization, and by simultaneously promoting company-wide knowledge management, the value systems of all employees are shared, fostering a sense of unity among them.

Another point that is shared with the research of Andrew is that while NTT and DoCoMo managed a balance among these dualities, the structures (decentralizing, delayering, and project forms of organization), processes (investment in IT, horizontal and vertical communications, and new human resource practices), and boundaries (downscoping, outsourcing, and strategic alliances) were also changed and managed at the same time. Specifically, the building of the delayered project-based organizations of the MBD and the GBD can be cited as structural changes. The high degree of decentralization of operational decisions in the traditional organization was also emphasized. As a change in processes, this point concerns the active adoption of new training efforts aimed at improving the competences and skills of employees for new products and services while also aiming for a share (Kodama, 2001) of values and mutual understanding in communication among all employees through the promotion of company-wide knowledge management (including in-house adoption of IT). As a change in boundaries, this point concerns the generation of new strategies and tactics that give birth to new products and services through the promotion of SC management with external partners and customers centered on the MBD and the GBD. As seen above, while triggering the bipolar concepts of thinking and acting that Andrew and others have characterized as dualities, NTT and DoCoMo have also actively implemented changes in structures, processes, and boundaries, enabling them to achieve innovations in new markets. Accordingly, even though the change model in these cases is included in the previous research results mentioned above, it provides the following new viewpoints in terms of its practical meaning.

Creation of an organization of a different nature

Top management members created an organization within the company for discontinuous transformation that was different in nature. This organization, consisting of different and capable members, was placed within the head office organization with the support of top management, and it was granted significant power with regard to strategic corporate planning for the future. The requirements of the leaders of this organization were innovative leadership, and the members of the organization were granted flexibility and autonomy. SCs with outside partners including customers emergently created strategies for the future and promoted experimentation and incubation. Based on thinking and action designed to break with previous creative thinking and networking (Nutt and Backoff 1997), they promoted entrepreneurial and time pacing strategies based on SC management. When a large corporation faces discontinuous transformation, revolutions in personnel such as the bold selection of staff is necessary to create an organization with a different nature. The key to success is the leadership provided by the top management team.

Radical change in organizational culture: the wedge effect

The new organizational culture held by an organization of a different nature drove wedges into the old organizational culture, which was influenced by inertia from the large corporation, and destroyed it completely. Conventionally, in corporate strategic innovation, a highly motivated new organization is established as a different organization within the company or a subsidiary, and is separated from the existing organization both physically and through their means of communication. The new organization promotes innovation at its own pace (Tushman and O'Reilly 1997) (Patterns 1 and 2 in Figure 9.1).

A particular case of pattern 2 concerns the development of the PlayStation, Sony's game machine. At the time, the majority of Sony's management team was opposed to developing a game machine and an associated sales business. Then CEO Mr Oga established a new company, Sony Computer Entertainment (SCE), and delegated considerable authority to Mr Kutaragi, developer of the PlayStation (and the current president of SCE and a former vice-president of Sony). A wide range of personnel from a variety of companies gathered at SCE to build a new business model that involved developing a new game machine and reforming the distribution of game software. Along with receiving the support of Mr Oga and many other Sony executives, SCE autonomously and dispersedly pursued the game business in a loosely-coupled relationship with its parent company Sony. As a result, SCE was born with a new culture and core competences that emanated from their entrepreneurship and were different from Sony's traditional culture. (The case of the PlayStation's development has points in common with the development of NTT DoCoMo's i-mode described in Chapter 3 and the innovation that occurs in corporate ventures by entrepreneurial organizations of a different nature. A difference in these cases of development, however, concerns whether the development is executed externally, as with a subsidiary following pattern 2, or internally, as with a new organization within the company following pattern 3.) Mr Idei, the previous CEO of Sony, made SCE a wholly-owned subsidiary of Sony and at the same time accorded Mr Kutaragi an exceptional promotion to become a vice-president of Sony. Besides developing game machines, Mr Kutaragi was also charged with technical strategies for digital appliances such as LCD televisions and DVD products. Mr Idei then tried to promote synergy by

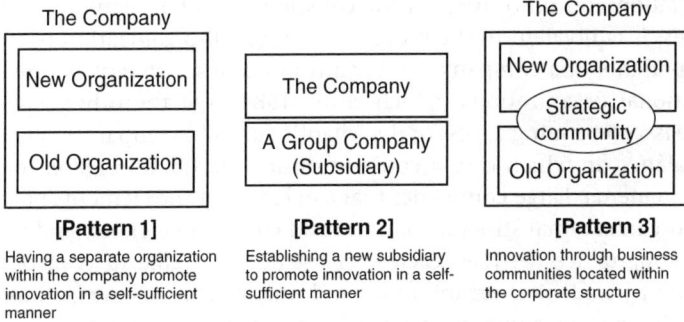

The Company	The Company	The Company
New Organization	**The Company**	**New Organization** Strategic community
Old Organization	**A Group Company (Subsidiary)**	**Old Organization**
[Pattern 1]	**[Pattern 2]**	**[Pattern 3]**
Having a separate organization within the company promote innovation in a self-sufficient manner	Establishing a new subsidiary to promote innovation in a self-sufficient manner	Innovation through business communities located within the corporate structure

Figure 9.1   Forms of strategic innovation in large companies
Source: Kodama (2003).

merging Sony's traditional core competences and SCE's core competences, but it is difficult to say at this stage that the merits of these efforts have achieved their maximum potential. (When Mr Idei resigned as CEO, Mr Kutaragi also resigned as Sony vice-president and moved to SCE where as president he is now devoted solely to PlayStation development.)

Although this manner of creating a new organization is very effective for new strategic innovation, it is not free of difficulties. The problem of pursuing innovation is an issue related to fusion and harmony between the cultures at the new and old organizations (Markides 1998). Even though the new organization might change its corporate culture and achieve innovation, for the company as a whole, the issue of innovation in the consciousness of employees who retain the old sense of values still remains. The author believes that a similar problem exists concerning the merging of Sony's and SCE's corporate cultures. It demonstrates how difficult it is to merge organizational cultures.

As the NTT and DoCoMo cases show, one method that can be used to overcome this obstacle is to bring the new organization and the existing organization into contact with one another by intentionally creating paradoxes in the corporation (Pattern 3 in Figure 9.1). Although conflicts are unavoidable, it is possible to turn conflicts into constructive and productive opportunities for change through the promotion of large-scale knowledge management between both organizations and by providing a communications arena for all employees, including the top management team, via knowledge management.

In this case, chaos and fluctuation were first caused in the corporation through the thinking and actions of organizations with different natures. A certain order in the entire company was then created through strategic integration and innovation in the consciousness of all employees. This process is equivalent to the process of urging self-organization between components of a company, i.e. organizations of a different nature and traditional organizations (Ulrich *et al.*, 1984). On the other hand, if there is a continuing excess of the 'chaotic status,' a company could lose its balance, in which case it could be difficult to obtain organizational achievements. Large companies that can establish the elements of strategy, organizational structure, culture and core competences, and maintain congruence between each element becomes able to control two different paradoxical organizations and finally achieve strategic innovation, though this only is viable if self-organization is achieved.

Integration of strategies

What we need to do in parallel with a revolution in employee consciousness is to integrate the paradoxical strategies in the two organizations. The new organization with a different nature and an entrepreneurial spirit pursues the feasibility of future business through creative and innovative-oriented experimentation and incubation based on new core competencies using internal and external core skills and technologies.

At the same time, however, based on accumulated core competencies, the traditional organization with an occupation ability-based, tight-coupling structure executes the current business using deliberate strategies that are well planned in terms of efficiency and certainty. This means that while the traditional organization is harvesting the blossoming flowers all at once, the organization with a different nature is planting the seeds of the flowers that will bloom in the future. The linkage between time pacing and event-based pacing is an important element with regard to capturing both time restrictions and expected results within a defined range. Through the integration of these two strategies, the organization is able to pay close attention to time linkages and is thus able to simultaneously address the needs of the business today and the nature of the business in the future.

Integrating strategic community management and business process management

SC management is ideal for cases in advanced technology and progressive service fields like those in the IT or multimedia industry, since these are cases in which business environment forecasts are difficult and which respond promptly to constantly changing environments. In other words, with SC management that promotes the fusion and integration of new knowledge and core competencies from internal and external partners

Strategic Community Management		Business Process Management
Adapts to unforeseen changes in the business environment	Adaption to environment	– Can foresee future business environments – Difficulty adapting to rapid change
Continually generates new community knowledge and competencies within the community, between communities, and in integrated communities (Enhanced knowledge management)	Knowledge and core competencies	Improves and upgrades existing knowledge
Main lead from middle management (Top management sometimes in between)	Leadership	Main lead from top management
Virtually networked	Organization	Straight-line hierarchical structure

Figure 9.2 Comparison of strategic community management and business process management
Source: Kodama (2003).

including customers, managers do not rely only on the company's own knowledge and core competencies but constantly monitor the wide range of knowledge and core competencies of external partners including customers, incorporate them quickly and on a timely basis into the company, and create a new body of knowledge and core competences that previously did not exist. As a result, they are able not only to avoid the core rigidity (Leonard-Barton, 1995) caused by experiences of success obtained from knowledge and core competences that were built and honed in the past with the company's own technology but also to respond appropriately to destructive innovation that might suddenly appear (Christensen, 1997). The innovative leadership of the community leader (mainly a middle manager, although cases exist in which a top manager may occasionally stand in between) fuses and integrates multiple virtually-networked communities and possibly create new community knowledge or core competences that previously did not exist (Figure 9.2). In other words, SC management can be considered a process in which knowledge management that mainly shared knowledge within the company or involved knowledge creation activities could become knowledge management that a wider networked community including customers and external partners further expanded and upgraded the quality and quantity of the knowledge.

Business process management, on the other hand, foresees changes in the business environment. Thoroughly enhanced efficiency and reforms in business operations inside a fixed system such as a traditional organization are accomplished via instructions decided by and handed down from top management. This approach, however, runs into trouble when prompt responses to rapid, unforeseen changes in the business environment or to the appearance of destructive innovations are required. The advantage of business process management is that there is a strong possibility that business environments will be foreseen, and once a measure is chosen, it can continue and remain unchanged until the expected target becomes successful. Business process management will exhibit its advantage in the course of incremental change in an orderly and top-down management organization in which the stability found in a traditional organization will be established. Conversely, it is said to be unstable management prone to miss the timing due to delays in action against a trigger, but the attempt of linkage with SC management was useful for constantly monitoring the market performance for the sake of the entire business operation, thus making it possible to take a prompt action against potential changes. Accordingly, SC management and business process management do not stand in opposition to each other. Instead, it will become increasingly important to find an appropriate balance between these two styles of management in order to achieve radical innovation.[1]

Leadership

In addition to the top management team, leadership is required in each layer of the two organizations, both the organization with the different nature and within the traditional organization. It is important that all layers of each organization (the top and middle layers) play their part and elevate leaders who demonstrate innovative thinking, who take action and execute strategies and tactics within their own organization, and who promote knowledge management and construct a management system within which many leaders can demonstrate achievement. A large corporation cannot achieve discontinuous transformation solely through the existence of a charismatic leader or the leadership of the top management team.

The project leaders of the organization with the different nature who continuously produce creative and emergent strategies that can form the basis for future corporate strategies require the leadership abilities necessary to the construction of new core competencies through the formation of strategic business communities with outside partners, including potential customers. It is vital that the company nurture many such project leaders who can then create new business in new markets and thus help maintain the company's advantageous competitive position. Tichy and Cohen (1997) calls this concept a leadership engine, and explains that the mechanism of raising leaders one after another in an organization not only establishes a continuous advantageous position in competition but is a practical element necessary for discontinuous change. The approach to leadership in this case study is similar to this idea.

The community system: a new management system for Japan

In Japan's current sluggish economy, the following new point of view is probably necessary as a new management system in large Japanese corporations of the 21st century.

As pointed out in this book, this viewpoint should be a mechanism that consciously incorporates heterogeneous organizations with an entrepreneurial spirit into existing traditional organizations and, centered on this new organization, forms SCs from both inside and outside the corporation to achieve innovation.

Until now, Japanese corporations, mainly manufacturers, in the second half of the 20th century built their international competitiveness while overcoming the rising value of the yen and two oil crises. Besides the seniority system, lifetime employment, and the loyalty and commitment exhibited by employees, other features of Japanese management that contributed significantly to this resilience was organizational knowledge creation activities based on tacit knowledge peculiar to Japanese corporations (Nonaka and Takenchi, 1995).

Although Japanese corporations of the past were able to raise productivity and quality control by avoiding heterogeneous or heretic human resources or groups and utilizing uniform human resources, they lacked the ability to consistently produce creative or radical innovations. To overcome this shortcoming, a new management point of view that actively takes advantage of creative strategies or tactics produced by heterogeneous human resources or groups and integrates these new strategies and tactics with the efficient operating skills and know-how that traditional organizations have accumulated over many years becomes necessary. To achieve this, while actively promoting knowledge management with heterogeneous organizations and traditional organizations, a process is needed whereby SCs that include customers and external partners are formed to fuse and integrate external knowledge and core competences with internal knowledge and core competences and thereby create and innovate new knowledge and new core competences.

Consequently, it will become increasingly important in the future for Japanese corporations to aim for a new 'community system' management that focuses not on American models such as restructuring, downsizing, or re-engineering but on forming SCs to arouse sympathy and resonate the diverse value systems of individuals, groups, and organizations, and to fuse and integrate high-quality intellectual capital.

In this section, the introduction of paradoxes was constructively understood to be the driving force behind organizational change, indicating one practical method for discontinuous transformation that uses paradoxes. Here, members of top management intentionally introduced paradoxes within the corporation in terms of strategies, organization, culture, competences and the like, and achieved strategic innovation through the use of knowledge management across the entire organization to control these paradoxes.

Managerial implications

SC and networked SC formation refers to the strategy and process of creating, sharing, and utilizing knowledge required by the corporation to acquire ongoing competitiveness. Knowledge creation occurs (or is facilitated) through SCs and networked SCs comprising actors who exchange knowledge from their different specialties. In other words, the author believes that actors of various management layers from not only the corporation but also partners including customers are the primary players involved in knowledge creation activities leading to innovation through strategic and conscious community networking. Specifically, as shown in the case studies in this book, it is possible not only to enhance business efficiency by organizationally consolidating and sharing knowledge assets possessed by individuals or corporations through the formation of SCs and networked SCs but also to give birth to value or innovation in the form of creative new products and services embodying the new knowledge.

How, therefore, do corporate managers form SCs and then networked SCs to create new knowledge? In particular, leaders and managers in charge of the company's future business must be bound by existing business frameworks and the paradigms of thoughts and behavior of their own past. It is important for them to be constantly sensitive to the potential needs of the market and its messages, and allow their own curiosity and power of imagination to come forth (Kanter, 2001).

They must also become actively involved in various unofficial communities (including spontaneous communities of practice for solving daily problems or improving work procedures within the company) that are hidden behind various industries including official organizations, companies, and different industries, and they must not fail to access information of a different nature from key persons in other companies or industries. Engaging in these practices will lead to important hints for new products or new business models that integrate new business ideas and various technologies.

When community leaders sense new ideas, they must not miss this chance to promptly develop the unofficial communities into an SC. It is then important for the community leaders themselves to link a number of SCs that they will commit to, and to launch the process of knowledge sharing and knowledge integration aimed at creating new knowledge. As the community leaders link the various SCs, they will no doubt face a variety of issues such as cross-cultural issues, contract negotiations, and challenges related to technology.

The author would like to mention important elements of management for leaders and managers at corporations as the formation of SCs and networked SCs gives birth to innovation. The conditions required by top and middle management in their aim to achieve innovation are an issue not only for Japanese corporations but also for many executives and managers in the corporations of other countries, including multinationals.

One element that is important for middle management is the necessity to understand and share context in the various SCs and networked SCs. The presence of a common vision, common interests, common merits, and common knowledge among the actors is essential. If the networked SCs' vision is too vague when they start, nothing will go well.

The second important element is that of improvisation in the formation of SCs and networked SCs. Like musicians playing jazz or surfers riding waves, middle managers must instantaneously execute practical decision-making so that they do not miss out on business opportunities. The third important element is the need for middle managers in SCs and networked SCs to embrace a deep commitment as they aim to realize their vision. The fourth important element is that of value shared among community members as resonance value mentioned above. The fifth important element concerns dialectical leadership with a sense of balance centered on community leaders.

It is also important for community leaders to engage in constructive discussions on the various issues within the networked SC and to use a productive, dialectical thought process to solve the issues. This is the dialectical leadership that is required of community leaders in the networked SCs, and the synergy of the dialectical leadership from each of the community leaders will give life to the capability of synthesis. To internalize this dialectical leadership, community leaders need a broad tolerance to understand their own patience and the values of diverse partners and customers. Dialectical leadership also requires mutual understanding on an equal level with subordinates, irrespective of authority.

Of course, these pre-requisites are not easy for middle managers. However, as middle managers engage in repeated practice and self-examination, including organizational learning from failures, the required skills and know-how become deeply embedded in the actors themselves as tacit knowledge and experience.

Next, the author would like to talk about elements that are important for top management. The first of these elements is to provide support for the activities of middle managers in SCs and networked SCs. To this end, appropriate executives in the top layer need to promote opportunities for dialog with middle managers while also gaining a deep understanding of middle managers' business activities and providing constructive support. If top management does not provide sufficient understanding and support, the 'strategic' part of the community will not exist and it will be nothing more than a mere community.

The second important element concerns the provision of a knowledge creation environment (Prahalad and Ramaswamy, 2004). The provision of an IT environment, especially in global business, is essential for supporting the formation of SCs and networked SCs and for efficiently promoting business activities. In addition, top management should review personnel and remuneration systems and actively adopt reward systems as ways to continuously maintain the positive results of middle managers engaged in knowledge sharing, knowledge integration, and knowledge creation within corporations spanning formal organizations.[2]

Conclusion

From the viewpoint of leadership and organizational development, the key issue for companies of the 21st century aiming to achieve innovation is how to nurture and produce many community leaders who possess the dialectical leadership based on the concepts of being creative and strategic, and the ability to act. And the formation of SCs that can continuously generate innovation via the capabilities of individual community leaders, the number of community leaders from each level of management, and the abilities of these leaders to exercise their skills, along with the networking of these SCs, determine whether or not a company is able to build synthesizing capabilities through dialectical leadership.

'How can corporations achieve innovation in a speedy yet reliable manner?' This is the greatest issue that innovative companies are facing in the 21st century. For example, on one side of this double-faceted issue is speed in introducing innovative new products and services to market ahead of the competition, while on the other side is expansion of the market for these products and services. To attain success, it is important for innovative companies to balance the various paradoxes in the SCs networked inside and outside the organization, including customers, and to exhibit practical abilities.

Through in-depth case studies in this book, the author presented one view on the proposition of what the capabilities of leading companies in the knowledge-based society are for SC-based firms that form dynamic innovative processes in SCs and network these SCs. In other words, one of the keys to producing innovation in a knowledge-based society is how companies can organically and innovatively network different knowledge created from the formation of a variety of SCs inside and outside the company, and acquire the integrative competences through dialectical leadership they need to generate new knowledge.

As community leaders, managers in the company who play important roles in producing dialectical leadership for the company use dialectical thinking and power to act to synthesize knowledge of good quality that was unevenly distributed inside and outside the company. To this end, it is important for community leaders to promote the speedy formation of quality SCs networked inside and outside the company, including customers, and to form an leader team made up of community leaders as soon as possible.

When we consider the greater sophistication and specialization of technology that has been occurring in recent years and the growing complexity of business models utilizing ICT, it is becoming increasingly difficult to create completely new knowledge and generate innovation just with the knowledge and core competences possessed by one company. (This is an issue directly confronting many innovators at leading-edge companies.) While the concept of networked SCs is considered to be one of the valid management methods for creating unknown future markets in a turbulent, dynamic environment, from now on we need to research this concept more thoroughly from both the theoretical and practical points of view.

Superior core technology in the leading-edge, high-tech fields of IT and e-commerce continues to spread throughout the world and undergo dramatic changes. Innovative companies that need to establish competitive advantage in the network economy must not retain full control over innovative processes under the conditions of conventional hierarchical mechanisms and closed autonomous systems. In other words, companies will from now on probably increasingly require a management that can, from a multiple variety of viewpoints, use networked SCs to synthesize superior knowledge that is open and spread out both inside and outside the organization, including customers.

Appendix: Research Methodology and Data Collection

I adopted a qualitative research methodology due to the need for rich data that could facilitate the generation of theoretical categories I could not derive satisfactorily from existing theory. In particular, due to the exploratory nature of this research and my interest in identifying the main people, events, activities and influences that affect the progress of innovation, I selected the grounded theory-based study of data interpretation, which was blended with the case study design and with ethnographic approaches (Locke, 2001).

The research data came primarily from longitudinal study during a 13-year period (1993–2005) examining new knowledge creation process with respect to new products and services development at a large company in competitive IT and multimedia business fields. This research paradigm, which was based on in-depth qualitative study, has some similarity to ethnography (Atkinson and Hammersley, 1994) and other forms of research (Lalle, 2003) that derive their theoretical insights from naturally occurring data including interviews or questionnaires (Marshall & Rossman, 1989). Especially, the author of this paper himself serves as a project manager of new product development in NTT and NTT DoCoMo, Japan's largest telecommunications companies. This experience provided the author with direct knowledge and detailed information with which the accuracy of the empirical analyses in this research was enhanced. Research data and insight are gained alongside or on the back of the intervention.

The data collected over the six years of the intervention have derived from work with practitioners involved in a large number and variety of customers and outside partner as well as internal organization members. During these interventions, the expressed experiences, views, actioncentered dilemmas, and actual actions of participants were recorded as research data in a variety of ways, including notes, internal and outside rich documents, etc. The theory that has emerged from this research has centered around the concepts of new knowledge creation process collaborated with outside partners and customers.

The data analysis for the research consisted of three stages: 1. developing in-depth case history of a big project's activities from the raw data that I could gain all the information, 2. open coding and subsequent selective coding the in-depth case history for the characteristics and origin of knowledge creation process, and 3. analyzing the pattern of relationships among the conceptual categories.

In the first stage of the data analysis, I constructed chronological descriptions of the project's activities with respect to knowledge creation process, describing how it came about, when it happened, who was involved, and major outcomes. Through this work, I completed an in-depth case history of the project.

The second stage of analysis involved coding the in-depth case history with respect to its characteristics, origin and effects. This was a highly iterative procedure that involved moving between the in-depth case history, existing theory, and the raw data (Glaser and Strauss, 1967). Data were subjected to continuous, cyclical, evolving interpretation and reinterpretation that allow patterns to emerge.

The grounded theory approach was adopted based upon the researchers' interpretation and description of phenomena based on the actors' subjective descriptions and interpretations of their experiences in a setting (Locke, 2001). This 'interpretation of an interpretation' strives to provide contextual relevance (Silverman, 2000). From the in-depth case history, I initially advanced first-order descriptions based on broad categories that were developed from the existing theory, and then refined these categories by tracing patterns and consistencies (Strauss, 1987). The analysis continued with this interplay between the data and the emerging patterns until the patterns were refined into conceptual categories (Eisenhardt, 1989). The third stage of data analysis was to examine the empirical in-depth case results across the selected categories and the theoretical literature, and to develop the logic of the conceptual framework and generate new theory.

The Matsushita and Fujitsu case studies are based on in-depth interviews with many senior managers of corporations that have formed networked SCs through internal and external collaboration, and on internal and external materials. From 2000 to 2003, the author worked as a project leader in product development at NTT DoCoMo. During this period, he gathered data through informal dialogs with Matsushita Electric and Fujitsu managers.

Based on the data obtained from field studies, the author first produced an in-depth cases concerning Matsushita and Fujitsu business. Next, based on this study, he performed analyses and observations from the viewpoint of boundary management. Various scholars (Eisenhardt, 1989; Pettgrew, 1990; Yim, 1994) have discussed the validity of case studies. Case studies make it possible to explain the relevance and cause-and-effect relationships of a variety of observations through deep and detailed insights with consideration given to qualitative information and subjectivity resulting from the peculiarities of individual cases and the difficulties of general analyses. Case studies not only compensate for the weaknesses of generalities but are also indispensable in new, creative theorization.

Notes

2 Theoretical Framework of the Research

1. Teece *et al.* (1997) point out that, in order to respond to market changes, the dynamic capability approach, as a dynamic process that constantly forms, re-forms, installs, and re-installs current resources, is in particular a source of competitive advantage. Though this is of course an important point in the business context, it is also important as a strategy-making process from the viewpoint of deliberately acquiring new capability for a corporation to create new markets and come out ahead of the competition. The cases of new product and service development at NTT DoCoMo concerning i-mode and FOMA, described in Chapters 3 and 4, and at NTT with optical fiber communications, cited in Chapters 4 and 5, were strategies that were formed not only to respond to environmental changes but to create a new environment as well.

2. Dialectical management is based on the Hegelian approach, which is a practical method of resolving conflict within an organization (Benson, 1977; Peng and Nisbett, 1999; Seo and Creed, 2002). Dialectic first appeared in the question and answer technique of Socrates and Plato's theory of ideas, and it became an approach to thinking about things that was discussed and developed through the history of philosophy. In particular, Hegel (1927) considered dialectic to be a law of dynamic development in cognition and existence, proposing the thesis, antithesis, and synthesis scheme of logic and the concept of 'aufheben' (to sublate). According to Marx (1930, 1967), Engels (1952), and others, Hegel's ideological dialectic developed in a practical methodology. They applied dialectic approaches to thinking to civilization and culture, produced thesis and antithesis with respect to propositions and historical fact, and proposed a methodology by which problem areas and conflicts were resolved through the synthesis of the two sides. The synthesis then became a new thesis, both of which were denied by antithesis, which produced another new thesis in a never-ending process; the process of historical development was proposed to be an eternal process. Dialectic, on the other hand, was also applied to organization theory, stimulating discussion based on absolute truths or morality in devotion to the community (Benson, 1977) or in the process of corporate reform (Van de Ven and Pool, 1995). In addition, Peng and Nisbett (1999) and Peng and Akutsu (2000) analyzed the psychological reactions that could easily result from two apparently contradictory propositions and, while risking crises that allow contradictions, proposed 'dialectical thinking in a broad sense' that judged parts of both propositions to be correct. Recently, Seo and Douglas Creed (2002) used a dialectical perspective to provide a unique framework for understanding institutional change that more fully captures its totalistic, historical, and dynamic nature, as well as fundamentally resolves a theoretical dilemma of institutional theory. Furthermore, Das and Teng draw on dialectics to provide an explanation for the instability and failure of strategic alliance (Das and Teng, 2000), and Rond and Bouchikhi also explored the characteristics and

contributions of a dialectical lens in understanding inter-organizational collaborations in strategic alliances (Rond and Bouchikhi, 2004).

3. Nisbett (2003) points out that, in contrast to the analytical thought of Westerners, Orientals exercise a dialectical thinking that is all-inclusive or holistic. As a practitioner himself, the author sympathizes greatly with the results of this research. In the reality of the business world, however, a number of aspects is involved, particularly in the areas of decision-making and conflict resolution, and the author believes that a fusion of the thought processes used by Westerners and Orientals is necessary. In other words, corporate leaders and managers need to internalize their different thought processes and exercise these skills at the same time or use one or the other as needed. This is the dialectical leadership that forms the main focus of this book.

4. There are many cases of incremental improvements such as newer versions for existing products where analyses of data on customer needs have been given important weight, and new products based on completely new concepts that very possibly emerged from strong desires among developers, customers, or experiences that were common with the market.

5. The concept of 'knowledge difference' is based on the author's many years of experience with development work in the fields of IT and info-communications and on dialogs with engineers at many partner enterprises. The same sorts of concepts were also obtained from dialogs with DVD development teams at Matsushita Electric in the field of home electronics and with developers of the Lexus brand automobile at Toyota Motors.

6. This matches the interaction-type opinion of conflicts in groups reported in the past. See S. P. Robbins (1974).

3 Dialectical Management in a Large Corporation

1. i-mode mobile phones are mobile phones capable of accessing networks and a wide variety of content via e-mail or Web browsers.

2. DoCoMo collects the content usage charge ($1 to $3 per month) from the end user together with the communication fee, and DoCoMo pays the usage fee to the IP delivering the content. In this charge collection system, the revenue of DoCoMo accounts for 9% of the usage fee. Though the collected fee is small for each end user, the greater the number of end users, the larger the amount of revenue accrued to the IP. It is in anticipation of these larger revenues that IPs are motivated to provide i-mode services with more content and thereby increase the number of end users using the content. The synergistic effect triggered by this positive feedback is a major driving force of i-mode. It is not rare for many IP vendors to realize monthly revenues of over $10 million.

3. Please refer to Kodama (2004) for DoCoMo's social and corporate visions (the concept tree).

4. Please refer to Kodama (2004) for DoCoMo's social and corporate visions (the 2010 Vision).

4 Managing Paradox in a Large Corporation

1. The International Telecommunications Union (ITU-T) classifies ISDN into N-ISDN (Narrowband ISDN) and B-ISDN (Broadband ISDN). Of this, the catch

phrase 'Now-ISDN' was coined by Mr. Ikeda, who used the 'N' in Narrow to mean 'Now.' This Now-ISDN concept was actively promoted primarily by the MBD among not only NTT employees but also the general public.

2. Figure 4.4 shows some of the measures promoted by the MBD as a priming engine stimulating the ISDN market. In addition to this, various terminal products were developed, investments were made in multimedia-related companies, and tie-up businesses were created with many content holders.

3. In terms of a specific case of this kind of strategic community management, to expand video networking services, the video business project leader formed several strategic business communities, first through the creation of a strategic business community dedicated to the development and sales of new videophone or videoconferencing technology, second through the formation of a joint venture with an American company to expand video networking services, and third to promote new virtual services such as distance learning and telemedicine using videophones. The promotion of virtual services at the same time was an attempt to jump start a video communication culture in Japan through the synergistic integration of these strategic business communities. Refer to Kodama (2000) for a case study of this project.

4. This matches the interaction-type opinion of conflicts in groups reported in the past (Robbins, 1974).

5. They rapidly changed the constitution of the frontline sales branch offices from an analog telephone type business framework (under the direction of the head office/routine work processes, etc.). In 1996, using the 'Yarima SHOW Multi Strategy' management innovation project, which espouses the principle that once started it will never again be possible to go back to the way things were, an effort was begun to convert all 200 branch offices nationwide to multimedia branches. This change had two strategic aims. One was a 'change in business style' wherein business at branch offices was changed from a telephone business to a multimedia business, while the other was a 'change in work style,' in which the work methodology itself was changed through the use of multimedia tools (Intranet, videoconferencing, groupware, etc).

6. Under the theme 'promoting multimedia in combination with existing services including ISDN for actual needs,' NTT was trying to tackle the multimedia business in a unified way. At a J Project meeting in July 1996, it was agreed that an NTT campaign theme known as 'Multi Net I.I.I' would be launched to promote the move to multimedia. The J Project greatly contributed to the sharing of the vision and the value system of the MBD and the top management team (about 20 board members) of the traditional organization under the president. On the other hand, a '100,000-person meeting' of NTT organizations and employees was held using multimedia tools. This meeting was not just a kick-off ceremony; the real intentions were (1) to have employees themselves actually feel they were a part of the multimedia movement and recognize that the organization was undergoing conversion from a telephone company to a multimedia company; (2) to recognize the real power of the NTT in-house network through simultaneous meetings in units of 10,000 employees; and (3) to become more aware of NTT's multimedia-related technologies and accumulate know-how. The '100,000-person meeting' was a new era in terms of the consciousness evolution (motivation or elevation of motivation) of all employees and the training of talented people through

the acquisition of skills via actual hands-on experience with multimedia technologies.

5 Dynamic View of Strategy in a Large Corporation

1. NTT DoCoMo to Conduct Trial of Multipoint Video Conferencing with FOMA. See Web site; http://bizns.nikkeibp.co.jp/cgi-bin/asia/frame-asia.pl?NSH_KIJIID=187570&NSH_CHTML=asiabiztech.html
2. NTT DoCoMo to extent its video services to FOMA. See Web site; http://www.japancorp.net/Article.Asp?Art_ID=3917 and also http://www.nttdocomo.co.jp/english/p_s/service/f/visualnet.html;
   The platform for the 'M-Stage Visual Net' service was selected on the 2003 R&D 100 Awards program (R&D Magazine in U.S.) as one of the 100 most technologically significant products introduced into the marketplace over the past year.; See Web site;
   (http://www.rdmag.com/scripts/awards.asp). The full list of winners in 2003 was published on September 2003 issue of R&D Magazine. The details of 'M-Stage Visual Net' regarding the technologies and service are described in Kodama *et al.* (2002) and Ohira *et al.* (2003).
3. Lookwalk NTT DoCoMo Users Get Video Conferencing. See Web site; http://www.3g.co.uk/PR/March2003/5054.htm
4. Very little research conducted in the field of paradoxical management has considered time fluctuations related to networks among organizations. Ford and Backoff (1988) described the paradox perspective of dualities in synchronic and diachronic organizations. If such paradoxes provide corporations the chance for innovation, the content and quality of innovation must greatly be influenced by the nature of the paradox conditions. Therefore, it may become more and more important to have the point of view that the paradox phenomenon is constructively and positively understood as being the motive power for the radical transformation of corporations indicated by Quinn and Cameron (1988).

6 Innovation Through Boundary Management

1. Hippel (1998, 2002) pointed out that a toolkit for customers in specified industries (custom LSI, CTI field, etc.) had been developed that the customer is able to use to transfer the solving of problems centered on custom products and applications to the customer side. The custom LSI toolkit enables customers themselves to develop, design and evaluate a prototype. In the case of LSIs, this device is equivalent to a so-called field programmable gate array (FPGA), which is an application-specific integrated circuit (ASIC) in the narrow sense of the word. Because the customer can program the details of the logic level of the electrical circuit, the desired functions can be realized. Since the program can be rewritten, the capability of the prototype can be checked freely on the customer side. With customer-as-innovator, which is being implemented in a very limited field at present, the product developer and manufacturer (the company side) renounces the effort to gain an accurate and detailed understanding of

the customer's needs and instead the whole of the innovation task related to needs data (from prototype design and trial manufacture to simulation and assessment, etc.) is shifted to the customer side. As a result, by repartitioning the task of developing goods and services into two sub-tasks with information related to needs on the customer side and information related to solutions on the company side, the toolkit approach enables the cost of transferring sticky information to be dramatically reduced. Then, as there is no longer any need for it to make a detailed understanding of the highly sticky information on customer needs, the company side can concentrate on routine work. On the other hand, the customer side progresses efficiently by learning how to use the toolkit by trial and error, and can really materialize by itself the necessary functions it wants. As to whether the process of developing system LSIs in accordance with the needs of the customer has somehow been shifted from the developer and producer (the side receiving orders) to the customer (the side that issues orders) by the evolution of system LSI toolkits, see Kodama and Ohira (2005c) concerning research involving case studies on the development of system LSIs for multimedia image processing.

2. A descriptor level that expresses the exchange of signals with the combination circuit that registers the required LSI.

3. Due to the appearance of gate arrays and the upgrading of the degree of abstraction of system LSI development design language in a background where interfaces such as this have appeared in the development and manufacturing processes in system LSI developments, as well as design support provided by electronic design automation (EDA) vendors centered in Silicon Valley and the perfection of EDA tools (special computer supported tools that are utilized for the automation of LSI design) for more efficient verification. When tools such as these had not yet been perfected, the Semiconductor Division carried out LSI design with gate-level descriptors (gate level descriptors are a method of designing descriptors by means of electronic semiconductor units such as AND gates and OR gates) and only specialist engineers of the Semiconductor Division with design experience (explicit knowledge) were capable of performing the design work. On the set side, architecture specifications have been prepared so that the data flow of the algorithms that constitute the system can be understood. Based on the specifications, the Semiconductor Division carried out the design at gate level. Consequently, this design method required much of the period and resources, but later the appearance of a hardware description language (HDL) brought about a change in the LSI design process. (HDL is a high-grade software language that facilitates the automation of gate-level design to be, the simplification of control circuit design, and the faster development of simulation.) HDL is a register transfer level descriptor. It is a better method of general description than the gate-level description, has design features for software description, and was able to broadly improve design efficiency. Moreover, freedom from design experience was achieved by summarizing the parts that relied on experience of the former Semiconductor Division in computer tools (CAD). The advent of this HDL and various types of EDA tools rapidly improved the efficiency and degree of perfection in LSI development.

4. Nikkei Electronics, '"Somehow after 10 years" is unforgivable,' November 2003.

7 Knowledge Creation Through the Networks of Strategic Communities

1. Merging and integrating different technologies refer to the integration of core technologies over a fixed broadband network and core technologies over a wireless broadband network. Although there are many examples of element technology development, I'll just describe a few. One technology development involves real-time conversion of the different signal protocols between a fixed broadband network and a wireless broadband network so that video and audio signals can be transmitted seamlessly between the two networks. (Of course, this requires a high level of quality so that it can be used in the provision of services.) A second development involves technology to convert different audio signal compression schemes. And a third development involves the development of a video streaming server and operation system for large-capacity broadband and wireless networks. (Technical details were not covered as they were outside the scope of the book.)
2. Fujitsu and NMS Communications Jointly Develop Wireless Video Gateway System for Mobile Handsets. See Web site: http://www.nmscommunications.com/nms/news.nsf/URLLookup/Fujitsu
3. NTT DoCoMo V-Live to begin its user paid service in cooperation with Packet Video. See Web site; (http://www.pv.com/press/view.asp?id=214); Regarding the details of technologies and applications, See the following the article; Ohira, H. Kodama, M. and Yoshimoto, M. (2003), 'The development and impact on business of the world's first live video streaming distribution platform for 3G mobile videophone terminals,' *International Journal of Electric Business*, 1, 1, pp. 94–105.
4. The service based on the CDMA2000 1x EV-DO network has been started from November 28, 2003 in Kanto, Chubu and Kansai area in Japan, and will be expanded to other major cities nationwide by end of March 2004. CDMA 1X WIN is based on the CDMA2000 1x EV-DO network that enables high-speed data communications at low cost based on a simple network infrastructure for data communications. By taking full advantage of its functionality and progressive 3G services, the service provides attractive features in every aspect, including content, fees, and handsets. See in detail; (http://www.mobiletechnews.com/info/2003/10/28/121552.html)
5. With Live Video Distribution, content captured live via cameras in various locations will be possible, enabling users to check up on their mobile phone car traffic information, weather and tourist information of various places on a real time basis. KDDI aggressively encourages Live Video Distribution services as well as applications for business solutions, taking advantage of a full range of CDMA 1X WIN features.
6. Several vendor companies in Japan and overseas have promoted studies in this product development. For the results of research in which the processes of development of each company's product were observed and analyzed in chronological order, see Kodama (2005a).

8 Innovation by Strategic Community-Based Firm

1. Substantial emergent strategy in a company is roughly deliberate, but the details of the strategy can be considered to be emergent. Instead, it can be

considered to be something close to entrepreneurial strategy (Mintzberg, 1978) that combines emergent with deliberate (Kodama, 2003).
2. Strategic discipline refers to a principle of action that has rules for actors who advance totally optimized management as a company in the midst of daily reform and improvement (for example, Toyota's continuous improvement, TQM activity, and so on) advanced by an organizational culture and corporate climate that enable the idea of new products (such as 3M's innovation). To maintain strategic discipline, it is necessary to stress the process of open discussion between actors and at the same time establish a clear decision-making process within the company.
3. In the field of empirical studies of strategic or organizational theory, there already is a large body of static snap-shot research based on detailed quantitative analyses. However, little qualitative research or process research has been conducted concerning time fluctuations in strategies or organizations, and there is also little field research into the formation of strategies stimulated by the values of actors. How would practitioners (especially top management and strategists) evaluate the analysis results, important as they may be academically, that were recognized to be logical, quantitative, and scientific in the narrow range of market structure and organizational behavior? What sort of strategy or organization could work effectively under any kind of environment or conditions? What individual relationships of cause and effect or mechanisms related to success and failure in the strategies or organizational structure have been executed for building a business model? What do top or middle management think about strategies or the organization and their positioning in the time spanning the past, present, and future? How should it be? How should people who work there be? These and other questions into the sort of knowledge-based view of the firm that should develop strategic theory or organizational theory from the viewpoint of human knowledge should yield insights that are different from existing static, quantitative empirical research.
4. Interpreted by the author from a dialog with Professor Amasaka of Aoyama Gakuin University (formerly manager of Toyota's TQM Promotion Division). Professor Amasaka calls Toyota's hierarchical task team the 'strategic stratified task team' (Amasaka, 2004).

9   Toward a Strategic Community-Based Firm

1. A similar report on the need for a balance between business process management and best practice (knowledge creation) is found in Brown (2000).
2. To promote knowledge management, the global corporation Buckman Laboratory has created an ICT environment where employees can share their various tacit and explicit knowledge and engage in creative activities. The results of the Issue-Driven Community's activities are linked to performance bonuses accorded to employees participating in this community (Buckman, 2004).

Bibliography

AERA (1999) *Gendai no Shozo* (in Japanese), 31: 62–6.

Allen, T. (1971) 'Communications, technology transfer, and the role of technical gatekeeper', *R&D Management*, 1: 14–21.

Allen, T. J. (1977) *Managing the Flow of Technology*, MIT Press.

Amasaka, K. (2004) 'Applying new JIT – a management technology strategy model at Toyota-Strategic QCD studies with affiliated and non-affiliated suppliers', *Proc. of the Production and Operations Management Society*, Cankun, Mexico, 1–11.

Ansoff, H. I. (1965) *Corporate Strategy*, New York, McGraw-Hill.

Atkinson, P. and Hammersley, M. (1994) 'Ethnography and participant observation', In N. K. Denzin, Y. S. Lincoln (eds), *Handbook of Qualitative Research*, 105–17, Thousand Oaks, CA, Sage Publications.

Barabasi, A. (2002) *The New Science of Networks*, Perseus Books Group.

Barlett, C. and Ghoshal, S. (2000) *Transnational Management*, Boston, MA, McGraw-Hill.

Barney, J. (1991) 'Firm resources and sustained competitive advantage', *Journal of Management*, 17(3): 99–120.

Bennett, R. (2001) ' "Ba" as a determinant of salesforce effectiveness: an empirical assessment of the applicability of the Nonaka-Takeuchi model to the management of the selling function', *Marketing Intelligence & Planning*, 19(3): 188–99.

Benson, J. (1977) 'Organization: a dialectical view', *Administrative Science Quarterly* 22: 221–42.

Brown, J. S. and Duguid, P. (1991) 'Organizational learning and communities-of-practice', *Organization Science*, 2(3): 40–57.

Brown, J. S. and Duguid, P. (2001) 'Knowledge and organization: a social-practice perspective', *Organization Science*, 12(6): 198–213.

Brown, S. J. (2000) 'Balancing act: how to capture knowledge without killing it', *Harvard Business Review*, 78(3): 73–9.

Brown, S. L. and Eisenhardt, K. M. (1979) 'The art of continuous change: linking complexity theory and time-paced evolution in relemtless shifting organizations', *Administrative Science Quarterly*, 42: 1–34.

Brown, S. and Eisenhardt, K. (1995) 'Product development: past research, present findings, and future directions', *Academy of Management Review*, 20(2): 343–78.

Brown, S. L. and Eisenhardt, K. M. (1998) *Competing on the Edge*, Boston, MA, Harvard Business School.

Bryson, J. and Crosby, B. (1992) *Leadership for the Common Good: Tackling Public Problems in a Shared-Power World*, San Francisco, Jossey-Bass.

Burgelman, R. A. (1983) 'A model of the interaction of strategic behavior, corporate context, and the concept of strategy', *Academy of Management Review*, 8(6): 61–70.

Burt, R. (1997) 'The contingent value of social capital', *Administrative Science Quarterly*, 42(2): 339–65.

Burt, S. (1992) *Structural Holes: The Social Structure of Competition*, Cambridge, MA and London, Harvard University Press.

Burtha, M. (2001) 'Working with leaders', *Knowledge Management Review*, 4(5): 7–8.

Buckman, R. H. (2004) *Building a Knowledge-driven Organization*, McGraw-Hill.

Business Week (2000) 'Feature article of i-mode', 17 January.

Busoni, S. and Prencipe, A. (2001) 'Exploring the links between products and knowledge dynamics', *Journal of Management Studies*, 38(8): 1019–35.

Busoni, S., Prencipe, A. and Pvatt, K. (2001) 'Knowledge specialization, organizational coupling, and the boundaries of the firm: why do firms know more than they make?', *Administrative Science Quarterly*, 46(4): 1185–200.

Carlile, P. (2002) 'A pragmatic view of knowledge and boundaries: boundary objects in new product development', *Organization Science*, 13(4): 442–55.

Carlile, P. (2004) 'Transferring, translating, and transforming: an integrative framework for managing knowledge across boundaries', *Organization Science*, 15(5).

Chakravarthy, B. (1997) 'A new strategy framework for coping with turbulence', *Sloan Management Review*, 38(2): 69–82.

Chesbrough, H. (2003) *Open Innovation*, Harvard Business School Press, Boston, MA.

Chrislip, D. and Larson, C. (1994) *Collaborating Leadership: How Citizens and Civic Leaders Can Make a Difference*, San Francisco, Jossey-Bass.

Christensen, C. (1997) *The Innovator's Dilemma*, Harvard Business School Press, Boston, MA.

Christensen, C. and Raynor, M. (2003). *The Innovator's Solution*, Harvard Business School Press, Boston, MA,

Clark, K. B. and Fujimoto, T. (1991) *Product Development Performance*, Harvard Business School Press.

Coleman, J.(1988) 'Social capital in the creation of human capital', *American Journal of Sociology*, 94: 95–120.

Cramton, C. (2001) 'The mutual knowledge problem', *Organization Science*, 12(3): 346–71.

Dacin, M., Ventresca, M. and Beal, B. (1999) 'The embeddedness of organizations: dialogue and directions', *Journal of Management*, 25, 317–56.

Das, T. K. and Teng, B. (2000) 'Instabilities of strategic alliances: an internal tensions perspective', *Organization Science*, 11(1): 77–101.

Davenport, T. H. and Prusak, L. (1998) *Working Knowledge*, Boston, Harvard Business School Press.

Davenport, T. H., Ge Long, D. W. and Beers, M. C. (1998) 'Successful knowledge management project', *Sloan Management Review*, Winter, 43–57.

DiMaggio, P. and Powel, W. (1983) 'The iron cage revisited: institutional isomorphism and collective rationality in institutional fields', *American Sociological Review*, 48: 147–60.

Dougherty, D. (1992) 'Interpretive barriers to successful product innovation in large firms', *Organization Science*, 3(2): 179–202.

Dougherty, D. (1996) 'Organizing for innovation', In S. R. Clegg, C. Hardy, & W. R. Nord (eds), *Handbook of Organization Studies*: Thousand Oaks, CA, Sage, pp. 424–39.

Doz, Y. and Hamel, G. (1998) *Alliance Advantage: The Art of Creating Value Through Partnering*, Boston, MA, Harvard Business School Press.

Duncan, R. B. (1972) 'Characteristics of organizational environmental and perceived environmental uncertainty', *Administrative Science Quarterly*, 17(2): 313–27.

Duncan, R. B. (1973) 'Multiple decision-making structures in adapting to environmental uncertainty', *Human Relations*, 26, 110–23.

D'Aveni, R. (1994) *Hypercompetition: Managing the Dynamics of Strategic Maneuvering*, New York, Free Press.

D'Aveni, R. (1995) 'Coping with hypersompetition: utilizing the new 7S's framework', *Academy of Management Executive*, 9(3): 45–60.

Eisenhardt, K. M. (1989) 'Building theories from case study research', *Academy of Management Review*, 14, 532–50.

Eisenhardt, K. M. and Brown, S. L. (1998) 'Time pacing: competing in markets that won's stand still', *Harvard Business Review*, March–April: 59–69.

Eisenhardt, K. M. and Sull, D. N. (2001) 'Strategy as simple rules', *Harvard Business Review*, 79, 106–16.

Eisenhardt, K. M. and Tabrizi, B.N. (1995) 'Accelerating adaptive process: product innovation in the global computer industry', *Administrative Science Quarterly*, 40(1): 84–110.

Engels, F. (1952) *Dialektik der Natur*, Berlin, Dietz.

Ford, F. D. and Bockoff, R. W. (1988) 'Organization change in and out dualities and paradox', In R. E. Quinn & K. S. Cameron (eds), *Paradox and Transformation: Toward a Theory of Change in Organization and Management*, Cambridge, MA, Ballinger, pp. 19–63.

Fuller, S. (2001) *Knowledge Management Foundations*, London, Butterworth-Heinemann.

Galbraith, J. (1973) *Designing Complex Organizations*, Addison-Wesley, Reading, MA.

Gersick, C. J. (1994) 'Pacing strategic change: the case of a new venture', *Academy of Management Journal*, 37: 9–45.

Ghemawat, P. and Costa, J. (1993) 'The organizational tension between static and dynamic efficiency', *Strategic Management Journal*, 14(1): 59–73.

Giddens, A. (1984) *The Constitution of Society*, Berkeley, University of California Press.

Giddens, A. and Pierson, C. (1998) *Conversation with Anthony Giddens Making Sense of Modernity*, Cambridge, Blackwell.

Glaser, B. and Strauss, A. (1967) *The Discovery of Grounded Theory: Strategies for Qualitative Research*, Chicago, Aldine.

Gomes-Casseres, B. (1993) *Managing International Alliances: Conceptual Framework*, Harvard Business School Note: 9-793-133.

Granovetter, M. (1973) 'The strength of weak ties', *American Journal of Sociology*, 78(6): 1360–80.

Granovetter, M. (1985) 'Economic action and social structure: the problem of embeddedness', *American Journal of Sociology*, 91: 481–510.

Grant, M. and Baden-Fuller, C. (1995) 'A knowledge-based theory of inter-firm collaboration', *Academy of Management Best Paper Proceedings*, 38, 17–21.

Grant, R. M. (1991) 'Resource-based theory of competitive advantage: implications for strategy formulation', *California Management Review*, Spring: 114–35.

Grant, R. M. (1996a) 'Toward a knowledge-based theory of the firms', *Strategic Management Journal*, 17(Winter Special Issue), 109–22.

Grant, R. M. (1996b) 'Prospering in dynamically-competitive environments: organizational capability as knowledge integration', *Organization Science*, 7(4), 375–87.

Grant, R. M. (1997) 'The knowledge-based view of the firm: implications for management practice', *Long Range Planning*, 30: 450–54.

Grant, R. and Baden-Fuller, C. (2004) 'A knowledge accessing theory of strategic alliance', *Journal of Management Studies*, 41(1): 61–84.

Greanleaf, R. (1979) *Servant Leadership*, New York, Paulist Press.

Hagel III and Brown, J. S. (2005) 'Productive friction', *Harvard Business Review*, 83(2): 139–45.

Hagel, J. and Singer, M. (1999) 'Unbundling the corporation', *Harvard Business Review*, 77(2): 133–41.

Hakansson, H. (1982) *International Marketing and Purchasing of Industrial Goods: An International Approach*, Chichester, John Wiley.

Hamel, G. (1996) 'Strategy as revolution', *Harvard Business Review*, July–August, 69–82.

Hamel, G. (2000) *Leading the Revolution*, Boston, MA, Harvard Business School Press.

Hamel, G. and Getz, G. (2004) 'Funding growth in an age of austerity', *Harvard Business Review*, July–August, 76–84.

Hamel, G. and Prahalad, C. K. (1994) *Competing for the Future*, Harvard Business School Press, Boston, MA.

Hargadon, A. and Sutton, R. (1997) 'Technology brokering and innovation in a product development firm', *Administration Science Quarterly*, 42, 716–49.

Hart, L. S. (1992) 'An integrative framework for strategy-making process', *Academy of Management Review*, 17(5): 327–51.

Hayes, M. J. and Abernathy, W. J. (1980) 'Managing our way to economic decline', In Tushman and Moore (Eds), *Reading in the Management of Innovation*, Marshfield, MA, Pitman, pp. 11–25.

Hedlund, G. (1986) 'The hypermodern MNC: a heterarchy?', *Human Resource Management*, 25: 9–35.

Hegel, G. W. F. (1927) *System Der Philosophie Erster Teil Die Logik*.

Heide, J. (1994) 'Inter-organizational governance in marketing channels', *Journal of Marketing*, 50(5): 40–51.

Henderson, R. M. and Clark, K. B. (1990) 'Architectural innovation: the reconfiguration of existing product technologies and the failure of established firms', *Administrative Science Quarterly*, 35(1): 9–30.

Hippel, V. (1998) 'Economics of product development by users: the impact of strictly local information', *Management Science*, 44(5): 629–44.

Hippel, V. and Katz, R. (2002) 'Shifting innovation to users via toolkits', *Management Science*, 48(7): 821–33

Hofer, C. W. and Schendel, D. (1978) *Strategy Formulation*, St Paul, Minnesota: West.

Hooper, A. and Potter, J. (2000) *Intelligent Leadership*, Random House Business Books, London.

Janis, I. L. (1982) Groupthink, 2nd edn, Boston: Houghton, Mifflin.

James, W. (1907) *Pragmatism*, New York, The American Library.

Jantsch, E. (1980) *The Self-Organizing Universe*, Pergamon Press, Oxford.

Kanter, R. M. (1983) *The Change Masters*, New York, Simon & Schuster.

Kanter, R.M. (2001) *Evolve! Succeeding in the Digital Culture of Tomorrow*, Boston, MA, Harvard Business School Press.

Kodama, M. (1999) 'Customer value creation through community-based information networks', *International Journal of Information Management*, 19(6): 495–508.

Kodama, M. (2000) 'Business innovation through customer-value creation – case study of a virtual education business in Japan', *Journal of Management Development*, 19(1): 49–70.

Kodama, M. (2001) 'New business through strategic community management: case study of multimedia business Field', *International Journal of Human Resource Management*, 11: 1062–84.

Kodama, M. (2002) 'Strategic partnership with innovative customers: a Japanese case study', *Information Systems Management*, 19, pp. 31–52.

Kodama, M. (2003) 'Strategic innovation in traditional big business' *Organization Studies*, 24(2): 235–68.

Kodama, M. (2004) 'Strategic community-based theory of firms – case study of dialectical management of NTT DoCoMo', *Systems Research and Behavioral Science*, 21(6): 603–34.

Kodama, M. (2005a) 'Knowledge creation through the networks strategic communities: case studies on new product development in Japanese companies', *Long Range Planning*, 38(1): 27–49.

Kodama, M. (2005b) 'New knowledge creation through leadership-based strategic community – a case of new product development in IT and multimedia business Fields', *Technovation*, 25(8): 895–908.

Kodama, M. (2007) 'Innovation through boundary management – case study in reforms at Matsushita electric', *Technovation*, 26(8).

Kodama and Ohira (2005c) 'Customer value creation through customer-as-innovator approach case study of development of video processing LSI', *International Journal of Innovation and Learning*, 2(2): 175–85.

Kodama, M., Tsunoji, T. and Motegi, N. (2002) 'FOMA Videophone Multipoint Platform', *NTT DoCoMo Technical Journal*, 14(3): 6–11.

Lalle, B. (2003) 'The management science researcher between theory and practice', *Organization Studies*, 24, 7, 1097–114.

Lawrence, P. and Lorsch, J. (1967) *Organization and Environments; Managing Differentiation and Integration*, Cambridge, MA, Harvard Business School Press.

Lawrence, T. B., Phillips, N. and Hardy, N. (1999) 'Watching whale-watching: a relational theory of organizational collaboration', *Journal of Applied Behavioral Science* 35: 479–502.

Leonard, D. (1995) *Wellsprings of Knowledge: Building and Sustaining the Sources of Innovation*, Boston, Harvard Business School Press.

Leonard-Barton, D. (1992) 'Core capabilities and core rigidities: a paradox in managing new product development', *Strategic Management Journal*, 13, 111–25.

Levitt, B. and March, J. B. (1988) 'Organization learning', in Scott, W. R., Blake, J. (Eds), *Annual Review of Sociology*, Annual Reviews, Palo Alto, CA, 319–40.

Lewis, W. M. (2000) 'Exploring paradox: toward a more comprehensive guide', *Academy of Management Review*, 25(6): 760–76.

Locke, K. (2001) *Grounded Theory in Management Research*. Thousand Oaks, CA, Sage. A.

Maccoby, M. (1996) 'Resolving the leadership paradox: the doctor's dialogue', *Research Technology Management*, 39(3): 57–9.

Malone, T. and Crowston, K. (1994) 'The interdisciplinary study of coordination', *ACM Computer Surveys*, 26, March: 87–119.

March, J. (1991) 'Exploration and exploitation in organizational learning', *Organization Science*, 2(1): 71–87.

Markides, C. (1997) 'Strategic innovation', *Sloan Management Review*, 38(2): 9–23.

Markides, C. (1998) 'Strategic innovation in established companies', *Sloan Management Review*, 39(3): 31–42.

Markides, C. (1999) *All the Right Moves: A Guide to Crafting Breakthrough Strategy*, Boston, Harvard Business School Press.

Marquardt, M. J. (2000) 'Action learning and leadership', *The Learning Organization*, 7(5): 233–40.

Martines, L. and Kambil, A. (1999) 'Looking back and thinking ahead: effects of priorsuccess on managers' interpretations of new information technologies', *Academy of Management Journal*, 42: 652–61.

Marshall, C. and Rossman, G. (1989) *Designing Qualitative Research*, London, Sage.

Marx, K. (1930) *Critique of Political Economy*, New York, Dutton.

Marx, K. (1967) *Writing of Young Marx on Philosophy and Society*, New York, Dutton.

McDonough, F. E. and Barczak, G. (1991) 'Speeding up new product development: the effects of leadership style and source of technology', *Journal of Product Innovation Management*, 8(3): 203–11.

Mintzberg, H. (1978) 'Patterns in strategy formation', *Management Science*, 24: 934–48.

Mintzberg, H. (1987) 'The strategy concepts I : five Ps for strategy', In G. R. Caroll & D. Vogel (eds), *Organizational Approaches to Strategy*, Cambridge, MA: Ballinger.

Mintzberg, H. and Walters, J. (1985) 'Of strategies deliberate and emergent', *Strategic Management Journal*, 6: 357–72.

Mintzberg, H., Ahlstrand, B. and Lampel, J. (1998) *Strategy Safari: A Guided Tour Through the Wilds of Strategic Management*, New York, The Tree Press.

Miyazu, J. (2003) *NTT Reform*, NTT Publishing.

Morgan, G. (1981) 'The systematic metaphor and its implications for organizational analysis', *Organization Studies*, 2(1): 23–44.

Nikkei Business, 'Special interview: self-reform is needed even more when times are good', *Nikkei Business*, 2003, 15 October.

NTT DoCoMo Technical Journal (1999) 'Feature article on i-mode service (in Japanese)', 7(2).

NTT Technical Journal (2003) 'Challenge to next generation video communication (in Japanese)', 15(4).

Nadler, D. A. and Tushman, M. L. (1989) 'Organizational framebending: principles for managing reorientation', *Academy of Management Executives*, 3: 194–202.

Nadler, D. A., Shaw, R. B. and Walton, A. E. (Eds) (1995) *Discontinuous Change: Leading Organizational Transformation*, San Francisco, CA, Jossey-Bass.

Nadler, D. A., Shaw, R. B. and Walton, A. E. (Eds) (1995) *Discontinuous Change: Leading Organizational Transformation*, San Francisco, CA, Jossey-Bass.

Nahapiet, J. and Ghoshal, S. (1998) 'Social capital, intellectual capital, and the creation of value in firms', *Academy of Management Review*, 23(2): 242–66.

Natsuno (2000) *i-mode Strategy* (in Japanese), Tokyo, Nikkei BP.

Nikkei Business (2000) Feature article of DoCoMo (in Japanese), 25: 26–39.

Nikkei Business (2005) 'Corporation: special interview (in Japanese)' 1312, October: 62–4.

Nikkei Sangyo Shimbun (1996) '100,000 people meeting and MultiNet I.I.I', 14 April: 8.

Nisbett, R. (2003) *The Geography of Thought*, New York, The Free Press.

Nohria, N. and Ghoshal, S. (1997) *The Differentiated Network: Organizing Multinational Corporations for Value Creation*, San Francisco, CA, Jossey-Bass.

Nonaka, I. (1991) 'The knowledge-creating company', *Harvard Business Review*, 96–104.
Nonaka, I. (1994) 'A dynamic theory of organizational knowledge creation', *Organization Science*, 5(1): 14–37.
Nonaka, I. and Konno, N. (1998) 'The concept of 'ba': building a foundation for knowledge Creation', *California Management Review*, 40: 40–54.
Nonaka, I. and Toyama, R. (2002) 'A firm as a dialectical being: towards a dynamic theory of a firm', *Industrial and Corporate Change*, 11(5): 995–1009.
Nonaka, I. and Toyama, R. (2003) 'The knowledge-creating theory revisited: knowledge creation as a synthesizing process', *Knowledge Management Research & Practice*, 1(1), 2–10.
Nonaka, I. and Takeuchi, H. (1995) *The Knowledge-Creating Company*, Oxford University Press.
Nonaka, I., Toyama, R. and Konno, N. (2002) 'SECI, ba and leadership: a unified model of dynamic knowledge creation', *Long Range Planning*, 33: 5–34.
Nutt, P. C. and Backoff, R. W. (1997) 'Organizational transformation', *Journal of Management Inquiry*, 6: 235–54.
Ohira, H., Kodama, M. and Yoshimoto, M. (2003) 'A world first development of a multipoint videophone system over 3G-324M protocol', *International Journal of Mobile Communications*, 1(3): 264–72.
Osterlof, M. and Frey, B. (2000) 'Motivation, knowledge transfer, and organizational forms', *Organization Science*, 11: 538–50.
O'Reilly III, C. and Pfeffer, J. (2001) *Hidden Value: How Great Companies Achieve Extraordinary Results with Ordinary People*, Boston, MA, Harvard Business School.
Orton, J. D. and Weick, K. E. (1990) 'Loosely coupled systems: a reconceptualization', *Academy of Management Review*, 15(2): 203–23.
Pam, S. L. and Scarbrough, H. (1998) 'A socio-technical view of knowledge-sharing at Buckman Laboratories', *Journal of Knowledge Management*, 2(1): 63–4.
Pascale, R. T. (1985) 'The paradox of corporate culture: reconciling ourselves to socialization', *California Management Review*, 27(3): 26–40.
Pascale, R. T. (1990) *Managing on the Edge: How the Smartest Companies Use Conflict To Stay Ahead*, New York, Simon and Schuster.
Peirce, C. S. (1898/1992) *Resonating and the Logic of Things*, Cambridge, MA, Harvard University Press.
Peng, K. and Akutsu, S. (2001) 'A mentality theory of knowledge creation and transfer: why some smart people resist new ideas and some don't', in Nonaka, I and Teece, D. (Eds) *Managing Industrial Knowledge-Creation, Transfer and Utilization*, London: Sage Publications, pp. 105–23.
Peng, K. and Nisbett, R. E. (1999) 'Culture dialectics, and reasoning about contradiction', *American Psychologist*, 54: 741–54.
Peng, K. and Nisbett, R. (1999) 'Culture dialectics, and reasoning about contradiction', *American Psychologist*, 54: 741–54.
Pettgrew, A. M. (1990) 'Longitudinal field research on change: theory and practice', *Organization Science*, 1(1):267–92.
Pettigrew, A. M. (2000) *The Innovating Organization*, London, Sage.
Popper, M. and Lipshitz, R. (2000) 'Installing mechanisms and instilling values: the role of leaders in organizational learning', *The Learning Organization*, 7(3): 135–45.
Porter, M. (1985) *Competitive Advantage*, New York, Free Press.

Porter, M. (1980) *Competitive Strategy: Techniques for Analyzing Industries and Competitors*, New York, Free Press.

Powell, W. and Brantley, P. (1992) 'Competitive cooperation in biotechnology: learning through networks?' in N. Noria and R. G. Eccles (Eds), *Network and Organizations: Structure, Form and Action*, Boston, MA, Harvard Business School: 366–94.

Powell, W., Koput, K. and Smith-Doerr, L. (1996) 'Inter-organizational collaboration and the locus of innovation: networks of learning in biotechnology', *Administrative Science Quarterly*, 41: 116–46.

Prahalad, C. and Hamel, G. (1990) 'The core competence of the corporation', *Harvard Business Review*, 68: 79–91.

Prahalad, C. K. and Doz, Y. (1987) *The Multinational Mission: Balancing Local Demands and Global Vision*, New York, Free Press.

Prahalad, C. K. and Ramaswamy, V. (2004) *The Future of Competition: Co-Creating Unique Value With Customers*, Harvard Business School Press.

Quinn, R. E. and Cameron, K. S. (Eds) (1988) *Paradox and Transformation: Toward a Theory of Change in Organization and Management*, Cambridge, MA, Ballinger.

Robbins, S. P. (1974) *Managing Organizational Conflict: A Non-traditional Approach*, Englewood Cliffs, NJ, Prentice Hall.

Romanelli, E. and Tushman, M. L. (1994) 'Organizational transformation as punctuated equilibrium: an empirical test', *Academy of Management Journal*, 3: 1141–66.

Rond, M. and Bouchikhi, H. (2004) 'On the dialectics of strategic alliances', *Organization Science*, 15(1): 56–69.

Rosenberg, N. (1982) *Inside the Black Box: Technology and Economics*, Cambridge University Press.

Rosenkopf, L. and Tushman, M. (1994) *The Co-Evolution of Technology and Organizations, Evolutionary Dynamics of Organizations*, Baum, J. and Singh, J. (Eds), Oxford University Press.

Rosenkopf, L. and Tushman, M. (1998) 'The coevolution of community networks and technology: lessons from the flight simulation industry', *Industrial and Corporate Change*, 7(6): 311–46.

Sawhney, M. and Prandelli, E. (2000) 'Communities of creation: managing distributed innovation in turbulent markets', *California Management Review*, 42: 24–54.

Seo, G. and Creed, W. (2002) 'Institutional contradictions, praxis, and institutional change: a dialectical perspective', *Academy of Management Review*, 27: 222–47.

Shannon, C. and Weaver, W. (1949) *The Mathematical Theory of Communications*, Urbana, University of Illinois Press.

Shenhar, A. J. and Dvir, D. (1996) 'Toward a typological theory of project management', *Research Policy*, 25(4): 607–32.

Silvermann, D. (2000) *Doing Qualitative Research,* Thousand Oaks, CA, Sage.

Spears, L. (1995) *Reflections on Leadership*, New York, John Wiley.

Stalk, G., Evans, P. and Schulman, L. E. (1992) 'Competing on capabilities: the new rules of corporate strategy', *Harvard Business Review*, March–April: 57–69.

Star, S. L. (1989) *The Structure of Ill-structured Solutions: Boundary Objects and Heterogeneous Distributed Problem Solving*. Huhns M. and Gasser l., (Eds), *Residing in Distributed Artificial Intelligence*, Morgan Kaufman, Menlo Park, CA.

Stein, B. and Kanter, R. M (1980) 'Building the parallel organization: toward mechanisms for quality of work life', *Journal of Applied Behavioral Science*, 16(1): 371–88.

Stewart, T. (1997) *Intellectual Capital: The New Wealth of Organization*, New York, Doubleday.

Storck, J. and Patricia, A. (2000) 'Knowledge diffusion through strategic communities', *Sloan Management Review*, 41: 63–74.

Strauss, A. (1987) *Qualitative Analysis for Social Scientists*, New York, Cambridge University Press.

Teece, D., Pisano, G. and Shuen, A. (1997) 'Dynamic capabilities and strategic management', *Strategic Management Journal*, 18(3): 509–33.

Thompson, J. D. (1967) *Organizations in Action*, New York, McGraw-Hill.

Tichy, N. M. with E. Cohen (1997) *The Leadership Engine: How Winning Companies Build Leader at Every Level*, New York, Harper Collins.

Tracy, L. (1989) *The Living Organization: Systems of Behavior*, NJ, Greenwood Publishing Group.

Turnbull, P. W. and Valla, J.-P. (1986) *Strategies for International Industrial Marketing: The Management of Customer Relationships in European Industrial Markets*, London, Croom Helm.

Tushman, M. L. (1977) 'Special boundary roles in the innovation process', and *Administrative Science Quarterly*, 22: 587–605.

Tushman, M. and Nadler, D. (1978) 'Information processing as a integrating concept in organizational design', *Academy of Management Review*, 3(3): 613–24.

Tushman, M. and Romanelli, E., (1985) 'Organizational evolution: a metamorphosis model of convergence and reorientation', *Research in Organizational Behavior*, 7(2): 171–222.

Tushman, M. L. and O'Reilly, C. A. (1997) *Winning Through Innovation*, Cambridge, MA, Harvard Business School Press.

Ulrich, Hans, Probst and Gilbert J. B. (1984) *Self-organization and Management Social Systems*, Berlin, Springer Verlag.

Van de Ven, A. H. and Poole, M. S. (1995) 'Explaining development and change in organizations', *Academy of Management Review* 20(5): 510–40.

Van de Ven, A. H. and Pool, M. S. (1988) 'Paradoxical requirements for a theory of change', In Quinn, R. E. and Cameron, K. S. (Eds), *Paradox and Transformation: Toward a Theory of Change in Organization and Management*, Cambridge, MA: Ballinger, pp. 19–63.

Vangen, S. and Huxham, C. (2003) 'Nurturing collaborative relations, building trust in interorganizational Collaboration', *The Journal of Applied Behavioral Science*, 39(1): 5–31.

Watts, J. (2003) *Six Degrees: The Science of a Connected Age*, W.W. Norton.

Watts, J. (1998) 'Collective dynamics of 'small-world' networks', *Nature*, 393(4): 440–2.

Weber, M. (1924/1947) *The Theory of social and Economic Organization*, Henderson, A. H., Parsons, T., (Eds), Glencoe, Ill. Free Press.

Weick, K. E. (1976) 'Educational organizations as loosely coupled systems', *Administrative Science Quarterly*, 21(1): 1–19.

Weick, K. E. (1982) 'Management of organizational change among loosely coupled elements, in Goodman', P. S. (ed.) *Change in Organizations*, San Francisco, CA, Jossey-Bass: 375–408.

Weick, K. E. (1989) 'Theory construction as disciplined imagination', *Academy of Management Review*, 14(4): 516–31.

Weick, K. E.(1969) *The Social Psychology of Organizing*, New York, McGraw-Hill.

Weiss, J. and Hughes, J. (2005) 'What collaboration? accept – and actively manage – conflict', *Harvard Business Review*, 83(3):139–45.

Wenger, W. (2000) 'Communities of practice: the organizational frontier', *Harvard Business Review*, 78: 139–45.

Wernerfelt, B. (1984) 'A resource-based view of the firm', *Strategic Management Journal*, 5:171–80.

Yin, R. K. (1994) *Case Study Research: Design and Methods*, 2nd edn., London, Sage.

Subject Index

Name Index